BOURKE MEMORIAL LIBRARY
CAYUGA COMMUNITY COLLEGE
197 FRANKLIN STREET
AUBURN, NEW YORK 13021

PRIVATIZING CORRECTIONAL INSTITUTIONS

PRIVATIZING CORRECTIONAL INSTITUTIONS

Edited by
**Gary W. Bowman
Simon Hakim
Paul Seidenstat**

With a foreword by
Warren Burger

Transaction Publishers
New Brunswick (U.S.A.) and London (U.K.)

Copyright © 1993 by Transaction Publishers.
New Brunswick, New Jersey 08903

All rights reserved under International and Pan-American Copyright Conventions. No part of this book may be reproduced or transmitted in any form or by any means, electronic or mechanical, including photocopy, recording, or any information storage and retrieval system, without prior permission in writing from the publisher. All inquiries should be addressed to Transaction Publishers, Rutgers-The State University, New Brunswick, New Jersey 08903.

Library of Congress Catalog Number: 91-45148
ISBN: 1-56000-055-4
Printed in the United States of America

Library of Congress Cataloging-in-Publication-Data
Bowman, Gary W., 1942-
Privatizing correctional institutions / Gary W. Bowman, Simon Hakim, Paul Seidenstat.
  p. cm.
  Includes bibliographical references and index.
  ISBN 1-56000-055-4
  1. Prisons—United States. 2. Privatization—United States. 3. Corrections—United States.—Contracting out. I. Hakin, Simon. II. Seidenstat, Paul. III. Title.
HV9469.B68   1992
365'.973—dc20

                                                                   91-45148
                                                                      CIP

In memory of David R. Meinster: a friend, a leader, a scholar, and above all, a genuinely nice person.

Contents

Foreword
  Warren E. Burger — ix

Acknowledgments — xi

1. Introduction
   Gary W. Bowman, Simon Hakim, and Paul Seidenstat — 1

2. Partial Privatization of Prison Operations:
   Let's Give It a Chance
   Warren I. Cikins — 13

3. Private Correction: The Delicate Balance
   Robert D. McCrie — 19

4. The Future of Correctional Privatization:
   Lessons from the Past
   Alexis M. Durham III — 33

5. The Privatization of Secure Adult Prisons:
   Issues and Evidence
   Dana C. Joel — 51

6. Bars on the Iron Triangle:
   Public Policy Issues in the Privatization of Corrections
   Michael Janus — 75

7. Federal Government Involvement in
   Private Sector Partnerships with Prison Industries
   Barbara Auerbach — 91

8. PRIDE of Florida: A Working Model for Inmates
   Judith Schloegel — 105

9. The Public-Private Partnership:
   A Challenge and an Opportunity for Corrections
   Norman R. Cox, Jr. and William E. Osterhoff — 113

10. Minimizing Liability with Private Management
    of Correctional Facilities
    Linda G. Cooper — 131

11. Privatization of Corrections: A Threat to Prisoners' Rights
    Harold J. Sullivan — 139

12. Proving Privatization Works
    H. Laws McCullough and Timothy S. Maguigan — 157

13. For Profit Jails: A Risky Business
    Todd Mason — 163

14. Low Cost, High Quality, Good Fit: Why Not Privatization?
    Wayne H. Calabrese — 175

15. Comparison of Privately and Publically Operated
    Corrections Facilities in Kentucky and Massachusetts
    Harry P. Hatry, Paul J. Brounstein, and Robert B. Levinson — 193

16. The Development, Present Status, and Future Potential
    of Correctional Privatization in America
    Charles W. Thomas and Charles H. Logan — 213

Contributors — 241

Index — 245

Foreword

I am happy to encourage experimentation in the employment of the private sector in promoting prison industries. I have long tried on focus public attention on this need. In a lecture at the University of Nebraska, Lincoln, cosponsored by the Nebraska Bar Association in 1981, I used the title, "More Warehouses, or Factories With Fences?" This was the culmination of more than twenty years of personal concern that went back to my childhood in Minnesota. I remember a visit as a Boy Scout to the Stillwater prison where some inmates were indeed "warehoused" even though Minnesota was a pioneer in prison production.

It is my hope, bolstered by years of observation beginning long before my 1981 speech, that we can take appropriate actions at all levels of government—including changing laws on the sale of prison products—to reverse this human deterioration. Many of the ideas in this volume will stimulate greater private sector involvement in bringing meaningful employment and training opportunities to the correction facility environment. This important problem, exacerbated by accelerating prison overcrowding in recent years, cannot be allowed to remain a serious threat to public safety. We are paying a huge price in public expenditures as well as human tragedy because of our lack of appropriate priority attention to this matter. The authors of this volume have my best wishes in raising greater public attention as well as allocation of resources (with great savings in the long run) to the role of the private sector in reversing current destructive trends in the treatment of the nation's wrongdoers. No *person* should leave a correctional institution without basic literacy and at least the beginnings of vocational training that will be salable in the employment market.

WARREN E. BURGER

Acknowledgments

This book would not have been possible without the dedicated assistance of many people. We would like to thank the Manhattan Institute of New York, which sponsored the project, and its director of research, Mr. Lawrence Mone, who assisted us throughout the process.

We would also like to thank Dean William Dunkelberg and the School of Business and Management of Temple University which made funds available for the project.

1

Introduction

Gary Bowman, Simon Hakim, and Paul Seidenstat

With more than one million people behind bars, the United States imprisons a larger share of its population than any other nation. Of every 100,000 citizens in the United States, 426 are incarcerated. The annual cost is $16 billion. In South Africa the rate is 333, in the Soviet Union the rate is 268, and in Europe the range is 35 to 120. From 1960 until 1975 the rate of imprisonment per 1000 arrests was quite stable at 113, and in 1975 the number of prisoners stood at 205,745. However, within five years the prison[1] population jumped by 25.5 percent, and by 1989 the number of prisoners reached 710,054. In 1989 the number of jail inmates was 395,553. America's population of detainees now surpasses a total of one million persons. The main reasons for the high incarceration rate in the United States is the adoption of federal and state mandatory minimum sentences, tightened parol eligibility criteria, and greater reliance on imprisonment. At the same time, the crime rate is higher here than in most other countries. For example, the murder rate is over seven times higher than in European nations, and there are six times as many robberies.

The result of the rapid increase in prison and jail populations is a serious overcrowding problem. In 1989, federal prisons were operating at 163 percent of design capacity. Federal prisons suffer the worst overcrowding; in 1987 they operated at 137 percent of designed capacity, while in 1989 they reached 163 percent of capacity. During the same period, the state prisons were at 105 and 107 percent, respectively. Prisons need to operate at most at 95 percent of capacity in order to allow for periodic maintenance and repairs and to permit special housing for protective custody, disciplinary cases, and emergency needs (U.S. Department of Justice, 1989).

Lawsuits, brought by inmate-plaintiffs requesting relief from overcrowding, are the immediate consequence of inadequate and insufficient jail and prison facilities. By judicial decree, thousands of inmates are released before their assigned sentences have been served so that overcrowding can be relieved. To comply with the court order, many longtime felons are assigned to unsuitable local jails and prisons that cannot provide for productive rehabilitation and employment activities in order to reduce recidivism.

It is obvious that the U.S. justice system is in disarray. Thomas and Logan (chap. 16) have calculated that just in order to meet the *growth* in demand for cells in 1989, one 700-bed jail and one 1,600-bed prison need to be opened every week. The total annual construction cost is $5.98 billion. Given the budgetary difficulties of states and counties, it is unlikely that the U.S. justice system can be easily rescued.

Conventional efforts appear not to be able to cope with the increasing shortage in beds or with inadequate rehabilitation services. A bold solution is required, and it may be in the hands of the private sector. Contracting out for limited services is not new and cannot yield major change. The few examples of construction and subsequent management of secured facilities appear to have been successful and could be expanded. However, close governmental monitoring is required.

One should not assume that privatization efforts have always been successful. Several small communities and counties have financed with high-yield revenue bonds the construction of prisons that were later rented to small private prison management companies to house prisoners from large cities. Some of the companies have also financed their own construction with high-yield "junk bonds" that were popular in the 1980s. The sole reason for these governments getting involved was to stimulate employment. For example, Washington, D.C. had entered such "rent-a-cell" agreements with private prisons in places like Crystal City, Texas where it housed some of its inmates.

Introduction

Several of these privatization efforts have failed due to lack of experience and/or insufficient financial resources of the contractors and local governments to meet the obligations of the high yield bonds. The leaders of economically depressed communities were so eager to boost employment that they conducted an insufficient investigation of the contracting companies (Mason 1991).

It is evident, however, that the experience with well-established capital-endowed companies has been better. At this early "infant" stage, the industry is characterized by small numbers of well-established experienced companies that enjoy economies of scale and scope in their operation and by still large numbers of small start-up firms. Most firms in the latter group are inefficient and under-capitalized, with small market share, suggesting high probability of failure. This is a usual phenomenon in an emerging industry. It is similar to the historical development of the automobile industry in the 1920s and 1930s and does not portend a gloomy future for the private correction industry.

The privatization planning process can be characterized by six stages: decision whether to privatize, establishment of goals, organization of the system, analysis of the legal/liability issues, preparation of the request for proposal (RFP), and evaluation and control.

Decision Whether to Privatize

The main reason for privatization is to reduce costs while maintaining the quality of service. Cost estimates of the existing system should include the direct cost of the operating agency, hidden costs carried by other governmental agencies, and opportunity costs of the fixed inputs (e.g., land and physical facilities). In effect, the planners basically need to compute the costs of the current governmental operation with the computation approach used by the private sector. The final outcome should be a maximum cost per bed the government would be willing to pay if it were to consider shifting financing, construction, and management to the private sector.

Establishment of Goals

Explicit goals and objectives and their relative weights are essential for successful privatization. The goals should reflect what the legislators and government officials wish the private company to attain and need to become part of the request for proposal (RFP).

Organization of the System

Review of the existing system is a basis for any consideration of its alteration. The planners should analyze the strengths and weaknesses of the current system and the roles of the various agencies involved.

Analysis of Legal and Liability Issues

State penal codes, institutional and welfare codes, and other state and local ordinances that may affect privatization efforts should be analyzed. This information may assist in determining the barriers to privatization and the type of liabilities governments may later assume. Based upon other privatization experiences the planners may derive the probabilities of such liability events and use them to adjust the costs estimates.

Preparation of the Request for Proposal (RFP)

The RFP sets the requirements for the contractor; it needs to be comprehensive, clear, and provide all the necessary information for the contractor to make a rational decision. The RFP should be clear about requirements for financial strength of the contractor, its prior experience in managing similar operations, and references from other agencies that have used its services. The contractor should be required to provide detailed plans with timetables once the award is made. A well-prepared RFP should guide potential applicants but not be too detailed, difficult, or full of red tape.

Evaluation and Control

The governmental system that will review and control the private contractor should be outlined in the RFP. Continuous monitoring is required to assure quality of service. Government holds ultimate responsibility for the arrestees, prisoners, and parolees, and all the funds are collected from the government. Government cannot relinquish responsibility and ultimate liability for the individuals in correctional institutions and must maintain close monitoring of the contractor.

Cost Considerations in Construction and Operation of Detention Facilities

Private Versus Public Financing

Public financing of prison and jail construction projects can be done through secured government bonds. The interest rate on public sector debt is lower than that available to the private sector because of perceived differences in risk and the tax free nature of such interest. However, the size of the differential depends upon the credit rating of the jurisdiction. In any case, any public bond issue requires a costly, time consuming referendum. A nonprofit corporation can still borrow through tax exempt revenue bonds at a rate higher than the municipal rate, but lower than the corporate bond market rates. The conclusion is that the public sector borrower enjoys only a slight advantage in interest rates. An important point is that the public sector debt, interest, and principal, is an obligation of the local government. The facility constructed and operated with those funds is not a commercial enterprise operated to generate revenue for debt retirement.

Construction

Corrections Corporation of America reports savings of 20 percent in construction costs over the government (Logan 1990). Examples of public sector construction costs include 58,000 for a maximum security bed, $46,000 for medium, and $26,000 for minimum security facilities (Brakel, forthcoming). The average construction period is two and a half years. In Houston, Corrections Corporation of America built a minimum security facility for the Immigration and Naturalization Service at a cost of $14,000 per bed in five and a half months. In a contract with Hamilton County in Tennessee, CCA has made capital improvements that included major renovations and construction of one new dormitory for $1.6 million at no charge to the county. The cost was covered by subsequent per diem management charges that were still lower than the county's operating costs. In Pennsylvania there had been a similar experience; in

1975 RCA Services was able to convert a state-owned building into the Weaversville Intensive Treatment Unit for Juvenile Offenders. In only ten days the facility was ready for operation. Building and architectural innovations that are instrumental in manpower savings in the operation stage are used by private correctional companies that are constructing facilities that they will also operate. Use of tiered cells, adjoining hallways, alarm systems, and closed circuit television are such examples. So far there have not been any claims that private contractors have sacrificed quality and built below public standards.

So, what is the secret, and why couldn't the public sector adopt the same methods? The answer is the profit incentive. The time-limited nature of contracts for managing prisons is a strong incentive to contain costs. Competition among private correction companies encourages utilization of the latest building methods and technological innovations.

Contracting Out

All but nine states contract out some correctional services. Such contracting runs the whole gamut from medical and psychiatric care, rehabilitation programs, classification of inmates, and food preparation to various data management functions. A 1984 national survey (Logan and Rausch 1985) showed that of fifty-two public agencies contracting for correctional facilities services, three out of four have experienced cost savings. Twenty-two of the largest contracts reported average savings of 26 percent compared to their own provision. Six agencies have reported a 16 percent higher average cost; however, some of these cases were contracts signed under court order pressure. The major reasons for savings accruing under contracting out are market competitive salaries, cash payments to suppliers, and more thorough search for low cost suppliers by private firms.

Private Management

The greatest savings and potentially the greatest nationwide expansion is in private management, possibly including construction of secured facilities. Current savings in private management are five to fifteen percent.[2] It is important to note, however, that in 1988 capital outlays by all states constituted only 12.9 percent of corrections expenditures while

Introduction

operations is the major bulk of the expenditures. It is in operations that there is the greatest possible savings through private operation (Bureau of Justice Statistics 1990). By law Tennessee requires that private management be cheaper than public sector costs in the preceding years.

Until the 1984 private operation was limited to nonsecurity institutions, and community-based facilities. Examples are halfway houses, holding centers for illegal aliens, and juvenile detention centers. Since then, state and local governments turned to private companies to operate medium and maximum security adult facilities (both jails and prisons). By 1989 there were over fifty private facilities with over 3,000 beds, and 2,500 additional beds had been approved for private operation. The success in such privately operated facilities is reflected by the fact that only a few states still forbid private management. On the other hand Alaska, Arkansas, Colorado, Florida, Maine, Massachusetts, Montana, New Mexico, Oklahoma, Tennessee, Utah, and Wisconsin have already passed enabling legislation. Arizona, Indiana, New Hampshire, and New Jersey are considering similar legislation (See chap. 5).

Governments usually pay a per diem for each prisoner. Some contracts allow for lower per capita rates as the number of inmates increases. For example, at the Bay County Jail in Panama City, Florida, CCA charges $31.01 for the first 310 inmates, $10 for the next twenty inmates, and $7.50 thereafter (Larson 1988). Indeed, accounting data shows that economies of scale exist in prison operation. As the size of the facility increases, average labor costs diminish, purchasing power rises, and labor is replaced by electronic monitoring. The length of the contracts is usually between three to five years. Most contracts require annual reviews, and fee negotiations. In most states government monitoring is quite intensive and includes site inspections, regular reporting, and immediate notification of unusual occurrences.

Cost comparison of private and publicly operated facilities is quite difficult. The many variables that need to be equated in order to enable fair comparison include the size of facility, length of detention, the security level, mixture of inmate services, and the oversight of the government. Thus, it is best to conduct a cost comparison for a facility which has shifted from public to private management. Apparently the only detailed case study that includes hidden costs is the Hamilton County Penal Farm in Tennessee.

CCA took over the management of Hamilton's minimum to medium prison in 1985 (Logan and McGriff 1989). There are two problems in making the comparison. The first is the hidden costs of a public corrections facility. The facility may use the services of other agencies or cover its expenses from a general fund. Examples of these costs include external administration overhead, legal services, successful legal claims, property insurance, staff training and others that are not part of the direct budget. These costs are estimated at 20 to 35 percent above direct agency costs. The other problem is compatibility of service rendered by the two operators. The Hamilton County comparison took into account those hidden costs that were estimated by the county's auditor. The conservative comparison revealed that private operation saved the county at least $107,440 in 1985-86 or 3.8 percent, 3.0 percent in 1986-87, and 8.1 percent in 1987-88, and still left profits for the contractor. The researchers summarized by stating that 5 to 15 percent savings can be easily defended. As to the second problem, the $5 million liability insurance provided an additional benefit. Other benefits include added training of their own staff who were employed by the contractor, new physical improvements, and improved, new, cheaper construction.

Another cost comparison example is the management of Marion Adjustment Center in St. Mary, Kentucky by the U.S. Corrections Corporation. It reported saving the state $400,000 a year. The direct cost to the state was estimated at $40 per inmate a day while USCC charged $25. In another case, CCA charged Bay County, Florida $29.81 to run its jail compared to self calculated cost of $38 which summed to an annual savings of $700,000.

Critics of privatization are concerned about possible deterioration of the quality of service. However, close monitoring of the operator, legislation which holds the contractor accountable, and selecting of reliable contractors appears to have prevented "cutting corners."

Issues in Privatization

In a study by Hackett et al. (1987), the authors clarified several legal issues and practical steps to be undertaken once a state or local jurisdiction decided to switch operations to the private sector. More recent works of Gemignani (1992), Kiekbusch (1992), and Cooper (chap. 10), have

Introduction

elaborated the issues in light of several more years of privatization efforts.

Is it legal for states and counties to contract with private companies for the operation of prisons and jails? A hidden issue is what happens to government liability when it contracts out. The answer is clear: it is legal unless specifically prohibited by state law. The U.S. Constitution, and federal laws do not prohibit private companies of managing all security types of correction institutions. The government can not shield itself from civil liability stemming from abridged prisoners rights. Government cannot totally divest itself of liability. However, as Cooper states in chap. 9, if a negligent action by the contractor is not related to the government's own negligence in that particular matter, then it does not create liability for the government. A detailed investigation of potential contractors, a proper contract that specifies all the contractor's obligations, and a bond or collateral reserve against any damage award may for all practical purposes shield the government from liability.

Another myth is the belief that private companies are restrained in the use of deadly force. In states that use the Model Penal Code the private contractor is limited in the use of deadly force to the facility itself. An escaped inmate becomes the responsibility of public law enforcement.

Unlike their public counterparts private employees in correctional institutions are allowed to strike. This fact requires that the contract specifies early notification of possible labor unrest or end of union's labor contract. Many private providers that took over entire management of facilities have hired the public employees, raised their pay, and provided better fringe benefits. In case of labor strike or any other emergency situations the state can send the National Guard to assist.

Conclusions

The serious and increasing overcrowding situation of prisons and jails needs imaginative and bold actions to avoid serious social problems and the deterioration of public safety. Regardless of efforts by the public sector, conditions in prisons have been deteriorating with no relief in sight. It is time to make a substantial change; over the 1980s private financing, construction, contracting out, and complete management have provided excellent indications that the private sector can be a capable provider of prison and jail services; costs are lower and the quality of services is higher. If adequate safeguards are provided in the selection and monitoring of private providers of correctional institutions at all levels, we will improve our obligation to public safety and improve services and work training to our inmates. The literature provides us with little theoretical or factual evidence against privatization of correctional institutions at all security levels. The major barrier to privatization appears to be posed by public workers' unions. However, many contractors who took over existing facilities hired their existing staff and worker satisfaction with the change appears high.

In chapter 2, Warren Cikins from the Brookings Institute describes the deteriorated condition of the justice system with particular reference to prisons. He briefly analyzes various solutions which have been suggested in the past, and outlines the private option and the political obstacles to implementing it. As a close associate of Chief Justice Warren Burger, he indicates the importance of private prisons and discusses the significant contribution that the private sector may have in training inmates, and changing their life-style habits.

Professor Robert McCrie from John Jay College of Criminal Justice follows in chap. 3 with historical description of correctional institutions in the U.S. He shows that private prisons are not a new concept and have existed in several forms since the eighteenth century. He argues that the experience gained with prisons for profit does not justify the opposition of the Civil Liberties Union or of the workers' unions. Professor Alexis Durham from Texas Christian University elaborates in chap. 4 upon McCrie's analysis by evaluating the cases of privatization. He examines the concerns of labor, abuses of inmates, and the source and resolution of disputes between the public and the private sectors.

Dana Joel reviews and evaluates in chap. 5 contemporary contracting out, privatization of prison industries, private construction of prisons, and private management of facilities. She provides private-public cost comparisons, addresses quality concerns, and briefly deals with government liability in case of contracting out.

Michael Janus, who is an associate warden of a federal correctional institution, examines in chap. 6 some often unconsidered indirect effects of privatization. He cautions about the symbolism associated with the introduction of profits to the correctional system. Janus is further concerned with possible influences which may be exerted by private vendors on legislators and other public administrators on funding distribution, definition of criminal acts, and length of sentence.

Barbara Auerbach from Criminal Justice Associates, a research concern in Philadelphia, Pennsylvania, reveals in chap. 7 the results of the study conducted for the National Institute of Justice on public/private partnerships in prison industries. She describes the nature, and problems of such partnerships, and makes suggestions for further development of these valuable opportunities for prisoners, governments, and the private sector.

In chapter 8, Dr. Judith Schloegel describes an actual implementation of private industries in Florida. Pride, a non-profit corporation, trains inmate workers and places them in jobs after their release. This successful effort appears to be a good model for transfer to other places.

Mr. Norman Cox, a private consultant, and Professor William Osterhoff from Auburn University continue in chap. 9 the investigation of public-private partnerships. They claim that limited partnership is possible; however they caution that the current climate of emotionalism and mistrust can be anticipated to continue into the future.

Chapters 10 and 11 raise the legal issues of liabilities and prisoners rights. Linda Cooper who is vice president for legal affairs with Corrections Corporation of America, the leading private contractor of corrections in the nation, clarifies in chapter 10 the legal issues that concern many governments which consider contracting-out correctional services. Well specified contracts and limited monitoring will minimize, according to Cooper, government liability.

In chapter 11, Professor Harold Sullivan of John Jay College discusses the topic of prisoners' rights in a private setting and considers the first and the eighth amendments to the Constitution. The author suggests safeguards to insure the protection of such rights under private management of prisons.

A book on privatizing correctional institutions would not be complete and comprehensive without the description and evaluation that the private companies provide. Chapters 12 through 14 present evidence on the experience of the "for-profit" private companies of medium and high security prisons and jails.

In chapter 12, McCullough and McGuigan from Pricor briefly describe minimum security adult and juvenile centers that were constructed, and are managed by the company. By 1991, Pricor was responsible for the operation and management of thirty facilities and programs in six states. Todd Mason of the *Wall Street Journal*, in chapter 13, gives evidence of some cases where privatization promoted typically by small firms is not proving to be as successful as promised. In chapter 14 Wayne Calabrese from Wockenhut's Correctional Corporation elaborates on savings accruing to public agencies of its own management of facilities and gives some tips on improving the contracting out process. Chapter 15 presents a detailed comparison of several matched pairs of privately and publically operated corrections facilities. The data were gathered and analyzed by a team of the Urban Institute which included Harry Hatry, Paul Brounstein, and Robert Levinson.

In the last chapter of the book Professor Charles Thomas from the University of Florida and Professor Charles Logan from the University of Connecticut summarize the main issues and concerns relevant in the evaluation of privatization. Their analysis includes the constitutional, liability, prisoners' rights, and quality concerns, and the cost and accountability issues. The chapter closes with clear prediction for the future of privatization.

Notes

1. Prisons are correctional institutions used to house offenders for a period usually longer than one year. Jails are mostly county facilities used to house pretrial detainees or misdemeanor offenders serving usually less than one year.
2. See Logan and Thomas in chapter 16.

References

Brakel, S. (1992) "Private Corrections" in Bowman, G., S. Hakim, and P. Seidenstat (editors) *Privatizing the Justice System*. Jefferson, North Carolina: McFarland Publishers.
Bureau of Labor Statistics. (1990) *Bulletin*.
———. (1988) *Justice Expenditure and Employment*. (July).
Gemignani, R. (1992) "The Public Sector's Responsibilities in Privatization of Correctional Services." In Bowman, G., S. Hakim, and P. Seidenstat (editors) *Privatizing the Justice System*. Jefferson, North Carolina: McFarland Publishers.
Kiekbusch, R. (1992) "The Privatization of Jails: A Corrections Management Perspective." In Bowman, G, S. Hakim, and P. Seidenstat (editors), *Privatizing the Justice System*. Jefferson,: McFarland Publishers.
Larson, Eric. (1988) "Captive Company." *Inc. Magazine* (June).
Logan, C. (1990) *Private Prisons: Cons and Pros*. New York: Oxford University Press.
Logan, C. and B. McGriff. (1989) "Comparing Costs of Public and Private Prisons: A Case Study." *NIJ Research in Brief Reports*, No. 216, (September/October).
Logan, C. and S. Rausch. (1985) "Punish and Profit: The Emergence of Private Enterprise Prisons." *Justice Quarterly* (September).
Mason, T. (1991) "Many For-Profit Jails Hold No Profit - Nor Even Any Inmates." *The Wall Street Journal*. (June 18).
U. S. Department of Justice. (1990) Bureau of Justice Statistics *Prisoners in 1989*.

2

Partial Privatization of Prison Operations: Let's Give It a Chance

Warren I. Cikins

The runaway situation with regard to prison overcrowding requires innovative planning and actions on the part of public officials at all levels of government if the nation is to prevent enormous social, economic, political, and public safety repercussions. Correctional officials have been striving mightily simply to avoid being run over by the stampede of new inmates being sent to their institutions. Far too little attention is being *given to the impact of the entire* criminal justice system on the correctional process. Legislators routinely enact anticrime proposals that will lead inevitably to greater prison population, without planning for or providing funds for the increased facilities needed.

The additional legislation requiring mandatory minimum sentences, the impact of sentencing guidelines that provide average determinate sentences that are greater than the prior average of indeterminate sentences, and the rising penalties for drug use and abuse, as well as drug distribution, all contribute to a condition of horrendous prison warehousing. This counterproductive development creates the vicious circle of prisons becoming greater crime "schools" that lead their inmates to perpetrate even greater crimes when they get out. Those who argue that prison should make the wrongdoer suffer mightily for his transgressions have certainly won the day. In prisons, violence is on the increase; idleness is rampant; corruption is growing within the system through the establishment of efficient drug distribution mechanisms. Those who are committed to humane treatment, those who believe in the possibility of rehabilitation, and those who simply recognize that enlightened self-interest requires giving inmates a chance to become literate and to be trained in a marketable occupation, find themselves embattled.

Since I first became involved in efforts to reduce prison populations in 1979, the prison population of the United States has doubled. I can only conjecture that, without my efforts and the efforts of others dedicated to the same objectives, it might have tripled. We observe, only half in jest, that if the same rate of incarceration continues or the rate increases somewhat, the number of people in prison in the year 2053 will be greater than those who are out of prison. Much of the political leadership of the nation over the years in both parties has chosen to inflame the passions of the American people rather than educate them about the causes of the problem and sound approaches to its being reduced.

Lest one despair of the future, it should be noted that a significant minority of elected officials, senior government officials, corrections professionals, religious leaders, business leaders, labor leaders, members of the media and academicians have recognized that the federal, state, and local correctional situation is in disarray and requires corrective actions. One of the most important persons in that regard has been retired chief justice Warren Earl Burger, who was known to have said, while Chief Justice, something to the effect that, if we had deliberately tried to, we could not have created a more incompetent and disordered criminal justice system. While this wide range of persons represents the whole spectrum of ideology and politics, its diversity is its strength. Creditable appeals can be made to persons from all sectors of society to gather together to help create a climate of acceptance of rational options to existing practices.

What are the options to these existing practices? In the hope of reducing prison population, numerous "intermediate" sentencing options have been devised by corrections specialists. They range from intensive supervision probation (ISP) programs, to such intermediate sanctions programs as house arrest, to electronic monitoring devices, to greater surveillance of probationers, to third-party supervision of community service, to "shock" incarceration or what is called "boot camp" correctional undertakings, to greater use

Partial Privatization of Prison Operations

of halfway house facilities, to victim compensation (often after victim/offender mediation), to intermittent incarceration.

Each of these techniques is being utilized in a number of states and localities, but the total number of persons involved is a small percentage of the number of persons incarcerated. There remains a strong need to convince the public, legislators, the media, the judiciary, and all those involved in the criminal justice system that these sanctions should be fully utilized. Until that development takes place, prisons and jails will continue to receive the preponderant number of those convicted of crimes, and these institutions will continue to become even more overcrowded.

If prison overcrowding is to be the dominant pattern well into the future, how do we plan to deal with it? Some scholars and practitioners argue that we should refuse to build more prisons because we will simply fill all the space we create whether we need it or not. This is an easy arrangement to accept, since it *avoids* the difficult effort of obtaining more funds, in general, for construction and public acceptance of the increased expenditure of public funds, in particular. What appears to be a progressive point of view on its face, however, leads to the unfortunate result of creating deteriorating conditions in existing prisons. It allows a misinformed public to have it both ways, urging a policy of being very "tough" on crime and avoiding the need to raise taxes to pay for the costs. An even more unfortunate development takes place in some states with more funds being allocated for prisons at the expense of education, environment, health, and other crucial needs.

It is this condition that leads me to look to the private sector to provide at least a partial answer. While I can see no necessary conflict between the profit motive and the provision of humane prisons built and operated by the private sector, some conventional criminologists seem unable to accept this possibility. It is not meant as an affront to many public correctional officers who are struggling valiantly to deal with impossible conditions to say that any visit to correctional facilities today leads one to argue that it would be no great challenge to the private sector to do better. One certainly does not have to advocate major upheaval of the correctional system to see a useful role for private involvement.

Private involvement can obviously ease overcrowding by making more facilities quickly available without the cumbersome and costly process of gaining public approvals. Many years ago when I worked for the Tennessee Valley Authority, one justification for the production and distribution of public power was that it could serve as a yardstick of economy and efficiency for the private sector, even though it was not anticipated that the public sector would exceed 5 percent of the total production. One can apply the same concept to endorse the role of the private sector in setting an example for the public sector in providing efficient and humane prison conditions.

There must be a major effort made to overcome the objections of some prison officials and labor unions to the utilization of the private sector. There must be safeguards established and monitored by state authorities that would ease the fear that pay and training would suffer, that profit considerations would lead to improper cost cutting, and that the private authorities would apply punishments inappropriately. At the same time, it should be made clear that the governmental "monopoly" on delivering correctional services is *not* necessarily constitutionally mandated, but, that in this area, as in so many others, the challenge of competition can improve the performance of *both* sectors.

While devotion to democratic processes is a treasured American principle, one might argue that with regard to the availability of prison space, we are not dealing with a principle, but a condition. To put it bluntly, the private sector offers state and local governments a way of financing prison and jail construction that avoids citizen approval of bond issues or jurisdictional debt limits. The most popular method is the lease/purchase agreement that involves the government leasing a facility with the option of purchasing. It is appealing to private sector investors, according to such investment houses as Merrill Lynch and Shearson Lehman. The governmental unit can move more rapidly and certainly, although whether this action is more economical is debatable.

Once the facility is built, the governmental entity is in a position to contract with a private correctional corporation to provide management of the facility. Such an arrangement may be established, whether or not the government is prepared to purchase the facility. Since this approach remains quite controversial, and widespread favorable experience has not yet been fully documented, the prudent approach would be to continue to focus on such minimum security needs or community-based facilities, youth correctional operations with low security needs, and other operations where the primary needs are for housing for a relatively short period of incarceration. It might also be feasible to experiment with private management of medium security facilities where the circumstances are most conducive to success. A great majority of the states and hundreds of counties are already exploring this option, with a small but growing number of governmental units actually "taking the plunge."

Those who oppose these developments have taken to the courts, as they should, to challenge their constitutionality, legality, and morality. They argue that only government can legitimately exercise the police power and that it cannot or should not be delegated to the private sector. They further maintain that the operation of correctional facilities is one of the central reasons why governments exist. With great finality, they assert that the government cannot escape liability when it delegates these activities to private prison owners or operators. The answer to that concern is that they are quite correct, but that the liability issue in no way precludes the utilization of the private sector. Both the state and the private operator are considered liable. Appropriate insurance should be made available to cover all private sector contingencies. Let us leave constitutional and legal questions to the courts to decide.

A more central question is whether the profit motive can be considered consistent with professional and humane treatment of inmates. Society is replete with examples of how the profit motive has measured up well to this requirement. To coin a phrase, one might call it "capitalism with a human face." If one wishes to, one can suggest or even cite a number of instances where the profit motive can run amuck. Does the same critic worry about existing prisons where drugs can easily be obtained, where training programs are undermined by drug dependency coupled with overcrowding, and where human brutality manifests itself without the profit motive being a factor?

Safeguards against all the real, imagined, or possible horrors that can take place in prisons must be undertaken, monitored, and enforced, whether the facility is public *or* private. One cannot evaluate the performance of the private sector with regard to some ideal of public prison operation, but rather against the reality of existing prison drug infestation, low pay and morale of many public employees, high turnover and poor training of many corrections officers, and the deteriorating possibilities of literacy training and meaningful job training of inmates in overcrowded prisons.

Those of us who worked closely with Chief Justice Warren Burger in the early 1980s in his efforts to create "factories within fences," or effective prison industries, welcome his return to this theme, a commitment of more than twenty years, after his invaluable contribution as chairman of the Constitutional Bicentennial Commission. In a keynote address to the National Conference of State Chief Justices on 21 January 1990, Chief Justice Burger characterized the jails and prisons of America as "institutions that penalize and punish but do not correct, improve, educate, or train." He has provided great leadership in attracting private sector interest and involvement in training inmates and teaching them life-style habits that will maximize their chances of returning to a law-abiding existence upon release.

Those corporations that have utilized prisoner personnel to produce products or provide services have done so in a manner that has been profit motivated at the same time as their efforts have contributed to social and societal objectives. There is no reason to doubt that private initiatives to construct and operate prisons have the same motivations. There is also no reason to rely on good faith alone; state and local authorities can establish a range of safeguards that should guarantee that profit motivated excesses are curbed and unprofessional behavior identified and dealt with.

This analysis is not meant to pit the private sector against the public sector. There are many dedicated public officials and corrections officers who are working against insurmountable odds to maintain civilized and efficient correctional institutions. In a climate where the public is clamoring for mandatory sentences, greater numbers of persons incarcerated, and longer terms of imprisonment, however, our correctional facilities are in danger of being totally overwhelmed. The entire criminal justice system, indeed, is in danger of being overwhelmed, as many judges are making quite clear. Prison overcrowding requires a continual search for innovative methods of reducing explosive pressures.

I must confess that I do become somewhat impatient with those criminologists who utter pious platitudes about the need to improve the way the public sector delivers correctional services, without offering any practical or pragmatic recommendations to meet the challenge. Intermediate sanctions do offer some real hope of reducing prison overcrowding, but a major effort must be mounted by all advocates of these sanctions to gain greater public acceptance of their application. Blueprints must be designed and implemented to educate federal, state, and local legislators about the virtues of these sanctions, the media must be enlisted to champion this cause, and religious, business, and labor leaders must convince their constituencies that these innovative methodologies are workable and morally acceptable. All sectors of society must become involved, and the private sector can and should make a meaningful contribution.

3

Private Correction: The Delicate Balance

Robert D. McCrie

In urban capitalistic societies citizens are expected to provide many services and requirements for themselves, and to do so to the greatest extent possible. In social-welfare oriented societies a similar ethos exists, though not to so great an extent. With the development of the modern city, urban services were initially provided by private means but over time, for various reasons, some of these services were assumed by the public. This transfer of a service from a private to a public provider did not occur easily. For example, firefighting services were provided by the government only when the private sector could not resolve the issue of whether an obligation existed to provide services to those who refused to pay for them (Chaudacoff 1975; Smith 1972; Conley and Campbell 1985).

Clearly, such services are provided for the public by the government due to historical, philosophical, and practical factors. Since its early history the United States at all levels of government has vacillated on the question: What is the role of government in the lives of its citizens, and what, therefore, are reasonable services that government should provide? Regardless of the debate on the quantity, quality, and nature of such services, a long-held tenet in American thought is that government spends more in providing these services than what the services would cost if provided by private enterprise. Thomas Jefferson argued that, all things being equal, the private sector manages services better than government does itself:

> Having always observed that public works are always much less advantageously managed than the same are by private hands, I have thought it better for the public to go to the market for whatever it wants which is found there, for there competition brings it down to the minimum value. (Caldwell 1944, 161)

Jefferson recognized in theory that cost looms as a significant differential between the public and the private sector; however, what services government should provide out of innate obligation is a different issue. The types of services government finds itself providing can change over time. For example, urban public transportation was provided by for-profit businesses that received a government-issued franchise to operate. Later, such businesses failed or were otherwise taken under the control of government and operated. Then, some transportation services—owned by government—granted management contracts to private organizations to run the systems. Hence, a system begun as a private service became publicly owned and operated, and then returned some operations to the private sector.[1] The debate on privatization is very lively, inasmuch as the word, understood as a public service transferred to private enterprise, first appeared in dictionaries only in the 1980s (Cellers 1988). Currently, private businesses and organizations provide a vast array of services in the U.S., from large projects, such as the operation of entire government energy facilities or space centers for the federal government,[2] to less philosophically questionable, more recreational services such as operating public golf courses for municipalities (Carlson 1991). Privatization seems to be breaking new ground in entering public service areas where they previously didn't exist. In Florida, a private company has been contracted to operate an elementary public school near Miami Beach (Holmes 1990). Further, the U.S. Postal Service has approved a contract to print postage stamps privately.[3] And the trend is not limited to the United States. Indeed, nations of diverse political ideology are at various stages of privatizing market sectors or considering the possibilities.

One category of services commonly provided by contemporary governments is embodied in the expression "the criminal justice system."

Private Correction: The Delicate Balance

Allen and Simonsen point out that three elements make up this collective group of services as encountered in the United States:

> The American criminal justice system is, in fact, many separate systems of institutions and procedures. The thousands of American villages, towns, cities, counties, states—and even the federal government—all have criminal justice 'systems' of sorts. Though they may appear similar in that all function to apprehend, prosecute, convict, and sentence lawbreakers, no two are exactly alike. . . . The criminal justice system is composed of three separate subsystems—police, courts, and corrections—each with its own tasks. (Allan and Simonsen 1989, 126)

Currently, American criminal justice services are widely perceived as traditional, essential, and, in many respects, inextricable parts of government's obligation to the public. But are they? Interest in the privatization of public services has spread to criminal justice activities, spurred by private and public initiatives (Donahue 1989). Indeed, a review of the origins of the three subsystems of criminal justice reveals that in some ways the private provision of such services antedated their being provided by government; in other ways privatization features coexisted with or were suppressed by the growth of public institutions. The current waxing of interest in aspects of criminal justice services privatization has roots in American colonial times, roots that originated in the Anglo-Saxon legal tradition and date from the period before laws were written.[4]

This chapter reviews historical, economic, and political antecedents for one aspect of the criminal justice system—corrections (McCrie 1992). Privatization, as a term, can cover five types of formal arrangements: sale of government-owned assets; abolition or relaxation of monopolies held by nationalized industries; the Build-Operate-Transfer agreement under which a private company agrees to build a major project and to operate it for an agreed-upon length of time; financing by customer fees—"pay for use"—rather than by taxes; and contracting-out of public services to the private sector.5 This chapter will concentrate on the contracting-out of private correctional services to supplement or replace their public counterpart. Similarly, prisons for profit may reflect a combination of two types of privatization, contracting-out and Build-Operate-Transfer for the penal facility itself.

The Distinction Between Public & Private Interests

Albeit small in numbers, private prisons and correctional programs have received extraordinary public attention in recent years (Donahue 1989; Keating 1985; Logan 1990; McDonald; Press 1987). Nevertheless, in many ways this current social phenomenon is firmly rooted in earlier privately operated forms. Excluding the consideration of jails and prisons for military and political purposes, the evolution of such institutions for criminal incarceration followed a pattern that increasingly reflected the growth of urbanization. Thus, in the seventeenth century, as the new nation grew, the requirements for jails and prisons increased.

> Crimes which in the Old World depended upon anonymity for their success were impossible in the American wilderness. Everyone knew everyone else; in fact, most were related by blood or marriage. Identification of criminals (or strangers who were watched for illegal behavior) was a simple matter, and flight to avoid prosecution meant living a precarious existence among compassionate Indians or being tortured to a slow death by tribes less friendly to white settlers. (Johnson 1988)

By contrast urban centers tended to deal with criminals by rapid dispatch: death, whippings, brandings, fines, financial restitution, public humiliation, transportation, and other punishments. Policing and corrections as known today are traced by organizational structure to the mid-eighteenth century. Previously, a constable with assistant constables provided the law enforcement during the day. In some communities, the constables received little pay depending upon fees from the service of legal documents to make a living. Constables interacted with the night watch, an obligatory service of all citizens. If the constables alone or with the aid of the watch took prisoners, the constables would present them to a magistrate at court as soon as possible. Jail might be one of the sanctions on the person arrested. In the eighteenth century extended periods of incarceration became an increasingly acceptable punishment in America. Deterrence and retribution were reasons for favoring extended imprisonment over more summary options and became the fashionable mode for dealing with criminality. The Marquis de Beccaria's *Essay on Crimes and Punishments* (1766), for example, emphasized the value of deterrence as a factor in prison confinement (Johnson 1988). Yet, even in the eighteenth century, continental and American observers saw that no simple relationship existed between the administration of harsh sanctions and crime reduction; nonetheless, the public penchant for incarceration for violent and property crimes became a routine sanction.

One common reason for incarceration was personal debt.[6] The individual imprisoned for failure to meet his or her financial obligations faced dire circumstances. Jailers demanded payment for their services in addition to the costs borne by prisoners for their food, clothing, firewood, and other necessities. Clearly, the prisoner incarcerated for debt faced the distressing situation of going deeper into debt for the very reason he or she was there. Work, if available, provided one means by which a prisoner might pay jail costs during incarceration.

Although appointed by government, a head jailer could be construed as being an independent operator of a for-profit enterprise functioning as a sole source government contractor. Often jailers provided employment for prisoners. The results of their efforts might be the production of items the jailer could sell; this was important for the impecunious prisoner. Prisoners could earn enough to buy their way out of debtors' prison and, possibly, to have sufficient money to exist briefly after being released from confinement. By contrast, wealthy prisoners could command a different ambiance: the best foods could be brought in; the prisoner might have a private bedroom with personal furnishings and ample heat; prostitutes, friends, and business or professional contacts could visit as they wished. For all of these accommodations, of course, a price had to be paid to the jailer, who depended on such income as an expected part of his compensation.

For much of the correctional history of the United States, prisoners have been expected to generate a profit for the institution or at least pay their own way if a profit wasn't feasable. That meant that, if prisoners could not produce saleable items within prison, they might be leased to private farms or businesses to generate income. This practice was particularly popular in the southern states beginning in the mid-nineteenth century. For instance, the Texas prison at Huntsville operated a cotton mill, beginning in 1854. During the Civil War convicts and free laborers produced products for public sale. Following the Civil War, the market for such cotton products declined; then the Thirteenth Amendment to the Constitution abolished slavery, creating a shortage of field hands for plantations, and prisoners took up the gap (Martin and Ekland-Olson 1987). In 1866, the Texas legislature approved a Board of Public Labor and directed its members to contract-out prisoners' services to the private community. Prisoners were organized to work on farms, railroads, in mines, and other private enterprises in addition to public work on roads and waterways. They were deemed "slaves of the state" in an 1871 decision, *Ruffin v. Commonwealth*[7] that was to justify their peonage for years to come. Texas experimented with privatizing the Huntsville prison because it was not generating a profit despite dual income from the cotton mill and the inmate leasing efforts. Prison conditions under the private initiative soon declined, and a legislative committee investigated alleged mismanagement and cruelty (Martin and Ekland-Olson 1987). The legislative investigation attacked the "infamous lessee system," which resulted in modification to the leasing system in which the state maintained control of the penitentiary and convicts but continued contracting arrangements with private interests beginning in 1883 (Martin and Ekland-Olson 1987). By 1885, thirteen states had turned part of their inmate populations over to private contractors; by 1923, no state continued the practice. (Kelly 1986)

What Need for Private Prisons?

In the latter nineteenth century in America, the concept of the jailer as an independent contractor subsided in urban prisons. The change in jails and prisons followed a similarly profound modification of policing. Prisons had gone through two philosophical experiments in the nineteenth century. The first model began in post-Revolutionary Philadelphia where a type of prison discipline espoused by Quakers was promulgated. Prisoners were sentenced to a confinement of complete silence, giving the convict ample time for penitence—hence the word "penitentiary." They were given large cells where they remained for the extent of their confinement. Even during church services prisoners would sit in laterally walled boxes that prevented them from seeing or speaking with others. Prisoners in the Walnut Street institution in Philadelphia did not work. Despite the sincerity and conviction of the Walnut Street staff, many prisoners committed suicide or had emotional breakdowns. The experiment had drawn much interest from abroad and had some influence on European jail reform but eventually was considered a failure. A variation of the Philadelphia model sought to incorporate work into the regime. In the Auburn, New York prison, communal work was reintroduced as part of the prisoner's daily activity, though such work was to be conducted in silence; prisoners were returned to their solitary cells at other times. This experiment also failed, but the concept of having prisoners work, if possible, became a norm for American prisons again thereafter.

As prison systems expanded throughout the states, admininistration of them was relegated to bureaucracies that sought a level of standardization; similar treatment for all convicts and minimum facilities became the pattern for state prisons administration. Wardens and staff were paid salaries set by the government, and the institutions sought to be as fully self-supporting as possible, providing much of their own food, clothing, and furniture. This pattern of government providing as many services as possible by its own personnel became the goal, and still is in many ways, in state and federal prisons. However, the high costs of operating such systems have never been exceeded by convict income despite persistent and intense efforts to make the system pay its own way.

Gradually in the twentieth century a trend began for the out-contracting of various services by jails and prisons. These institutions had long out-contracted for medical, dental, and psychological services. Now the facilities were seeking outside sources for food preparation and educational services. More recently, governments have been willing to contract out for an increasing part of the incarceration program including total facility design, construction, and management.[8]

Why might units of United States government at federal, state, and local levels consider contracting-out a service that had for so many years been inextricably linked philosophically to what government is supposed to do? Clearly, several fundamental changes in society made such a shift possible.

The rapid increase in the incarceration option was one leading factor. Incarceration has been increasing steadily in the United States, by absolute numbers and on a population-adjusted basis; further, the United States distanced itself in this regard from other developed nations. Although statistical comparisons of one nation's crime data with another are invariably risky propositions, analysts generally accept the premise that far more individuals are incarcerated in the United States than in other industrialized nations for which data are available. By 1970, the number of persons incarcerated in the United States by this measurement increased at a rate much faster than that experienced in selected other nations. Mathiesen, a Norwegian criminologist, compares the growth of crime in the U.S. with England/Wales, Italy, and West Germany.

In 1970, the United States exceeded the incarceration levels of these nations with about 180 prisoners per 100,000 population; by 1985, it was almost 320, an increase of about 78 percent in fifteen years. By 1990, the relative and absolute number of prisoners in the United States had grown even more (Mathiesen 1990). Other nations also experienced a prison systems growth. Italy increased from over forty to over seventy per 100,000 for the same period of time, an increase of about 75 percent. England/Wales also increased during this same period of time from under eighty to almost one hundred per 100,000, but this change represents a greater increase if compared with its low point in 1974. West Germany shows a decline in the number of prisoners on a population adjusted basis (Mathiesen 1990).

The pressure of increased incarceration overwhelmed the ability of many governmental areas to meet requirements. Federal and state prisons were filled beyond their capacity, and legally active prisoners and advocates sought early release of some prisoners to make room for others more recently sentenced. The public thus reluctantly but unwaveringly tended to approve increases in cell capacity to meet the steadily growing number of inmates being shuttled toward prison gates.

Meanwhile, a new model of prison management had come into vogue: the concept of the prison as a rehabilitative environment. The idea wasn't new; juveniles in particular had always been considered likely candidates for rehabilitation. Juvenile prisoners generally had been separated from adults since the nineteenth century, and their environment often provided work, trade skills, education, and psychological support to help the young convict break the destructive pattern and assume a conventional role in society. Now this group of services would be offered to adult prisoners, some of whom had experienced early incarceration in juvenile facilities. The great surge of rehabilitatively oriented penal financing commenced during President Johnson's tenure. The "Great Society" program threw financial resources at problems to solve them; prison management and recidivism were two of these issues. The great phase of rehabilitative incarceration had begun. Large numbers of prisoners in the United States and elsewhere received training, counseling, and increased support on release from their institutions. Similarly, other industrialized nations picked up the rehabilitative vogue in their comparatively smaller-scaled programs.

After sufficient passage of time to assess results, the conclusion from such intensive efforts was not encouraging. Mathiesen, asks the question, "Does prison have a defense in rehabilitation?" His answer may be put very briefly: "An overwhelming amount of material, historical as well as sociological, leads to a clear and unequivocal *no*." (Mathiesen 1990, 47) In a volume of papers entitled *Are Prisons Any Better? Twenty Years of Correctional Reform*, over a dozen U.S. contributors generally reach negative conclusions on the prospects of reducing crime or recidivism from correctional measures as practiced in the past generation. The authors of the study conclude, "(T)he prison system in the United States is in disarray. . . . Everyone appears to be afraid to take the risks that are necessary to depart from existing approaches and chart a new course for prison reform" (Murphy and Dison 1990, 163).

Thus a confluence of three factors has enabled privatization of correctional facilities to emerge as an acceptable operational concept: the growing cost of incarceration; the failure of costly, extensive, and well-intentioned rehabilitative experiments; and the willingness of government and the public to consider privatization of incarceration.

America's previous experience with private prisons was a failure, breeding inhumanity and provoking public outcry. Presumably, a new era of prison privatization would not repeat the outrages of the past because of the contemporary climate of judicial activism: a judge can order changes in a facility because it fails to meet agreed-to standards, constitutional or other legal guarantees of the inmates, or for other reasons. Indeed, at least one private prison contractor requires that the contracting agency maintain agents on the site to monitor contract compliance.

Today, the prison-for-profit industry remains small, representing perhaps only twenty or thirty private correction facilities, depending on the definitions of private and correctional.[9] The most notable company is the Corrections Corporation of America (CCA), based in Nashville and begun in 1983 by founders and investors who had earlier started Kentucky Fried Chicken.[10] This corporation reported its first profit in the fourth quarter of 1989 and now owns or operates four county jails, two juvenile detention centers, two penal work camps, two alien detention units, and two minimum-security state prisons.[11] To date, CCA has been highly lauded for the professionalism of its services. The managers and executives of CCA include numerous correctional officials with broad experience. Pricor, also based in Nashville, operates five correctional facilities and issued shares to the public in a stock offering floated in 1989. Other major corporations interested in the prison-operating industry include Wackenhut, a publicly held security guard company, and Bechtel, a privately held contractor that seek to construct and operate two Texas prisons. A score or more of other private organizations established for profit currently operate facilities or hope to do so when they can receive contracts.

Most of this discussion has concerned adult prison programs. This includes low and medium security centers, jails, and temporary detention centers and services for such organizations as the U.S. Immigration and Naturalization Service and the Customs Service. The private sector seems more successful at obtaining newer types of custodial facilities, like the INS and Customs contracts, instead of conventional jails and prisons with their decades old procedures and staffing relationships. However, for the industry to succeed on a grand scale, greater numbers of contracts for conventional facilities must be received by the fledgling industry participants.

Juvenile facilities in America have often been operated by not-for-profit institutions such as church and other charitable groups since at least the early eighteenth century. Facilities for juveniles that are operated by the private sector tend to be small, residential, education-oriented, and flexible in programming (Fox 1985). Such facilities may be better operated by private initiatives than by government, although many government managers currently underwrite such programs. Pricor is seeking to expand its juvenile correctional management programs following its public offering of stock in 1989.[12] Another "market segment" in which the private sector is active concerns home monitoring of offenders. Under such a system, usually a nonviolent, first-time offender is sentenced to remain within his/her residence for specified times. The offender is monitored electronically by a cuff that is "interrogated" periodically by a nearby central processing unit that sends a prerecorded message to a monitoring center if anticipated signals are not received (Goss 1990). In many cases the system is installed and monitored by private sector businesses, though monitoring by police is an option. A monitoring service may call the police to arrest the offender who is not apparently within the prescribed area and possibly incarcerate the individual for violating the system.

The years ahead will provide "no escape" from the growing needs of incarceration facilities (DiIulio 1991). Less than two percent of the market for adult prisoners is currently served by for-profit services; further, many areas of the country apparently are uninterested in the privatization option, or are determined to keep it as a demonstration program to countervail the power of governmental employees' unions and established relationships. CCA endeavored to operate the entire prison system for the state of Tennessee in the 1980s; however, the state government did not agree to the proposal. Private prisons have run credibly well to date, so future growth is expected, but how robust a future? Continued growth depends upon the leaders in the field managing their businesses with efficiency, integrity, and profitability. It is conceivable that some governmental managers could layer on additional requirements to the operations of these facilities without providing additional commensurate income to the contractor, resulting in unforeseeable profitability. Such a development could ring the death knell to this fragile industry. Although it should be in the interests of government executives to see that private contractors make a profit, in reality that is not a typical attitude enunciated by government contracting agents. An unintentional confederation of tight-fisted contracting agents, government workers' unions, and judicial advocates pushing for costly and unanticipated program modifications could destroy prison privatization before it celebrates the end of its second decade. Given the fact that prisons for profit now exist in the United States, albeit at a minor level, the question may be raised, should the phenomenon exist at all? Confinement represents one of the most particular powers of government. Economic or cost-cutting issues aside, does government have the right—morally or philosophically—to jettison a service that seems to be such an inherent responsibility of the collective public?

DiIulio, an academic interested in prison issues, burlesques the concept of private prisons or even a private correctional system:

> Suppose that CCA has made it really big. They have proved that they can do every thing the privatizers have promised and more. The corporation decides to branch out. The company changes its name to CJCA: the Criminal Justice Corporation of America. It provides a full range of criminal justice services: cops, courts, and corrections. In an unguarded moment, a CJCA official boasts that "our firm can arrest 'em, try 'em, lock 'em up, and, if need be, fry 'em for less." Is there anything wrong with CJCA? . . . Implicit in the "farming out" of such responsibility is a denial of the group's moral integrity. (DiIulio 1991, 199-200)

Surprisingly, perhaps, no vast public sector has emerged to express shock or shame at the concept of prisons for profit. Private for-profit organizations offer an extensive variety of services to government that are taken for granted. Objections to privatization of prisons on principle continue to characterize some critics, though clearly most public-interest groups have taken a wait-and-see attitude toward the concept. Only prison guards' unions, other similar government employees' unions, and the American Civil Liberties Union have systematically opposed the concept of prisons for profit. All research to date indicates that privatization lowers costs to the taxpayer, even taking into consideration hidden expenses for program administration. Other issues remain to be evaluated in the years ahead. Legal challenges have not restrained private prison operations to date. An unanswered question for the future relates to the inherent conflict in this type of service: private prisons make money by making sure that prison beds are filled. Thus, at present, no incentive exists for private prisons to take any actions that might reduce the recidivist rate thus lowering revenues in the future for these private contractors. But then again, the wardens and jailers in the U.S. for the past century haven't had much incentive to do this either.

Notes

1. An example might be the subway system of New York which started as a for-profit enterprise franchised by the city government. Two competing systems prospered for many years. When bankruptcy eventually threatened, the city purchased the assets, combined the two with a third subway company, and eventually ran the system as a public service. The next phase was to turn the operation over to a quasi-public independent operation which had the mandate of managing systems and turning a profit from all managed assets.
2. An example would be the Savannah River Project operated by a private contractor for the Department of Energy, or Cape Canaveral operated by a private contractor for the National Aeronautical and Space Administration.
3. Not only was the contract given to a private company, but that organization through a subcontractor had the work partially done in Canada.
4. Hammurabi produced the Babylonian Codes, about 2000 BC, the first written rules for internal, nonmilitary conduct. It is not known if nonmilitary police existed to carry out the codes, if so, they could be history's first police. In subsequent millennia history was marked with examples of societies which sought to mitigate the strength of the army from sapping internal liberties. Police originated, in part, from this need.
5. In some cases communities are more interested in having private corporations do the design and construction of the facility, but not its later management. This is because it is widely perceived by government executives that, given the opportunity,

a private firm is likely to be more efficient than a government planning and construction management agency.
6. Incarceration for debt continued until the early nineteenth century in American cities. The death by starvation of at least two debtors in Philadelphia, turned the judicial tide against locking up people who couldn't pay their bills.
7. *Ruffin v. Commonwealth*, 62 Va. 790, 796 (1871).
8. Sometimes government is willing to sell a prison to help solve a budget crisis. The private corporation which "buys" the prison then leases it back to government at a previously agreed-to rate that guaranties profit to the "buyer."
9. Many nonprofit organizations that provide services to the correctional sector build in profits for their work, though technically the organizations are tax exempt.
10. Annual report of the Correctional Corporation of America.
11. CCA financial press releases.
12. Offering memorandum of Pricor.

References

Allan, H.E., Simonsen, C.E. (1989) *Corrections in America: An Introduction.* 5th ed. New York: Macmillan, 126.

Caldwell, L.K. (1944) *The Administrative Theories of Hamilton and Jefferson.* Chicago: University of Chicago Press, 161.

Carlson, E. (1991) "Privatization Lets Small Firms Manage Everything From Libraries to Golf Courses." *Wall Street Journal*, April 2, B1.

Cellers, M.P. (1988) "*The History and Development of Private Prisons in the United States.*" Unpublished Ph.D. dissertation, Philadelphia: Temple University, 4.

Chaudacoff, H.P. (1975) *The Evolution of American Urban Society.* Englewood Cliffs, NJ: Prentice-Hall.

Conley, P.T. and P. R. Campbell. (1985) *Firefighters and Fires in Providence.* Providence: Rhode Island Publications Society.

Dean, S.C. (1986) "Electronic Monitoring and Control: Rapidly Changing World. *Corrections Today*, July: 36-38.

DiIulio, J.J., Jr. (1991) *No Escape: The Future of American Corrections.* New York: Basic Books.

Donahue, J.D. (1989) *The Privatization Decision: Public Ends, Private Means.* New York: Basic Books.

Fox, V. (1985) *Introduction to Corrections.* Englewood Cliffs, NJ: Prentice-Hall.

Goss, M. (1990) "Serving Time Behind the Front Door—Electronic Monitoring Programs Provide Prison Alternatives." *Corrections Today*, July, 80.

Healey, B.(1991) "The First US Stamp Made Outside the US." *New York Times.* March 29: A10.

Holmes, S.A. (1990) "In Florida, a Private Company Will Operate a Public School." *New York Times.* December 7: 1.

Johnson, H.A. (1988) *History of Criminal Justice.* Cincinnati: Anderson Publishing.

Keating, J.M., Jr. (1985) *Seeking Profit in Punishment: The Private Management of Correctional Institutions.* Washington, DC: AFSCME.

Kelly, D. (1986) Statement before the Subcommittee on Courts, Civil Liberties and Administration of Justice, Committee on the Judiciary, U.S. House of Representatives. *The Privatization of Corrections.* Nov. 11. Washington, DC: U.S. Government Printing Office, 23.

Logan, C.H. (1990) *Private Prisons - Cons and Pros*. New York, Oxford University Press.

Martin, S.J. and S. Ekland-Olson (1987) *Texas Prisons - The Walls Came Tumbling Down*. Austin: Texas Monthly Press.

Mathiesen, T. (1990) *Prison on Trial: A Critical Assessment*. Newbury Park, CA: SAGE Publications.

McCrie, R.D. (1992) "Three Centuries of Criminal Justice Privatization in the United States." Bowman, G., S. Hakim, and P. Seidenstat (editors). *The Privatization of the Justice System*. Jefferson, NC: McFarland Publishers.

McDonald, D. ed. (1990) *Private Prisons and Public Policy*. New Brunswick, NJ: Rutgers University Press.

Murphy, J.W. and J.E. Dison, editors. (1990) *Are Prisons Any Better? Twenty Years of Correctional Reform*. Newbury Park, CA: SAGE Publications.

Press, A. (1987) "A Person, not a Number: Slowly, Private Prisons are Finding Their Niche." *Newsweek*, June 24: 63.

Smith D. (1972) *Report From Engine Company 82*. New York: Saturday Review Press.

4

The Future of Correctional Privatization: Lessons from the Past

Alexis M. Durham III

In 1976 RCA Services, a private company, assumed control of the Weaversville Intensive Treatment unit located in North Hampton, Pennsylvania. This facility was designed to handle male delinquents. Although the private sector had long been involved in providing a wide range of correctional services, such as linen, food, medical, and program services (Camp and Camp 1984), this was the first modern institution for serious offenders to be completely operated in what has become an increasingly lengthy line of such institutions in the American correctional system.

The early 1980s were characterized by vigorous debate regarding the propriety of expanding private sector involvement in the correctional system. Advocates argued that private industry could assume responsibility for various aspects of the penal system with greater administrative efficiency, resulting in significant cost savings (Logan and Rausch 1985; Fenton 1985; Hutto 1990). Such cost claims are of special interest in light of the rapidly increasing prison population. The prison population more than doubled in the decade of the eighties, and now exceeds 800,000 inmates (*Bureau of Justice Statistics, 1992,* 2). States, as well as the federal government, scurried to create adequate space to house new prison admissions. As of the beginning of 1990 more than 5.5 billion dollars had been allocated to new prison construction (Camp and Camp 1990, 34). Such capacity-increasing efforts have had at best limited success. Thirty-eight states are under court order for institutional crowding and conditions related to crowding (Camp and Camp 1990, 6).

During the last five years of the 1980s a number of privately owned or operated correctional facilities were opened. The Corrections Corporation of America alone operates approximately twenty facilities nationwide. Although early institutions tended to be detention centers or minimum security facilities, interest in private operation of higher security level institutions has been growing, and corporations such as CCA now control several such facilities.

Nonetheless, the appropriateness of private sector involvement in owning or operating adult penal institutions is far from settled. The American Bar Association, American Civil Liberties Union, National Sheriff's Association, American Jail Association, American Correctional Association, American Federation of State, County, and Municipal Employees, and AFL-CIO have gone on record either as opponents of such privatization, or as voices asking for a moratorium on further expansion of the private sector's involvement in adult corrections. Data on the effectiveness of private facilities, in areas such as cost effectiveness for instance, are still sparse, and do not permit confident predictions about the ultimate wisdom of private sector involvement in corrections (Logan 1989). Some of the issues remaining unsettled will not be answered conclusively until private companies have had a fair chance to show what they can accomplish. This seems to suggest that we must be content to wait until the chips fall where they may before making a realistic assessment of the prospects of private sector correctional involvement.

There are, however, several reasons why such an approach is less than entirely satisfactory. First, if private industry is not able to accomplish its objectives valuable time and effort that might well have been invested elsewhere will have been squandered. Second, there are historical data that may provide insight into the likely success of private sector initiatives in corrections. Finally, the lessons of that historical record may be used either to support foreclosure of further pursuit of private avenues for handling correctional problems, or to anticipate and avoid such problems.

This paper represents an effort to contribute to the ongoing discussion regarding the merits of private sector participation in corrections. Contrary to the common understanding, correctional privatization is far from being a modern innovation. The nineteenth century was a period of heavy involvement of private industry in the execution of correctional responsibilities. The record of this involvement provides insight into a wide range of dilemmas that may have relevance to the modern interest in privatizing corrections. This discussion examines four such potential problem areas, and describes some of the American experience relevant to these problems. We begin with consideration of the current concern with cutting the costs of corrections, then turn to examination of problems associated with free labor and business, abuses of inmates, and resolution of disputes between government and private contractors.

Cutting Correctional Costs

According to the former Director of the National Institute of Justice

> The overall interests of business and prison are basically different. Yet through careful planning and negotiation of key issues such as security and production, those goals can coalesce to create a workplace environment operating at a profit for business while offsetting prison costs and providing work experience for inmates. (Stewart, in Sexton et al. 1985, 1)

This view fits nicely with the general conservative enthusiasm for privatization that emerged during the early years of the Reagan administration. Various public services, such as trash removal, transportation and health services, have been privatized during the past few years, ostensibly in an effort to conserve precious resources. With regard to crime and justice, Reagan's attorney general created a task force to examine violent crime. One of the recommendations contained in the final report was that private sector operation of correctional institutions be examined as a possible alternative to conventional government penal operations (Cox and Osterhoff 1991, 231).

This interest is certainly not peculiar to the twentieth century. New York was one of the first states to enlist the private sector in running various aspects of its correctional system in an effort to control costs. New York's nineteenth-century Auburn prison, which became the most significant model for the developing penal systems of other northern states, used private contractors from the very beginning of its operation

(McKelvey 1977, 21). The primary motive for permitting such involvement was cost. The New York legislature was vigorous in its insistence that Auburn not only be self-supporting, but that it actually produce a revenue surplus (Lewis 1965, 178-79). The prison keepers were subjected to steady pressure to secure advantageous contracts with private companies. Contracts were secured, but the period from the mid-1820s to the early 1840s was characterized by uneven profitability. The passage of the Labor Law of 1842 seriously debilitated private contracting for prison labor at Auburn. The same was true of Sing Sing prison.

Southern states generally did not develop penitentiary systems until much later than their northern counterparts. Nonetheless, southern states were also concerned with reducing the costs of their new systems of incarceration. Louisiana, one of the earliest southern states to open a penitentiary, opened its first institution in 1835. In less than a decade the state legislature decided that the cost to the state of running the facility was unacceptable. In contrast to the initial New York experience, which involved merely leasing the labor of convicts to the private sector, Louisiana leased its entire penitentiary to McHatton, Pratt, and Company. The company paid nothing for the five-year lease. The state was satisfied to be free of the costs of operating the facility (Carleton 1971).

Virginia's experience was in many ways similar to that of New York and Louisiana. "Virginia persisted in its efforts to run a profitable prison . . . Though Thomas Jefferson and George Keith Taylor had both conceived high purposes of the moral uplift of the prisoners, the more dominant factor soon became frankly economic" (Keve 1986, 28). Before the end of the nineteenth century's first decade the position of facility agent was put up for bid. The agent was given the right to market prison-made goods in a private company store (Keve 1986, 33). However, it was not until the severe penal crowding typical of the post-Civil War south that real incentives were created for heavy use of the private sector in Virginia. After being appointed superintendent in 1879, S.C. Williams phased out all state operation of industrial shops in the penitentiary. In addition, inmates were contracted out to businesses that actually removed the inmates from the prison. Prisoners were sent to privately constructed and owned facilities, where they were put to work for the contractor. The state retained the burden of clothing the convicts, and the contractor paid the cost of feeding and housing the convict, as well as paying a daily fee for the convict's labor (Keve 1986, 73).

Post-Civil War concerns with the costs of incarceration touched the West as well as the South. At the close of the war the Texas legislature created a Board of Public Labor and charged them with the responsibility for cultivating private involvement in various aspects of correctional operation. Inmates were quickly contracted out to private plantation owners, who put the convicts to work on their land (Martin and Ekland-Olson 1987). But Texas went further than Virginia. "The prison in Huntsville was still not operating at a profit. With hopes of remedying this problem, the state leased the entire penitentiary operation to private interests" (Martin and Ekland-Olson 1987, 6).

On the Pacific coast, California pursued a similar path. In 1851, before California had a state penitentiary system, two entrepreneurs proposed to provide land and build a prison for the state. In addition, they would be responsible for the facility's operation. LaMott describes the reaction of state legislators.

> In looking over the offer, the legislators had one thing in mind, and that was money. A senate committee discovered that of twenty "commodious and well-adapted" state prisons in the East, only four yielded a profit. They reported with dismay that the average deficit was more than $100,000 a year. Acutely aware of the chronic exhaustion of the California state treasury, the senators fell over each other in their haste to accept Vallejo's munificent offer. (1961, 9-10)

In 1851 the legislature granted the two businessmen a ten-year lease.

Thus, nineteenth-century state legislatures across the nation were vigorously interested in the cost advantages of turning over various aspects of their correctional systems to the private sector. How far they went in engaging private industry was influenced by a host of general factors, such as their respective crowding problems, state system costs, and general economic well-being, as well as by more specific factors such as the special problems experienced in the South resulting from the demise of the slave economy.

The experiences of some of the states with the private sector did confirm the expectation that the private sector could reduce the financial burden of state penitentiary systems. New York legislators were quick to notice the profits made in Connecticut and Massachusetts, and to pressure the Auburn and Sing Sing keepers to be more energetic in finding ways to generate revenue (Lewis 1965, 179). Kentucky transferred the prison in Frankfurt to private hands in 1825, and managed to create an ongoing profitable relationship with a series of companies (Sellin 1976,

141-42). Florida realized an annual gain of more than $300,000 in 1911 from its lease with the Florida Pine Company (Sellin 1976, 156). Even in New York, which essentially destroyed its lease system with the Labor Law of 1842, profits were generated during most years in the 1830s (Lewis 1965, 186).

However, the revenue enhancement obtained through private sector engagement was not without a variety of economic and non-economic costs. It is to some of these difficulties that we now turn our attention.

Labor and Business Concerns

From the very outset of the American experience with private sector involvement in corrections concerns were raised about the impact of such involvement on the free market economy. Shoemakers protested the manufacture of shoes in New York's Newgate Prison in 1801, prompting the passage of the first piece of New York legislation regulating prison-produced goods. By the 1830s both business and free labor succeeded in getting a more comprehensive law passed, and in 1842 the previously mentioned Labor Law of 1842 was enacted. This statute prohibited private contractors from using inmate tradesmen in a trade unless they had learned their trade before coming into the prison. In addition, inmates were to be employed only in industries that would not damage free industries (Lewis 1965, 197).

In Louisiana, free workers protested the lease system because it consumed jobs on farms, plantations, and railroads. A minority report read at the state Democratic Convention in 1883 noted "That the employment of convicts outside the walls of the Penitentiary is detrimental to the interests of the honest labor portion of the ... State ... that it brings this species of slave labor in competition with honest industry to the great pecuniary profit of the penitentiary lessee, but with disastrous results as far as the honest free labor of our state is concerned" (in Carleton 1971, 39). The final majority report condemned the lease system and called for its replacement with a system of public works. Despite this call for abolition, the battle continued to rage for two more decades. Leasing did not disappear from Louisiana until 1901.

Tennessee's prison in Nashville opened in 1831. It was intended to be profit-producing, and it did produce profits during its first twenty years of operation. By mid-century, however, free workers vigorously protested the impact of the prison industry system on free labor. In his 1853 annual speech to the legislature Governor Johnson added his voice to the protests (Cody and Bennett 1987, 830). Yet no immediate changes were made, and during the post-Civil War period economic difficulties created enormous financial pressures. As a result, a four-year lease was awarded to a private furniture manufacturing company. A series of leases were subsequently awarded, despite the continuing opposition of free labor. The situation deteriorated until free miners stormed the lease prisons in 1891, releasing more than 400 inmates (Cody and Bennett 1987, 838). This dramatic protest motivated the legislature to finally end the traditional leasing system.

Of course, labor was not alone in having concerns about leasing.

> Protests were heard from business as well as free labor. As early as 1872 a competitor of the Tennessee Coal, Iron, and Railroad Company charged that convict labor gave that company a $70,000 advantage over mines that depended on free labor. The convict lease system, argued a Northern member of the American Iron and Steel Association, was the major reason the South could produce such cheap iron. (Ayers 1984, 194-195)

McKelvey notes that companies in midwestern states were also troubled by prison contracting.

> Presidents of wagon factories, shoe, furniture, and stove companies, chiefly from Wisconsin, Michigan, Iowa, and Missouri—all at that time lacking anticontract laws—gathered in Chicago in 1886 to hold their convention. Here they frankly unveiled their interest in eliminating the unfair competition of their rivals. (McKelvey 1977, 120)

The experiences in these states were not atypical. As the nineteenth century drew to a close and the new century began, state after state began to shut down their contracting and leasing arrangements (McKelvey 1977, chap. 5). In 1885 three-fourths of prison inmates were involved in productive labor, the majority of whom were working in contract or leasing systems. Fifty years later only 44 percent were involved in such labor, and almost 90 percent worked on state rather than private work programs (Barnes and Teeters 1959, 535).

Although some of the conditions that spawned business and labor dissatisfaction in the nineteenth century were peculiar to that time period, modern interests are concerned about the impact of privatization on both free labor and public employment. The AFL-CIO, for instance, has expressed its opposition to privatization (Ryan and Ward 1989, 22). The lack of enthusiasm for privatization on the part of public employees is reflected by the energetic resistance of the American Federation of State, County and Municipal Employees. It is concerned that the number of employees used in corrections will be reduced, and that the salaries of corrections employees will be diminished (Dudek 1987). Advocates of this view claim that this is exactly what transpired when the Florida's Okeechobee facility was turned over to the Eckerd Foundation (Ryan and Ward 1989, 33).

Abuses of Inmates

One of the concerns raised by modern critics of correctional privatization is that profit-motivated firms will make decisions that enhance profits at the expense of the rights and well-being of inmates.

> We see the potential for serious abuse in the delegation of the control and custody of prisoners. No one but the state should have the awesome responsibility or power to take away an individual's freedom; freedom should not be contracted to the lowest bidder. (Elvin 1985, 51)

Advocates of privatization argue that abusive practices would not be in the long-term interests of private contractors, and would thus be avoided. Jeremy Bentham was perhaps the first to assert that the well-being of inmates would be protected under a private system. Of private contractors he noted

> The more orderly and industrious the prisoners, the greater amount of his profits. He will, therefore, teach them the most profitable trades, and give them such portion of the profits as shall excite them to labour. He unites in himself the characters of Magistrate, Inspector, Head of Manufactory, and of a family; and is urged on by the strongest motives faithfully to discharge all these duties. (Quoted in McConville 1987, 228)

McConville summarized Bentham's view by noting that "Within the constraints of his contract, therefore, Bentham considered that the public welfare, the welfare of the prisoners, and the financial interest of the entrepreneur would be united" (1987, 228).

The historical record, however, casts significant doubt upon this position. In Flanagan's view, "Corruption of public officials and abuse of prisoners were the seeds of destruction of the early contract systems of prison labor" (1989, 43). In his discussion of nineteenth-century practices Keve notes that "With private contractors greedy for profits and government failing to provide or to enforce standards of prisoner management, treatment of contracted prisoners across the country ranged from shabby to brutal" (1986, 73). Considerable evidence exists consistent with Keve's assessment.

Virginia was one of the relatively few southern states electing not to lease its facilities to the private sector. They were satisfied to grant contracts for inmate labor only. Inmates were, however, contracted to companies that relocated inmates outside penitentiary walls in various work camps. Conditions in these camps were dismal, nonetheless "contractors persistently avoided any recognition of the degraded conditions and high death rates in the work camps" (Keve 1986, 75).

Beyond private prison labor programs, private management of entire state institutions was also troubled by abuses. Texas provides an excellent case in point. In 1875 a legislative commission investigated the Texas system. A site visit to the privately operated Huntsville facility revealed children as young as nine years old mixed in with hardened adult offenders. The commissioner discovered that the private operators did not provide adequate food or medical care to the inmates. "Sleeping arrangements were described as 'decidedly filthy' and infested with vermin. Writers of the report were 'at a loss for terms too sufficiently strong to condemn as inhuman and unfit for the purpose, the place in the Penitentiary miscalled a hospital'" (quoted in Martin and Ekland-Olson 1987, 6). In addition, the committee found that despite specific stipulations in the Texas Penal Code regarding permissible punishments for inmate disciplinary infractions, the Code was regularly ignored. For instance, it was stipulated that whipping was never to be used without special authorization. In fact, "Whippings were frequently administered that left inmates 'scarified in a most shocking manner'" (Martin and Ekland-Olson 1987, 7). The findings of the committee led to the reestablishment of state control over the penitentiary.

Texas is not a unique example. Like Texas, by statute California was supposed to develop a written list of institutional rules, rules to be enforced by the prison commissioners. Such new rules were never promulgated, and there was no effort to see that the old rules were enforced. Punishment within San Quentin was brutal, relying heavily upon flogging. Food consisted of "spoiled beef, maggoty hams, wormy flour, rusty mackerel, and coarse brown bread" Lamott 1961, 45). The facility was seriously overcrowded. As a result of such practices, as well as other offenses, the lessee ultimately was forced to give up his contract (Lamott 1961, 51).

In 1884 the pressures of overcrowding led Tennessee to lease out its entire convict population to the Tennessee Coal and Iron Company. State convicts were held both in the Nashville Penitentiary as well as in work sites across the state. A state board of health physician reported on the condition of inmates held in the work sites:

> Of their treatment the state knows nothing; the company cares nothing, except the amount of money that can be made out of them, and of that they seem to have rather a good opinion, as they show an evident preference for that sort of slave labor over the paid work of free men. (Quoted in Sellin 1976, 161)

An 1889 legislative prison commission investigation of the privately operated convict dwellings found them to be "rough board shanties unfit for the habitation of human beings" and that inmates were subjected to "cruel and inhuman whippings with a heavy strap on the naked backs of convicts for failure to get out the tasks . . . and for nearly everything" (quoted in Chaneles 1985, 107).

An 1893 legislative inspection of the prison system found prisoners still living in pitifully inadequate and filthy housing. Furthermore, the "prisoners were furnished with shoes but no socks, drawers or night shirts as required by law, notwithstanding the bitter cold weather in winter" (quoted in Chaneles 1985, 108). The commission found desperately inadequate food, and the continued use of brutal punishments. Such neglect, abuses, and punishments led to an average of over 130 murders annually in Tennessee's lease system, according to a prison committee report in the mid-1880s (Chaneles 1985, 112). Tennessee eventually abandoned its contracting practices, though more as a response to the objections of free labor than to abuses of convicts (Cody and Bennett 1987).

Advocates of modern private involvement in corrections argue that these kinds of abuses can be avoided through the adoption of careful monitorship mechanisms. In Texas, for instance, facilities run by the Corrections Corporation of America have a state monitor working daily on the premises. However, such control mechanisms are not new. When California first turned over its system to the private sector, the enabling legislation of 1852 required state monitors. However, systematic monitorship was quickly eliminated in cost cutting efforts. The subsequent 1856 leasing legislation also provided for state monitors, and stipulated that they would reside at the prison and report to the Board of Prison Commissioners. The monitorship system did not survive. "Within a year, the legislature eliminated the daily monitors as an unnecessary expense" (McAfee 1987, 856). The historical record thus suggests that even legislative adoption of monitoring mechanisms does not guarantee that they will be maintained as devices to control abuses of inmates.

Disputes with Private Companies

As in any contractual arrangement disputes may arise between the contracting parties. When such disputes involve conflicts between private business and state interests the hazards associated with such disputes may exceed those typical of disputes between private business concerns. The importance of certain kinds of public responsibilities has resulted in a variety of dispute limitations that do not apply in the private sector. Police and fire departments, for instance, are typically prohibited from striking because of the dangers to the community associated with a collapse of such services. In a similar vein, if transfer of responsibility for penal institutions is not carefully executed, the consequences may be disastrous. Beyond inconvenience and the assumption of unanticipated costs, both public safety and inmate well-being may be at stake.

Examination of the historical record reveals that such disputes were neither uncommon nor without serious consequences. For instance, by the middle of the nineteenth century Auburn Prison was heavily dependent on its carpet shop for revenue. The shop was contracted out to a local businessperson, Josiah Barber. In 1851 Barber refused to make the required labor payments to the state, claiming that business conditions had rendered fulfillment of the conditions of the contract impossible. The state provided Barber with several extensions, and secured the increasing debt through claims on Barber's equipment. When no further payments appeared forthcoming the state decided to cancel the contract and try and recoup some of its losses by liquidating Barber's assets. Unfortunately, due to rug industry conditions the equipment was unsalable. Moreover, contract termination would create problems beyond the loss of revenue. The shop closure would leave idle more than 300 inmates, creating significant institutional management dilemmas. The state had little choice in how to resolve the issue:

The outcome clearly revealed the inability of the institution to defend its position if an important contractor fell into arrears. Despite Barber's indebtedness, the inspectors intervened in his favor. He was awarded a new contract requiring him to pay less for his inmate labor than before, containing nothing on the subject of security for his old obligations, and awarding him the free use of convicts for three months. (Lewis 1965, 265)

The dependency of the state, which had been the result of the shift of responsibility to the private sector, left the state unable to resolve the dispute in a satisfactory manner.

Virginia's experience was similar. By law the state retained the power to remove inmates from the care of private companies if contractual conditions were not met. But the reality of the situation was not so simple. Keve points out that "once the state had become dependent on the contract system, it was trapped. With the penitentiary having filled up, it was virtually impossible for a contract to be canceled" (1986, 78). As in New York, the state's reliance upon the private sector gave private companies the advantage in disputes over contractual issues.

Louisiana had a somewhat different, but equally unfortunate, experience. Samuel James had purchased the convict lease from Huger and Jones, the original lessees. In 1875 the state filed a lawsuit against James for two years nonpayment of the fees for inmate labor. Despite this suit, James continued to withhold payments, and in addition, continued to work convicts outside prison walls in violation of state law (Act 22). The reality of the situation was simply that James was politically very well-connected. Gubernatorial pressure was applied to delay government processing of the suit. The case ultimately went to an arbitration committee in 1879, and the amount owed was set at more than $44,000. Nonetheless it was not until 1881 that payments began to be made (Carleton 1971). Thus, despite clear grounds for cancellation of the lease, including failure to pay the state the convict fees specified in the lease, the major's political contacts incapacitated the state's ability to recover such fees.

Of course, not all disputes involved failure to fulfill contractual financial conditions. In California the contractor awarded San Quentin subcontracted the facility to an entrepreneur named John McCauley. McCauley took full advantage of the opportunity to squeeze as much out of the arrangement as possible:

Money was, in fact, the single and entire key to McCauley. He ran the prison like the forced-labor camp that it was. By the end of 1857 the life of the San Quentin convict

The Future of Correctional Privatization

>had fallen several steps from even the low condition it had occupied under Estell. McCauley ignored the physical needs of the convicts, ignored the orders sent down from Sacramento, ignored the suggestions of his own prison officers, ignored everything but his profit, and left the prison a wealthy man. (LaMott 1961, 52-53)

A legislative committee visited the prison in 1858, and found conditions so appalling, and in such blatant violation of the contract, that the legislature hurriedly passed a bill declaring the contract void, and restoring the prison to state control (LaMott 1961, 56-57). This resulted in a series of court battles and political machinations. In the end, despite the profound violations of the original contract, the state supreme court returned control of the prison to McCauley. The state was forced to pay more than $200,000 to secure the agreement of McCauley to abandon all future claims on the prison (LaMott 1961, 66). What had initially been intended to be a cost-effective solution to California's penal needs turned out to be an expensive debacle that resulted in severe abuses of inmates and widespread public embarrassment.

In Nebraska an investigation of penitentiary conditions revealed "shocking conditions, including the total neglect of sanitation, the improper association of women and boys as well as the insane with the rest of the population, and the use of physical torture as a penalty for failure to complete the labor tasks" (McKelvey 1977, 223). Despite these obvious violations, it took two years before the contract could be terminated, and even then the state was required to buy out the contract.

Thus, disputes between contractors and states attempting to cancel contracts were not rare. Clear contractual provisions provided no assurance that the elements of service agreed upon would be provided by the private company. In addition, violations of contracts did not always result in simple contract cancellation, even when legislative action formed the legal authority for cancellation. Service dependency, political influence, and court battles severely limited state ability to discard agreements that had been violated by private businesses.

Conclusions

This discussion has examined three main issues in the debate over correctional privatization: labor and business concerns, abuses of inmates, and settlement of disputes between government and private contractors. It has presented material from the American historical experience in an effort to document the very real nature of the potential hazards raised by critics of the modern privatization movement. Consideration of these issues has also brought to light other associated issues, such as the practical difficulty of terminating contracts when the state has become dependent on private companies.

It is important to be cautious in making judgments about the implications of this historical record. There is considerable temptation to examine the record, observe the many problems with private sector involvement in corrections in the nineteenth century, and to conclude on this basis that modern privatization is necessarily doomed to fail. It may well be doomed, but some of the problems experienced in nineteenth-century initiatives were the product of unique historical circumstances. For instance, institutional overcrowding motivated many southern states to turn to the private sector for help. This crowding was to no small extent the result of changes in southern society produced by the demise of the slave economy. Examination of postwar penal statistics for southern states shows enormous proportions of blacks in penal systems that had typically been white while slavery was still in effect (e.g., Carleton 1971, 13). The influx of blacks into southern penal systems produced population increases that were difficult for the devastated postwar state economies to handle. Such conditions are obviously not factors in the modern movement.

It can also be argued that the horrible conditions inmates were forced to endure were a product of an era characterized by judicial reluctance to become involved in the operation of the correctional system. After all, most of the important court cases establishing inmate rights were decided only in the last thirty years. Inmates now have legal protections unavailable to their nineteenth-century counterparts.

Many states experienced abuses of contracts that essentially obviated the advantages sought through relations with the private sector. However, the failure of nineteenth-century monitoring mechanisms can be credited with some of the abuses. Modern methods of management and oversight may result in far more effective monitoring of contractors.

Finally, some of the difficulties encountered by states can be traced to their failure to draw up adequately specific contracts. Some analysts argue that modern expertise can produce contracts of sufficient precision to avoid the damaging lawsuits and negative judicial rulings that cost the states significant resources (McAfee 1987).

The Future of Correctional Privatization

Nonetheless, although there are time period-specific conditions which may account for at least some aspects of the nineteenth-century experience, there are still reasons for concern that similar difficulties may arise during the current initiative. For instance, although the demise of the slave-based economy is not relevant to current conditions, institutional crowding similar to that which resulted from the end of slavery is indeed a current problem. As noted earlier, almost 80 percent of the states are under court order regarding institutional conditions, most relating to crowding. Billions of dollars have been committed to supporting the increasing size of the American correctional system. Crowding and the costs associated with a burgeoning prison population are relevant factors in the modern privatization debate. States are seeking relief from both, and as in the nineteenth century, private initiatives have appeal as a potential solution.

With regard to the inmates' rights argument, it is true that inmates have legal rights that were not available in the nineteenth century. However, it is far from clear that the availability of such rights has resolved the abuse issue. Numerous states have been the target of inmate suits that have forced them to make considerable adjustments in their practices. Yet many of these suits have taken than a decade or more to produce results (e.g., Ruiz v. Estelle in Texas). Thus, even where the state, and not a private company, has been involved, the increased access to the courts and availability of new legal protections has not guaranteed inmates effective protection from abuses. Will this become an even greater problem in systems utilizing private companies to execute correctional responsibilities? Will the substantial economic costs incurred through inmates' rights suits be even greater where the private sector is involved?

Although states presumably do possess greater expertise in drafting adequately comprehensive and specific contracts than was the case during the last century, such specificity is no guarantee that expensive litigation can be avoided. In fact, it can be argued that the inclinations toward and incentives for litigation are greater now than at any time in American history. Furthermore, privatization-related litigation has already been initiated (Cody and Bennett 1987, 848). In addition, contractual specificity regarding various obligations does not assure that such obligations will be met. It is worth recalling that California's contracts in the 1850s included explicit provisions regarding monitoring. In practice, monitoring was nonexistent (LaMott, 1961).

With further regard to monitoring, it may indeed be true that the technology to monitor private facilities is now relatively sophisticated. Again, this does not assure effective monitoring in practice. For instance, according to one analyst, at the Corrections Corporation of America jail in Chattanooga "government oversight is sometimes spotty. Only one county official serves as 'liaison' at the Chattanooga jail, and he was absent the day a visitor made a tour" (quoted in Weiss 1989, 40). It is worth noting that the Corrections Corporation of America is one of the leading companies in the private corrections industry.

Thus although there are reasons to believe that the twentieth-century privatization movement need not result in ultimate disaster, and it can be hoped that lessons will be learned from earlier experience, there nonetheless remain serious reasons for concern. The relative lack of understanding of the historical record displayed by academicians, policymakers, and citizens in the debate does not suggest that the lessons that can derived from this record have been or will be learned and applied. Furthermore, if Matthews is correct in noting that for its advocates "privatization has become elevated to the level of theology" (1989, 6), there may be little interest in scrutinizing this record carefully. Nonetheless, until further attention is accorded to this historical experience it seems likely that at least some of the errors committed in the nineteenth-century experiment with correctional privatization will recur in modern efforts.

References

Ayers, E.L. (1984) *Vengeance and Justice*. New York: Oxford University Press.

Barnes, H. E., and N.K. Teeters. (1959) *New Horizons in Criminology*. Englewood Cliffs, NJ: Prentice Hall, Inc.

Bureau of Justice Statistics. (1992) "National Update." Washington, DC: U.S. Department of Justice.

Camp, C.and G. Camp. (1984) *Private Sector Involvement in Prison Services and Operations*. Washington, DC: National Institute of Corrections.

———.(1990) *The Corrections Yearbook*. South Salem, NY: Criminal Justice Year book.

Carleton, M.T. (1971) *Politics and Punishment*. Baton Rouge: Louisiana State University Press.

Chaneles, S., ed. (1985) *Prison and Prisoners: Historical Documents*. New York: Haworth Press.

Cody, W.J. and A.D. Bennett (1987) "The Privatization of Correctional Institutions: The Tennessee Experience." *Vanderbilt Law Review*, 40: 829-49.

Cox, N.R., Jr. and W.E. Osterhoff. (1991) "Managing the Crisis in Local Corrections: A Public-Private Partnership Approach." In J.A. Thompson and L.G. Mays (eds.), *American Jails-Public Policy Issues*. Chicago: Nelson Hall.

Dudek, D. (1987) "Going Private . . . Paying Less?" *State Legislatures*. March: 26-29.

Elvin, J. (1985) "A Civil Liberties View of Private Prisons." *The Prison Journal* 65(2): 48-52.

Fenton, J. (1985) "A Private Alternative to Public Prisons." *The Prison Journal* 65(2): 42-47.

Flanagan, T. J. (1989) "Prison Industry and Labor." In L. Goodstein and D.L. MacKenzie (eds.), *The American Prison-Issues in Research and Policy*. New York: Plenum Press.

Hutto, D.T. (1990) "The Privatization of Prisons." In J.W. Murphy and J.E. Dison (eds.), *Are Prisons Any Better? Twenty Years of Correctional Reform*. Newbury Park, CA: Sage.

Keve, P. W. (1986) *The History of Corrections in Virginia*. Charlottesville: University of Virginia Press.

Lamott, K. (1961) *Chronicles of San Quentin*. New York: David McKay Company, Inc.

Logan, C.H. (1989) "Proprietary Prisons" In L. Goodstein and D.L. MacKenzie (eds.), *The American Prison: Issues in Research and Policy*. New York: Plenum Press.

Lewis, W.D. (1965) *From Newgate to Dannemora*. Ithaca, NY: Columbia University Press.

Logan, C.H. and S.P. Rausch. (1985) "Punishment and Profit: the Emergence of Private Enterprise Prisons." *Justice Quarterly* 2(3): 303-318.

Martin, S.J. and S. Ekland-Olson. (1987) *Texas Prisons: The Walls Came Tumbling Down*. Austin: Texas Monthly Press.

McAfee, W. M. (1987) "Tennessee's Private Prison Act of 1986: An Historical Perspective with Special Attention to California's Experience." *Vanderbilt Law Review* 40: 851-865.

McConville, Sean. (1987) "Aid From Industry? Private Corrections and Prison Crowding." In S.D. Gottfredson and S. McConville (eds.) *America's Correctional Crisis*. New York: Greenwood Press.

McKelvey, B. (1977) *American Prisons: A History of Good Intentions*. Montclair, NJ: Patterson Smith.

Ryan, M. and T. Ward. (1989) "Privatization and Penal Politics." In R. Matthews (ed.), *Privatizing Criminal Justice*. London: Sage: 52-73.

Sellin, T. (1976) *Slavery and the Penal System*. New York: Elsevier.

Sexton, G.E., F.C. Farrow, and B.J. Auerbach. (1985) *The Private Sector and Prison Industries*. Washington, DC: National Institute of Justice.

Weiss, R.P. (1989) "Private Prisons and the State." In R. Matthews (ed.) *Privatizing Criminal Justice*. London: Sage.

5

The Privatization of Secure Adult Prisons: Issues and Evidence

Dana C. Joel

The prison population "boom" of the last decade has created a crisis within this country's correctional system. At the end of 1990, federal and state prisons housed a total of 771,200 inmates in a system designed to hold between 586,500 and 641,800. Presently, federal and state prisons hold 800,000 inmates, more than twice the number held in 1980 (Bureau of Justice Statistics [BJS], 1991).

Recent statistics show an alarming increase in the prison population within just the last year. From June 1989 to June 1990, as many as 80,000 inmates were added to the nation's prisons, the largest annual increase in recorded history (BJS 1990). At the close of 1988, the number of admitted prisoners required 800 additional beds per week; only six months later, the number had risen to 1,800 (BJS 1989).

The growing number of offenders at the state level is particularly disturbing. More than doubling over the last decade, the most recent inmate count topped 690,000 in a system designed to hold a maximum of 598,000 (BJS 1991). In the early part of 1970, not one prison was under court order (DiIulio 1989). In 1987, 33 states were under court order (*Newsweek* 1986, in Savas 1987). Today, all but five states contain at least one facility under court order or consent decree. Nine states are under court order for crowding conditions within their entire prison system (National Prison Project, in *State Legislatures* 1990).

Many states, despite budget constraints and declining year-end reserves, are trying to build their way out of the prison crisis, spending more on prison construction than ever before. Proposing close to $3 billion to build and expand facilities for fiscal 1990 (Pagel, 1989), state budgets for correction facilities are growing faster than any other budget item (National Conference of State Legislatures, in Edsall 1989).[1]

Even this recent surge in spending has not provided cells fast enough to house the daily stream of admitted offenders. It takes several years to build a new prison, not including the time spent winning legislative and voter approval. Many states turn to the local jails for available space, but the localities, also struggling with a rising inmate population and shortage of funds, do not have the capacity to handle the state's overflow.

Finding prison space fast enough is not the only dilemma. The costs to hold prisoners behind bars are staggering. Taxpayers pay $60,000 to $80,000 per bed for construction, and another $12,500 to $18,000 per bed annually for operation and maintenance (BJS 1988), the latter alone exceeding the amount it would cost to send an offender to college. Within this nation's federal, state, and local systems, society pays a total of $20 billion a year for corrections (DiIulio 1990).

Under pressure by the federal district courts to relieve prison crowding as quickly as possible, many states release prisoners long before they have completed their sentences in order to allow for incoming prisoners. At least sixteen states operate pre-release programs (C. Camp and G. Camp in Thomas and Hanson, 1990), dismissing over 18,600 sentenced offenders into the streets (National Institute of Justice [NIJ] and American Corrections Association [ACA] 1988). Recent studies show that as a result of this "revolving door" policy, an alarming number of these prisoners go on to commit further crimes.

The *Orlando Sentinel* reported, for example, that from February 1987 to March 1989, one out of four pre-released inmates in Florida was rearrested. During that period, a total of 2,180 crimes were committed by these recidivists, including eleven murders or murder attempts (Holton and Vosburgh 1989). Similarly in Oklahoma City, government officials attributed a three-month, 36 percent jump in the crime rate to the state's early-release program (Williams 1986).

The "solution" to release inmates early serves neither the community—who despite spending an exorbitant amount of tax dollars on prisons are sharing the streets with pre-released offenders, nor the government—which must allocate limited resources to supervise the growing number of released prisoners. The escalating recidivism rates indicate the latter is not being achieved.

In short, the government's provision of corrections in the face of the prison population explosion has been sorely inadequate. Federal courts and state executive officials increasingly are demanding improved service and quality within the state prison system (Mullen et al. 1985). At the same time, legislative delays and bureaucratic red tape are preventing correctional agencies from availing prison space fast enough to accommodate incoming prisoners, let alone improve conditions. All the while, costs to the taxpayer to build and operate the facilities are skyrocketing. To quote Charles H. Logan, a sociologist and author of the book, *Private Prisons: Con's and Pro's*, "Faced with overflowing and aging facilities, with court orders demanding immediate reforms, with already straining budgets and voter rejections of prison construction bond issues, and with mandatory sentence laws. . . government authorities are ready to consider many different options to help relieve the strain" (Logan 1990).

In search of a viable solution to this seemingly insolvable problem, a growing number of state and local governments are turning to the private sector to provide some answers. Since the early 1980s, numerous jurisdictions have been "contracting out" to private, for-profit firms the financing, construction, and management of prisons, believing that proprietors can build facilities faster and operate prisons more efficiently than the government. Because the private sector is less constrained by the large web of government bureaucracy and costly regulations, "privatization" advocates reason, private operators will be able to respond more rapidly, flexibly, and directly to the needs of the correctional system.

Privatization: World Appeal

"Privatization" refers to the transfer of a traditionally performed government function from the public sector to the private sector. Privatization by no means has been limited to this country. The world is witnessing the achievements of the privatization movement, as governments around the globe have been loosening their grip, allowing market forces to operate. In fact, the most dramatic examples are beginning to occur with the collapse of communism in what was the Soviet Union and throughout Eastern Europe. Cutting themselves free from the confining ropes of centralized government, the countries within the former Eastern bloc are leasing or gradually selling government-owned property to private purchasers and allowing private businesses or cooperatives to produce and sell goods.

Western Europe has been selling off state-owned industries to private investors within the last decade. Most notably, Great Britain under the Thatcher administration sold off numerous government-owned assets, including Jaguar Motors, British Aerospace, British Petroleum, and Britoil (Butler 1987) and more recently, British Airways and British Steel (Fixler et al. 1989).

The privatization effort in the United States is attributed to President Ronald Reagan, influenced in large part by Prime Minister Margaret Thatcher and her success at diminishing the size of Great Britain's government. Reagan, however, was not altogether as successful. Despite his priority to reverse the expansion of government—which had been growing steadily since the turn of the century and accelerating since the Great Society of the 1960s—Congress impeded the passage of most privatization initiatives. The limited successes to privatize federally owned enterprises included the sale of Conrail in 1987 for roughly $1.6 billion, and federal loan assets for $5.5 billion (Fitzgerald 1988). Nonetheless, Reagan was successful in introducing to Americans across the country the notion that under market competition, the private sector could provide many public services more efficiently and inexpensively than government monopolies.

While efforts to loosen government control at the federal level became deadlocked in Congress, the privatization impetus trickled down to the state and local levels, fueled by deteriorating government services (Benenson 1985) and budget constraints. Taxpayers from both political parties, given a choice between cutting spending or raising taxes, in many jurisdictions rejected both in favor of privatizing many traditional public services (Fixler et al., 1989).

At the local level alone, more than $100 billion in public service contracts were awarded to private firms in 1987, up from $65 billion in 1982 and $22 billion in 1972 (Moore 1988). With at least 180 different types of public services contracted out (Savas 1987), cities and counties have increased the number of awarded contracts within the last decade from 63 to 444 for street repair; from 9 to 337 for data processing; and from 5 to 142 for park maintenance (Fitzgerald 1988). Other frequently privatized services include solid waste collection, utility billing, legal services, public relations, automobile towing and storage service, and ambulance service. On the state level, health care services are most widely privatized, with corrections following close behind (Touche Ross 1989).

Proponents of privatization believe that services provided by the private sector generally will be more efficient and less costly than under government operation.[2] By competing in the open market, they argue, firms will want to provide the best of quality at the lowest possible cost to gain an edge over their competitors.

Supporters contend that government institutions, unlike private entities, do not operate under market incentives. While a private institution profits by minimizing costs, a public entity profits through growth and spending. By its very nature, its survival depends on budget expansion. Success is not measured by the ability to keep costs down, but by the ability to keep costly promises made to a very large constituency (Poole in Logan and Rausch 1985).

As Harvard professor John D. Donahue, a critic of prison privatization, notes, "As a general rule, organizations confronting competition will generally be more efficient than organizations secure against challenge. Workers and managers in a positions to benefit, directly or indirectly, from efficiency improvements will generally be more energetic in reducing costs than those with no such prospects. And lower costs, in a competitive market will generally translate into lower prices" (Donahue 1989). But how does this translate into the provision of correctional services?

Privatization of Corrections

Privatization of corrections can take many forms. Among them are the contracting out of prison services, prison industries, facility construction, and private management.

Contracting Out Services

Contracting out services is the most common form of privatization for corrections; all but nine states currently contract out various correctional services to the private sector. The most typical of these include medical and psychiatric care, food, drug treatment, staff training, and inmate counseling (Cikins 1986). Several jurisdictions more recently have contracted out rehabilitation programs, classification of inmates, data systems management, and payroll and accounting (Chi 1989).

Few studies have been conducted comparing costs of privatized correctional services with those which are government operated. However, a 1984 national survey found that out of fifty-two agencies contracting out correctional services to the private sector, three out of four experienced cost savings. Furthermore, among the largest of these contracts, twenty-two agencies reported that it cost them on average 26 percent less than if they had provided the same service. Six agencies reported that it cost them on average 17 percent more. However, some of these less cost-efficient private operators were providing services for facilities under court order and were, therefore, under pressure to enhance their services (Camp and Camp in Logan and Rausch 1985).

Prison Industries

Private business has become increasingly interested in prison labor during the past decade. Prompted by state and federal measures lifting some restrictions to private sector use of prison labor, a dozen states contract out the work of an estimated 1,000 convicts. Over twenty firms, ranging from small business to multinational corporations, provide jobs for inmates (Sexton et al. 1985).

For instance, Best Western International, Inc. employs over thirty Arizona prison workers to operate the hotel's telephone reservation system. Four years after the Best Western program began in 1981, inmates had paid over $182,000 in taxes, contributed over $187,000 to the government for room and board, and paid at least $112,000 in family support (Sexton et al. 1985).

Similarly, Trans World Airlines, Inc. hires young offenders from the Ventura Center Training School in California to handle over-the-phone flight reservations. During its first year of operation, inmates had paid over $13,000 in taxes, $15,000 for room and board, and $11,000 to victims for restitution (NIJ 1985).

In most cases, the state correction system provides the working facility for the private firm. The firm manages and trains the inmates and releases their earnings to the care of the state. The wage rates, in most instances, are negotiated between the state agency and the private firm.

Private Construction and Financing

With forty-five states under court order for crowded prison conditions, state correctional agencies are under enormous pressure to provide more prison space as quickly as possible. A growing number of states are turning to the private sector to build prisons, recognizing that private firms can mobilize resources and staff quickly to provide necessary prison space. There are currently eight states contracting with private companies to build at least sixty correction facilities totaling 10,750 beds (*Corrections Compendium* 1989).

One example is the Houston Detention Center for illegal aliens, built and operated by Corrections Corporation of America (CCA), a leading prison management firm. In 1984, CCA won the contract with the federal Immigration and Naturalization Service (INS) to build a 68,000 square foot detention center to hold 350 illegal aliens. In only five and a half months at a cost of $14,000 per bed, construction was complete. Based on the average time it takes the INS to construct a facility of comparable size, it would have taken two and a half years to complete at $26,000 per bed (Brakel 1989).

Speed is not the only appealing aspect of private construction. Because private firms free from government red tape are much less limited than the government in choosing sites for prisons and can obtain a variety of different materials for building, the private provider can be much more flexible. In 1986, the U.S. Corrections Corporation met the state of Kentucky's urgent request for a 200-bed minimum security facility. The Kentucky-based firm purchased an old seminary in rural St. Mary's. Within only one week after the contract was signed, the Marion Adjustment Center opened. The private owner and operator of the detention center, U.S. Corrections Corporation, in July 1990 renewed its contract for another three years (National Criminal Justice Association [NCJA] 1987).

Private firms also are showing a greater interest in innovative architectural designs and technology than government, enabling them to improve security. For example, some firms are designing facilities with adjoining hallways or tiered cells to improve the oversight of prisoners. Others are installing video equipment. These innovations allow the prison operators to upgrade surveillance techniques while saving taxpayer dollars for unnecessary manpower (Brakel 1989).

Besides designing and building facilities, more than a dozen private firms finance the project as well, most notably through lease-purchase agreements. Traditionally, the government finances facility construction by appropriating cash (the pay-as-you-go approach) or by issuing general obligation bonds. The former method places the whole financial burden of construction on the state's annual budget; the latter method requires voter approval and is restricted by debt limitations. Private financing through lease purchasing, however, spreads the cost of construction over a long period of time and does not require voter approval.

One of the major constraints preventing jurisdictions from financing prison construction is public opposition. In the 1980s, an average of 60 percent of all local referenda for jail bonds was rejected (Fitzgerald 1988). Sincerely interested in cracking down on offenders, the public is very anxious to throw lawbreakers behind bars. They just oppose bars in their backyard. Numerous surveys convey the public's contradictory sentiment. Forty-three percent of Floridans polled in 1985, for example, responded that they were "extremely concerned" about crime. When asked which services should receive more government funding, however, prison construction was the twelfth and last choice (Donahue 1989).

Lease purchasing would enable jurisdictions to build prisons without issuing voter referenda. While opponents argue that this is nothing more than an accounting gimmick to avoid public scrutiny and accountability, supporters counter that lease-purchasing arrangements are all the more accessible to public view. As law professor Samuel Jan Brakel observes, "Public oversight is preserved in other ways—most notably via a contract that may be more specific and more (visible) than typical public accounting mechanisms" (Brakel 1989).

Under a lease-purchase agreement, a private firm agrees to build a prison, and the state signs a long-term lease for the prison. Early payments of rent by the government are used to fund the construction. When the government entity completes the payment obligations—the debt and finance charges—it receives title to the facility. The private firm benefits from tax advantages and cash flow from the lease payments. The state government often benefits from faster construction because voter approval is not required and debt limit constraints do not apply. In most cases, lease purchasing must be approved by the legislature.

Private Management Of Prisons

The private sector's role as manager of correction facilities until a decade ago was limited to the operation of "secondary" or community-based facilities, such as halfway houses, detention homes, and holding centers for illegal aliens awaiting deportation. Approximately thirty-nine states (Ring 1986), as well as the federal Bureau of Prisons and Immigration Naturalization Service, contract out to private firms the operation of these nonsecure facilities. In addition, roughly 66 percent of all state juvenile detention centers are privately run.

In the early 1980s, government officials in several states began turning to private firms to run more secure adult prisons and jails. Currently, over a dozen states contract out one or more of these "primary" facilities to the private sector (Logan 1990). There are over forty such facilities totaling over 15,000 beds. An additional 5,400 beds have been approved for future private operation (Thomas 1991).

While most private "primary" institutions are minimum security, proprietors within the last few years have begun to house medium and maximum security prisoners, as well. For example, the Silverdale Detention Center in Hamilton County, Tennessee operated by CCA holds both minimum- and medium-secure inmates. Under the terms of CCA's contract to operate New Mexico's Women's Prison, the firm manages the state's entire first-time female offenders—minimum through maximum security. Similarly, the U.S. Corrections Corporation's Marion Adjustment Center, although classified by the state's attorney general as a minimum security prison, contains a maximum-secure wing holding capital murderers and rapists (Logan 1990).

Only a few states, such as Washington state, explicitly forbid by statute the contracting out of prison management to the private sector (NCJA 1987). Fifteen states actually have passed enabling legislation. These include Alaska, Arkansas, Colorado, Florida, Maine, Massachusetts, Montana, New Mexico, Oklahoma, South Dakota, Tennessee, Utah,

Virginia, Wisconsin, and Wyoming. (Brakel 1988b and Fitzgerald 1988 and American Legislative Exchange Council 1991). Four other states—Arizona, Indiana, Pennsylvania, and South Carolina—are considering similar legislation (American Legislative Exchange Council 1991). Private prison management is by far the most far-reaching form of prison privatization—and the most controversial. While other forms of prison privatization are equally important and frequently discussed, the remainder of this chapter will focus only on the private management of prisons.[3]

The Contractual Process

When a state or local government chooses to contract out a prison's operation to a private vendor, it issues a formal request for proposal (RFP), specifying its performance criteria and general qualifications. Respondents to the RFP, in most cases, must present their company's previous experience in related fields, staff qualifications, programs they would implement, and financial history. An RFP sets the terms later to be used in negotiating a contract. In addition, it assures that the bidding process is fair and open to any proprietor that wants to compete for the job (Hackett et al. 1987).

The selected firm and the government entity negotiate the terms of the contract, including the "price" the government will pay the proprietor for managing the prison. In many cases, although depending on the terms of the particular contract, the government pays a per diem fee for each inmate. Some contracts apply a sliding scale, lowering the price as additional prisoners are admitted. For example, at the Bay County Jail in Panama City, Florida, CCA charges a daily fee of $31.01 per inmate for the first 310 inmates. For the next twenty inmates, the fee drops to approximately $10, and for all additional inmates, the price drops still further to roughly $7.50 (Larson 1988).

The duration of contracts can vary, although most range from three to five years. Almost all contracts require review and annual fee renegotiations. CCA holds a thirty-two-year contract with Hamilton County, Tennessee to manage the Silverdale Detention Center. The contract is renewable every four years, while the terms of payment are renegotiated every year (Logan 1990). As is the case with most contracts, the county can terminate the contract at any time if officials have reason to believe required standards are not being met.

Private providers are monitored extremely closely and regularly by the government. While the process may vary from one jurisdiction to another, most require periodic reporting; on-site inspections; and immediate notification in cases of inmate escapes, injuries, illnesses, or deaths (Hackett et al. 1987).

There is no universal procedure governments use for contracting out and monitoring private operation. States' standards and requirements will vary, depending on their definitions of quality and on the specific needs of their correctional systems and institutions. In some states, standards are defined by statute; in others, they are devised through contractual agreements.

Despite this procedural diversity, jurisdictions increasingly are coming face to face with the same issues and concerns. Questions pertaining to the legal and technical aspects of prison privatization, which used to impede privatization initiatives, are now being addressed through specific legislation and within the terms of the contract. At the same time, jurisdictions confronting the same issues are learning from one another and consequently, are tailoring similar RFP's and contractual provisions, and monitoring standards to iron out potential wrinkles. In the process, jurisdiction are perfecting and standardizing these measures and are ensuring greater accountability.

Battling It Out: Opponents, Proponents and the Search for Empirical Evidence

This is not to say that prison privatization has exhausted its supply of critics. On the contrary, the subject continues to be as divisive as ever. Opponents, who believe the profit motive has no place in corrections, fear that the prison environment inevitably will deteriorate under private management. They claim private operators will cut corners to keep costs down which, in turn, will lower quality standards and jeopardize the prisoners' welfare. Moreover, they argue that private operators will develop into a powerful special-interest group, successfully lobbying lawmakers for more and longer sentences.

Members of the American Federation of State, County, and Municipal Employees (AFSCME), one of the largest divisions of the AFL-CIO comprised of state and local civil-service employees, are the staunchest and most powerful critics of prison privatization. In the northeast region of the country where labor unions are strongest, AFSCME has been particularly effective in preventing privatization.

Proponents of privatization claim that private operators, not restricted by bureaucratic red tape and cumbersome government restrictions, are able to make decisions more quickly and to adapt to changing needs more freely. In addition, they contend private firms can acquire supplies faster and cheaper, purchasing by bulk and paying by cash rather than credit. Proponents believe there is potential for considerable cost savings and improved performance, as private firms apply more innovative and entrepreneurial skills.

Throughout the 1980s, the prison privatization debate was limited in large part to theoretical arguments such as these. Because evidence on private prisons was sorely lacking, empirical evaluations have had to borrow from the experience of other industries. For example, Samuel Jan Brakel presented a compelling comparison of Robert Charles Clark's study on for-profit health care to prison privatization (Brakel 1988a). While these studies have been vital in perpetuating the prison privatization debate, there are obvious disadvantages to applying the conclusions of another public service to that of corrections.

Graduating beyond its early "road-test" days, prison privatization gradually is establishing its own track record. Several articles and studies have been written in just the last few years that go beyond theory to document some of the actual results of privately run prisons. The following section includes some of both evidence and general theory in presenting the key issues of the prison privatization debate.

Cost Savings

One of the most appealing aspects of contracting out to the private sector, in general, is the potential cost savings to the government. Approximately 96 percent of all local governments contract out more than one type of public service, saving taxpayers millions of dollars annually (Moore 1988). E.S. Savas, a leading expert in privatization, reports that the private sector saves the government on average 35 percent collecting garbage, 60 percent building and maintaining roads, 50 to 60 percent operating urban bus services, and anywhere from 25 to 88 percent operating wastewater treatment plants (Savas 1987).

Prison privatization, compared to these other services, is in its embryonic stage. While privately run prisons reportedly have saved anywhere from 3 to 40 percent (Savas 1987), reliable cost-data is sparse and conclusions, therefore, are varied.

One reason is that comparing correctional costs among different prisons is a difficult and complex procedure. Costs vary enormously—regardless of whether the prisons are privately or publicly run—depending on the facilities' location, number of beds and staff, age, level of security, and type of housed offender (Logan 1989).

For example, a 1985 report on federal INS detention centers lists seven publicly operated facilities and their corresponding per diem costs. The costs range from $17.65 per inmate (for a 334-bed facility in El Centro, California) to $68.14 (for a 224-bed facility in New York City) (Ring 1986).[4]

The task is even more complicated when comparing privately run to government-run prisons. Besides the inherent "apples and oranges" dilemma, there is also a problem with government's "hidden" costs—those costs that are excluded in the government's correctional budget-reporting process but included in the private sector's ledgers. Unlike the private sector, which has the incentive to include all costs in order to recover expenses, the government has no such incentive. Consequently, important cost items frequently are omitted from government correctional budgets, such as depreciation, debt service, personnel expenses, garbage collection, transportation, overhead, and many others (Logan 1989). This is not necessarily an intentional oversight. Various expenditures incurred by prison operations often fall outside the corrections budget. They are, therefore, easily overlooked when the government assesses correctional expenditures. For example, liability costs generally are paid out of the state or county attorney's budget. Similarly, fringe benefits and pensions usually are paid from a general fund. These are all costs that must be accounted for by the private operator (Logan 1989).

Writer Randall Fitzgerald reports, for example, that the INS saves more money through privatization than it actually reports. While CCA calculates both construction and operation costs, the INS does not include construction (Fitzgerald 1988).

Despite the lack of a reliable and standardized accounting method to determine actual costs, some states require private providers to set fees below the "likely full cost to the state" to assure cost savings to the government. Tennessee requires that private firms charge a per diem rate 5 percent below the government's per diem cost (Brakel 1988). Similarly, Texas requires a 10 percent cost savings (Robbins 1989). Before governments mandate such savings, they should devise a more fair and accurate method of assessing what the "likely full cost" actually is.

A path-breaking study conducted for the National Institute of Justice does this by accounting for these hidden costs and other accounting discrepancies. Charles Logan and County Auditor Bill McGriff compared the costs of the CCA-operated Hamilton County Penal Farm with the costs that would have been incurred had the county continued to operate the facility. Using conservative county cost estimates, they concluded that CCA saved the government at least 4 to 15 percent annually over a three-year period (Logan and McGriff 1989).

Supporters of prison privatization believe that proprietors save taxpayers' money by adopting innovative, low-cost techniques. Opponents, on the other hand, contend that it is not possible to be innovative in corrections because, whether a government agency or a private firm, the "basic service" is the same—to shelter and feed prisoners. The number of technological "alternatives" to providing that service, they argue, is severely limited (Donahue 1989).

But number of private businesses that are employing innovative, cost-saving techniques illustrates the private sector's ability to be flexible and creative in providing the "basic service." For example, Buckingham Security, Ltd. of Pennsylvania, which operated the Butler County Jail from 1985 to 1985[5] lowered utility costs by using fluorescent light bulbs instead of the usual incandescent bulbs, and by routinely checking showers for running water. In addition, the firm saved money by shopping for better bargain prices and by purchasing supplies in bulk. Food was purchased by the U.S. Department of Agriculture which sold surplus food to the jail at below-market prices. While this alternative also had been an option under the county's operation, the government had rejected it (NCJA 1987). Within the same year that Buckingham assumed management, the company renovated the high-security facility, employing inmates to do the construction and generating additional savings to the county.

Other proprietors claim they save money as a result of low start-up costs (NCJA 1987) and their more frugal approach to purchasing supplies. Unlike the government that acquires materials through the more costly time-consuming bidding process and pays by credit, contractors can shop around among discount stores, purchase goods in bulk, and pay directly with cash. Don Hutto, CCA's Executive Vice President and former Virginia corrections commissioner, recently commented that "[The government] buys supplies on low bid, but low bid doesn't mean low price" (Larson 1988).

Extremely labor-intensive, prisons spend about 80 percent of all operation costs on salaries. How private operators control and minimize labor costs is critical to the firm's survival. Contractors generally achieve their greatest savings by eliminating unnecessary overtime and reducing overinflated benefits, such as sick leave and retirement, typically paid to unionized government workers (Logan 1990).

If private employees' benefits tend to be lower than government's, how is it that there exists a pool of qualified labor from which the private sector can hire? Why is it that private managers are able to find experienced and qualified employees? Besides the fact that many employees find the working conditions much more favorable in private prisons (Ring 1986), many also are attracted to the opportunities for promotion virtually nonexistent under government operation and for the more generous pay raises. CCA, for example, bases promotions on job performance, typically rewarding deserving staff with an eight percent wage increase (Larson 1988).

Opponents warn that contractors will cut costs by reducing key personnel. But this has not been the case. In fact, some private providers have added staff, recognizing the need for more employees to control the increasing number of prisoners. When CCA won the contract for the Silverdale facility, management increased the number of employees from fifty-eight to seventy-two (Ring 1986).

Opponents also frequently warn that the private sector will lower employees' salaries. While private firms are not under the same pressures and demands from unionized civil service workers that the government is, private employees' wages as a rule remain competitive with government's. Moreover, Buckingham Security's employees received higher wages than their previous government workers (Logan 1990), as currently do most of CCA's employees. When CCA assumed operation of Bay County Jail, the 70 out of 75 employees that stayed on (Logan 1990) received a 7 percent pay increase, as well as a $500 bonus (NCJA

1987). CCA also gives employees the option of sharing company profits by buying into the employee stock ownership plan (Larson 1988).

Quality

To quote John Donahue, professor at Harvard's John F. Kennedy School of Government and a prison privatization critic, the quality of privately run prisons will depend on "the existence of lively and realistic competition . . . the degree to which quality can be monitored; and the government's ability and inclination to reward, penalize, or replace contractors on the basis of performance" (Donahue 1988). Donahue questions whether these criteria can be met under private operation. Yet these criteria exist only when the private sector is present; they are nonexistent under a government monopoly.

No one disputes the advantages of competition. Opening the market to competition assures that proprietors will attempt to offer the best at the lowest possible cost. The present owners and managers of the Marion Adjustment Center won their contract by out-performing the original winner of the contract. Kentucky rewarded U.S. Corrections Corporation with the contract to manage the minimum secure prison only after the original bidder failed to secure the location of the facility as agreed to in the contract (Chi 1989).

Critics contend that "perfect" competition does not exist among private providers, because there are too few private operators. But while some argue the "industry" at present is no more than an oligopoly, it by no means has reached its saturation point. At approximately ten years of age, prison privatization (of "primary" facilities) is in its youth. Start-up costs are relatively low, and firms can enter the market fairly freely (Logan 1990). As long as significant barriers of entry do not exist, the pool should continue to grow. At any rate, competition can exist among a limited number of firms; competition cannot exist under a government monopoly.

It is also possible for government and the private sector to "compete" against each other by opening the bidding process to government agencies, as well as private firms. "Competition can be sharpened even further," writes Savas, "when the public and private sectors both deliver the same service in the same jurisdiction . . . [This form of] competition has been successful in producing operating efficiencies and costs that are remarkably low by national standards" (Savas 1987).

The government agency's monitoring process also ensures a high level of performance. As discussed in a previous section, evaluation procedures are becoming more standardized, including frequent on-site inspections; monitoring of food, health, security, and correctional programs; and continuous review of evaluation reports (Hackett et al. 1987). Certainly, no such watchdog exists (except in cases where court orders are enforced by special masters) with this degree of oversight over government operations. Some may argue that the general public supervises the government's performance. But given the public's overall detachment and apathy toward the daily affairs of prison operations, the argument would not hold.

Finally, contracts allow the government the flexibility to choose among a pool of providers. Most contracts are not longterm but expire after three to five years. In most cases, expired contracts have been renewed, but the government always has the option to contract with another operator. Therefore, it is in the proprietor's interest to provide the highest possible quality of performance.

Some opponents worry that a practice called "low-balling" will ensue. Low-balling occurs when a bidder wins an initial contract by suppressing prices below the market rate. Over time, when the contractor believes the government is totally dependant on his service, he raises the bid far above the market price to recover costs. His security is knowing that the government would incur larger costs if it terminated the contract and tried to provide the service itself.

This is, in large part, a theoretical problem that realistically could occur in the absence of a pool of competing providers. The greater the competition, the less secure a bidder is in low-balling, because the government always has the choice of awarding another contractor.

In the absence of "lively" competition, there are safety measures to assure against low-balling. As part of the monitoring process, the government should keep a close watch on all of the contractor's costs. As the cost of a particular segment of corrections rises, the government should be aware of this (Ring 1986). Increased bids, therefore, will be accountable. Illegitimate increases will be distinguishable from real market-based increases. As another precaution, the government should avoid rewarding a contract automatically to the lowest bidder. (Logan 1990)

Although prison privatization is in its infant stage, there has not been any evidence of low-ball bidding. INS, the oldest government entity to contract out prison operation, has not reported experiencing this problem (Logan 1990). Nor is there evidence of low-balling among other privatized services (Savas 1987).

Theory Aside

There are numerous documented examples of operators who substantially improved the facility's conditions under private management. CCA's Silverdale Detention Center is one such example. The institution's contract monitor, who also served as the facility's warden prior to CCA's contract, reported to researcher Samuel Jan Brakel that CCA had made improvements in the five following areas: the physical plant, the classification system, the staff treatment of inmates, the disciplinary system, and the medical care. Through his own extensive research of the facility, Brakel added to the list of "substantial gains," including the recreational programs and facilities, religious and other counseling services, inmate grievance and request procedures, and legal access" (Brakel 1988).

CCA also upgraded the quality of Florida's Bay County Jail. Under government control, there had been several lawsuits pending against the county for crowded conditions, fire safety violations, and poor medical care. Seven months after CCA signed the contract, the lawsuits were dropped as a result of the notable improvements, such as a new 174-bed work camp and a rehabilitation program at no extra charge to the government, among others (NCJA 1987).

A recent study prepared by the Urban Institute (see chap. 15) compares quality levels between the private Marion Adjustment Center and the public Blackburn Correctional Complex, both located in Kentucky. Based on surveys and interviews with prison staff and inmates, as well as personal visits and review of agency records, the researchers compared the quality of the two comparable prisons by breaking down total service into the following segments: prisons' physical condition, escape rates, security and control, inmates' physical and mental health, adequacy of programs, and rehabilitation (as determined by recidivism rates). The study concludes that "By and large, both staff and inmates gave better ratings to the services and programs at the privately-operated facilities: escape rates were lower; there were fewer disturbances by inmates; and in general, staff and offenders felt more comfortable at the privately-operated facilities."

Liability

Questions concerning liability—such as which party is liable under private operation, does "state action" exist, and can liability costs shift from one party to another—have been an extremely important component of the prison privatization debate. Civil rights and abuse cases within the correctional system are pervasive. In 1989, 18,389 prisoner civil rights suits were filed in federal courts, up from 6,600 in 1975 (Thomas and Hanson 1990). No matter how cautious private operators are, they are not immune to the same types of legal challenges.

Privatization critics fear that contracting out will expose the government entity to liability charges for which it is not accountable or in control. Previously, privatization supporters argued that by contracting out, liability would shift from the government sector to the private sector, thereby shielding the government.

The Medina v. O'Neill case (586 F. Supp. 1028 [S.D. Texas 1984]), however, changed that way of thinking. The case involved a prison guard hired by a private firm under contract with the INS. The guard had shot two inmates, killing one and severely wounding the other. The decision by the federal district court was that the private entity performed as an agent of the government which provides a constitutionally mandated service. "State action" did exist, and the government, therefore, was liable (Brakel 1989).

Since the case, the consensus among most legal scholars is that because the government entity retains ultimate authority and responsibility for the contractor, contracting out constitutes "state action" (Logan 1990). There is ambiguity in situations where the private contractor is providing segments of the service that would not have been provided by the government. Professors Charles Thomas and Linda Hanson conclude, "Notwithstanding the United States Supreme Court's widely analyzed efforts to clarify these requirements, the circumstances under which private persons or entities will encounter civil liability for constitutional torts are not easily defined" (Thomas and Hanson 1989).

To protect both potentially liable parties, almost all private providers carry liability insurance. CCA carries $15 million in liability insurance for the Bay County Jail, as is required under the terms of the contract (Fitzgerald 1988). Similarly, the U.S. Corrections Corporation carries insurance to cover up to $1.5 million per incident (Logan 1990). In addition, many contracts include indemnification clauses which shift all liability costs to the private contractor. In several states, contractors are required by law to carry insurance and to sign indemnification provisions (Ring 1986).

Exploiting the Political Process?

Opponents of privatization—who at least acknowledge the probable continuing trend of privately operated prisons—envision a future corrections industry of politically entrenched private operators with the lobbying power to influence government policy. Specifically, they fear that the private sector's penetration in corrections potentially would create a strong lobby group pushing for longer sentences to incarcerate more individuals.

It is hard to imagine how private providers of corrections would gain more political power than do the private providers of any other public service. Do private firms that handle solid-waste disposal in landfills lobby against recycling? Or, as E.S. Savas poses, do operators of day-care centers lobby as a political force against birth control and abortion (Savas 1987)? Were private vendors able to mobilize to politically influence the length of prison sentences, it would only be because they had the support of the general public which has advocated longer sentences for more than a decade.

Privatization of prisons is not meant to replace the government's provision of corrections, but to provide an additional source with additional and improved capacity. Nor do private operators have control over the release of prisoners. In almost all cases of release—whether for furlough, probation, or permanent discharge—decisions are made by the government entity. Most jurisdictions handle all "good behavior" decisions. For those that do not, standard procedures are used and closely monitored (NCJA 1987).

The critics' premise assumes that private operators will be desperate for inmates to fill their cells—a difficult situation to imagine. The day when there is a shortage of prisoners seems light years away. But should the rising prison population taper off, the private operator—more so than the government—has enormous flexibility to adjust to changes in the prison population. Facing a decline in the number of inmates, the firm could save money by cutting back on staff and eliminating certain services that are not necessary with fewer prisoners—such as elaborate recreational programs, purportedly provided as a crowd-control mechanism against inmate violence.

Conclusion

America's correctional system is rapidly deteriorating. Government spending for corrections is growing faster than ever, yet prisons are not being built quickly enough to house the ballooning inmate population. Meanwhile, states are feeling pressure from the federal courts to find more prison space. When they miss court-imposed deadlines to provide such space, the states often find it necessary to release offenders before their sentences are served. And the federal government, less able to rely on the bulging county jails to hold federal offenders, are also struggling to find more cell space.

Privatization of prisons can help alleviate this crisis. More than thirty-five federal, state, and local jurisdictions are tapping the innovations of the private sector, awarding contracts to build, finance, or operate adult secure facilities.

In the early 1980s, during prison privatization's early road test days, observers questioned whether the private sector could succeed in providing service traditionally performed by the government. Opponents predicted that contractors would fail to save the government money, the quality of prisons and inmate care would decline as vendors cut corners to save money, and problems concerning liability would eventually turn agencies away from private operation.

Over the past decade, however, the achievements of private operators have put to rest many of these concerns. Concerns about liability are being sorted out in the terms of the contracts. Most importantly, vendors are proving they can save money while improving the quality of facilities.

Notes

1. In fiscal 1990, state budgets for correctional facilities rose by 14.2 percent.

2. Seventy-seven percent of state government officials responding to a Touche Ross survey listed cost-savings as an advantage of contracting out. Sixty-one percent of the states responded to the survey (Touche Ross 1989).
3. For the remainder of this chapter, "prison privatization" will refer to the government contracting out "primary" prisons to private management.
4. The other listed per diem costs are $17.65, $19.08, $20.73, and $33.13 (Ring, 1985).
5. Buckinghams Security's contract to operate Butler County Jail was not renewed due to political and successful efforts of AFSCME to terminate the private operator's contract. The powerful labor union threw its state-wide support behind two candidates for county commissioner who opposed prison privatization. As was later agreed by players on both sides of the issue, Buckingham Security was the victim of "labor and county politics." For a more detailed account of this situation see Logan (1990, 36-37).

References

Abell, R.B. (1989) "Beyond Willie Horton." *Policy Review* 47, Winter.

Benenson, R. (1985) "Privatizing Public Services." Congressional Quarterly, Inc., *Editorial Research Reports*, July 26.

Brakel, S.J. (1988a) "'Privatization in Corrections: Radical Chic or Mainstream Americana?" *New England Journal on Criminal and Civil Confinement* 14, 1, Winter.

———.(1988b) "Prison Management, Private Enterprise Style: The Inmates' Evaluation." *New England Journal on Criminal and Civil Confinement* 14, 2, Summer.

———.(1989) "Privatization and Corrections." Reason Foundation, *Federal Privatization Project*, January.

Bureau of Justice Statistics, U.S. Department of Justice (1988) *Report to the Nation on Crime and Justice*, Second ed., March.

———.(1989) press release, "Prison Population Jumps 7.3 Percent in Six Months." September 10.

———.(1990) press release, "Prison Population Grows 6 Percent During First Half of the Year." October 7.

———.(1991) *Prisoners in 1990*, May.

Butler, S.M. (1987) "Privatization: Lessons from British Success Stories." The Heritage Foundation, *The International Briefing* 15, February 12.

Chi, K.S. (1989) "Prison Overcrowding and Privatization: Models and Opportunities." The Council of State Governments, *The Journal of State Government* 62, 2, March/April.

Cikins, W.I.(1986) "Privatization of the American Prison Systems: An Idea Whose Time Has Come?" *Notre Dame Journal of Law, Ethics and Public Policy* 2, 2.

DiIulio, J.J., Jr. (1989) *Prison Overcrowding and Judicial Intervention* (Unpublished).

———.(1990) "Prisons for Profit?" *Commentary* March.

Donahue, J.D. (1988) "Prisons for Profit: Public Justice, Private Interests." Economic Policy Institute.

———.(1989) *The Privatization Decision: Public Ends, Private Means*. New York: Basic Books.

Edsall, T.B. (1989) "States' Prison Programs Are Fastest-Growing Cost." *Washington Post*, August 8.

Fitzgerald, R. (1988) *When Government Goes Private: Successful Alternatives to Public Services*. New York: Universe Books.

Fixler, P.E., Jr. R.W. Poole, Jr. and L. Scarlett. (1989) *Privatization 1989: Third Annual Report on Privatization.* Reason Foundation.
Hackett, J.C. H.P. Hatry R.B. Levinson J. Allen K. Chi and E.D. Feigenbaum. (1987) "Contracting for the Operation of Prisons and Jails," National Institute of Justice, U.S. Department of Justice, *Research in Brief,* June.
Holton, S. and M. Vosburgh. (1989) "Special Report: Crime Before its Time." *The Orlando Sentinel,* August 13-16.
Larson, E. (1988) "Captive Company." *Inc. Magazine.* June.
Logan, C.H. and S.P. Rausch. (1985) "Punish and Profit: The Emergence of Private Enterprise Prisons," *Justice Quarterly.* September.
Logan, C.H. and B.W. McGriff. (1989) "Comparing Costs of Public and Private Prisons: A Case Study." *NIJ Reports.* National Institute of Justice, U.S. Department of Justice, September/October.
Logan, C.H. (1989) "Proprietary Prisons," *The American Prison: Issues in Research and Policy.* Lynne Goodstein and Doris L. MacKenzie (editors). New York: Plenum.
Logan, C.H. (1990) *Private Prisons: Cons and Pros.* New York: Oxford University Press.
Moore, S. (1988) "Privatization in America's Cities: Lessons for Washington, Part I." The Heritage Foundation, *Backgrounder,* 652, May 31.
Mullen, J. K.J. Chabotar and D.M. Carrow. (1985) *The Privatization of Corrections.* National Institute of Justice, U.S. Department of Justice, February.
National Criminal Justice Association. (1987) "Private Sector Involvement in Financing and Managing Correctional Facilities." *Special Report,* April.
National Institute of Justice, U.S. Department of Justice. (1985) "The Privatization of Corrections." *Issues and Practices,* February.
U.S. Department of Justice and American Correctional Association. (1988) *National Directory of Corrections Construction,* second edition, April.
Pagel, A. (1989) "Military Bases—Sites for Prisons?" *Corrections Compendium,* January/February.
Public Employee Department, AFL-CIO. (1990) *Privatization Update,* Winter.
Raspberry, W. (1988) "What Is the Purpose of Prison?" *Washington Post,* November 22.
Ring, C. (1986) *Report Relative to Prisons for Profit.* Legislative Research Council, The Commonwealth of Massachusetts.
Robbins, I.P. (1989) "'Dungeons for Dollars': Private Enterprise Sees Money in Jails." *Legal Times,* November 27.
Savas, E.S. (1987) *Privatization: The Key to Better Government.* New Jersey: Chatham House Publishers.
Sexton, G.E. F.C. Farrow and B.J. Auerbach. (1985) "The Private Sector and Prison Industries." *Research in Brief.* National Institute of Justice, U.S. Department of Justice, August.
State Legislatures (1990), March.
Thomas, C.W. and Suzanna L. Foard (1991) "Private Correctional Facility Census," Center for Studies in Criminology and Law, University of Florida. (Unpublished survey), November.
Thomas, C.W. and L.S. Calvert Hanson. (1989) "The Implications of 42 U.S.C. 1983 for the Privatization of Prisons." *Florida State University Law Review.* 16, 4, Spring.
_____.(1990) "Access to Qualified Immunity by Private Defendants in 42 Section 1983 Damage Suits: The Implications for Correctional Privatization," (Unpublished paper presented at the Academy of Criminal Justice Sciences annual convention), March 17.

Touche Ross and Company. (1989) *State Government Privatization in America.*
Williams, S.D. (1986) "Good Time/Early Release: Out Before Their Time." *Corrections Compendium*, July.

6

Bars on the Iron Triangle: Public Policy Issues in the Privatization of Corrections

Michael Janus

Within the last several years, there has been a surge of interest in the area of privatization of corrections in the U.S. This surge represents the culmination of a variety of historical circumstances that include: increasing inmate populations at all jurisdictional levels (local, state, federal), increasingly "tight" governmental budgets, increasing court intervention in the administration of corrections, disenchantment with the government's ability to perform any task effectively, and a corresponding fondness for private sector values.

Privatization of corrections has come to have a variety of meanings. Privatization is used to refer to private funding of the construction of correctional institutions, as well as the contracting out of individual services (to date, primarily food and medical services). There has also been an effort to "privatize" correctional industries. Finally, the most controversial meaning of privatization refers to the management of entire adult facilities by private corporations. The substantive questions surrounding privatization of corrections are typical of the privatization debate in other areas: Is it cheaper? Is it better? Are there any legal barriers to privatization?

Criminal justice is unique in that symbolic and public policy issues are important factors in the privatization debate, above and beyond substantive issues. Criminal justice is an area in which symbolism plays an important role. If pursued on a large scale, privatization of corrections will introduce a new motive (profit) into an area that in modern times has been solely under the control of the public sector. The symbolic and public policy implications of corporate involvement in corrections have yet to be explored in detail. The key question is "Whether the introduction of the profit motive affects the symbolism, and in turn, public policy in corrections, and in criminal justice as whole."

Private involvement in corrections can effect symbolism in corrections in two important ways. First, it can serve to distance the state from the inmate (and vice versa), by introducing an intervening actor. Second, privatization introduces an important new political actor into the fundamentally symbolic public decisions that take place in criminal justice decisions.

It is the purpose of this paper to separate the potential substantive and symbolic impacts of private corrections, and provide a detailed focus on the symbolic and public policy implications of prisons for profit.

Substantive Reality in Corrections

Obviously, there is a substantive side to the criminal justice effort, that which is depicted in most criminal justice texts. This set of tasks reflects the activities of the police, prosecutors, courts, and corrections to respond to the mandates of the law. Increasing crime rates through the sixties and seventies, largely reflective of the aging of the baby boom generation, have put extraordinary pressure on the players in this system to respond to the flow of activity through the network. In some cases, particularly at the front end of the system, considerable discretion exists to offset the impact of this increased workload. The police have discretion to arrest. The prosecutor and courts use plea bargaining to offset the large numbers of defendants. However, corrections officials have little discretion in the handling of their charges. They can not turn away inmates, and with the exception of some provisions of good time, they have little say about the amount of time that inmates will spend in the system.

Add to this lack of discretion, a general lack of recognition for the tasks relegated to those who manage offenders, the end product of the system. Consistent with the notion of banishment, one of the earlier forms of reaction to deviance, the general public has little interest in what happens to convicted offenders, and reacts primarily to escapes or stories of brutal mistreatment of offenders. There is a history of almost constant opposition to the placement of correctional institutions in most localities.

Reflecting this basic public attitude, legislators often overlook corrections budgets in favor of more recognizable and attractive alternatives such as increased police and enforcement budgets. These low budgets, in conjunction with an overall low image of "guards," low starting salaries, bad working conditions, aging prisons, and dramatically increasing inmate populations have left many correctional systems in bad shape. As policy makers face court orders to relieve overcrowding and improve conditions (thirty corrections agencies are currently under court order according to Camp and Camp (1986, 23), the high expense of confining inmates becomes increasingly apparent.

It is under these conditions that policy makers have expressed an interest in privatization. Some observers have pointed out that governments are attempting to rid themselves of the burden of corrections by shifting the load to the private sector:

> Since corrections has a limited constituency, even the most conscientious political tactician who addresses corrections issues faces a fruitless situation.... If a politician can sidestep the entire correctional arena, he can avoid a major political pitfall and a frustrating no-win emotional battleground.... So it is little wonder that elected officials perk up when private groups offer seemingly expedient solutions and propose to take over 'the problem' by removing it from the public arena. (Anderson et al. 1985)

The largest share of the debate concerning private corrections centers around the substantive issues, specifically will private enterprise be more cost effective? It is at this level that most of the general discussion of government "contracting-out" can be brought to bear. Proponents claim that private enterprise is inherently more efficient (see Savas 1982 and Bennet and Johnson 1981). Arguments that point out the lack of competition, the mass of red tape, the inefficient economies of scale, and various other factors ingrained in the governmental way of business are offered by these groups in support of contracting out.

Opponents of contracting out (see Hanrahan 1983) cite contractors low-balling (submitting initially low bids and raising prices as the government becomes dependent on the contractor's services), the lack of genuine competition, and the use of contracts to subvert personnel ceilings, among other issues, as major inefficiencies in contracting out. Both sides submit numerous cases as evidence, most of which are either anecdotal or scientifically insufficient, supporting their arguments.

Similar debates surround the privatization of corrections. Proponents of privatization point out the potential for increased innovation and efficiency. The reasons for this increase in efficiency include better economies of scale, more flexible personnel policies (the ability to hire and fire), more effective procurement policies, and more timely reaction to needs. See the testimony of Richard Crane, vice president of Corrections Corporation of America (1986, 32-53) and Gruber (1986) for a thorough summary of these claims.

Of course, opponents of privatization are skeptical. They do not believe that costs can be kept lower without serious impact on the quality of correctional service. They believe that the areas that proponents of privatization claim are most ripe for cutting (such as personnel and training), are already stretched paper thin in the publicly operated system. They also point to the relative lack of competition in the private corrections business. This lack of competition, they say, will result in very little actual competition and lead to a high probability of contractors monopolizing the corrections arena, eventually leading to uncontrollably high prices. (See Gruber 1986 and Keating 1986 for a more detailed development of these arguments.)

Once again, however, the objective evidence is lacking. No major adult medium- or higher-security level facility has gone private. Probably the most comprehensive evidence exists from the American Correctional Association's evaluation of the takeover of the Okeechobee Boy's School in Florida by the Eckerd Foundation. The ACA report did not find any compelling evidence that Eckerd had improved cost or quality of service (National Institute of Justice, 1985). In fact, the report noted some evidence in the other direction. However, it is clear that many of Eckerd's problems resulted from a difficult transition from public to private, a phenomenon not unexpected even by the most fervent supporters of privatization. The Okeechobee experiment still needs to face the test of time.

The ACA report also highlights the difficulty of making public-private correctional comparisons. The nature of public and private accounting and budgeting makes cost comparisons difficult. For instance, private costs (on a per diem basis) must be all inclusive, while public costs often include only operating expenses and exclude capital depreciation. The private sector includes their building and capital equipment as assets; such a position is rarely taken in regard to public accounting. On the other hand, private rates often do not include monitoring costs, while public figures include administrative overhead (the public equivalent of contract development and monitoring). Government agencies usually self-insure, but do not include claims in their operating costs, while private firms are forced to pay large sums for liability insurance. There are other cost and accounting issues, depending on the type and scope of the comparison. What is generally recognized is the lack of solid evidence in this area. (See Gruber 1986, 61-82; Legislative Research Council 1986, 63-68; and National Institute of Justice 1985, 79-81).

Beyond cost is the issue of effectiveness. One of the major problems here is defining what effectiveness is for corrections. On the most basic level, incarceration itself is a major goal, but there is some question as to what degree deterrence, rehabilitation and punishment can be incorporated into the private-public comparison. Perhaps all evaluators can do at this point is address the "process" of incarceration rather than the overall "outcome" of incarceration. (See Roberts and Powers 1985 for a discussion of this issue.)

Another set of substantive arguments revolves around legal issues. Included in these issues are the authority to delegate corrections to private entities (enabling legislation), the ability of the government to avoid civil rights lawsuits, the ability of the government to delegate law enforcement powers to privately compensated individuals, and the necessity of writing and monitoring very specific contract arrangements. These issues have been discussed by a number of authors. (See for instance Robbins 1986; Gruber 1986; and National Institute of Justice 1985). The general consensus is that legal issues can be carefully worked out at the operational level; but that caution is advised.

The Importance of Symbolism in Criminal Justice

Crime is clearly the domain of the government in modern society. In fact crime does not exist outside of its definition by agents of the state;

there is no crime without law, (*nullen crimen sen lege*). In an operational sense, it is also clear that a criminal becomes a criminal only when he or she is so defined by agents of the state through the enforcement and adjudication process. This process is more than a rhetorical game; it is the key to the actions that govern the way our society reacts to deviance.

The notion that criminal justice is both substantive and symbolic is a fundamental building block of criminal justice theory. Emile Durkheim is well known for developing the symbolic importance of criminal justice policies for the stability of society (1975). In his functional analysis, the labeling of certain acts and actors as officially deviant helps to enforce the solidarity of societal values.

Herbert Packer (1968) also addresses the importance of symbolism when he discusses the crime control and due process models of criminal justice in *The Limits of the Criminal Sanction*. When viewed as crime control, criminal justice is at its most "efficient." Maintenance of order is the ultimate goal. Defendant's rights are obstructions to the attainment of this goal. When viewed as due process, fairness is the ultimate goal. Rights of the accused are seen as the cornerstone of the process. Obviously, our current system contains threads of both of these models. Policy is formed with both of these goals in mind, and this policy is tempered by the decisions of the courts.

Legislative decisions regarding the machinery of criminal justice are made largely at the symbolic level. The customer of these decisions is undoubtedly the general public. Deviant behavior, or more importantly, the fear of certain kinds of deviant behavior, generates decisions to criminalize an activity, as well as funding efforts relating to certain enforcement activities. Executive branch decisions emphasize the direction and strength of enforcement efforts, providing symbolic background for the policies of a particular administration. The courts generally referee these activities.

A classic example of the importance of symbolism is the Federal criminal justice response to drug abuse in the United States over the last decade. First, the Reagan administration shifted enforcement priorities from the Carter administration's emphasis on white collar and organized crime to illegal sale and use of drugs. Then the Congress, reacting to increasing public concern and publicity, passed the Comprehensive Drug Act of 1986, severely increasing penalties for drug sales and use, and funded 1.7 billion dollars for enforcement activities. This despite the widely held opinion that enforcement has had little impact on reducing the flow of illegal drugs in the U.S.

In spite of a limited flirtation with private contracting for corrections and the use of convict labor, (Dilulio 1986) all of the major players in the social response to crime in the U.S. have been public officials, either elected or civil service. The introduction of private interests with a profit motive has the potential to effect the symbolism in the criminal justice system. Private involvement can impact the symbolic function of criminal justice in two ways. One is the larger issue of the propriety of turning over the very basic governmental responsibility for incarceration to profit-oriented entities. The other is the operational impact of private influence on the symbolic aspects of public policy making.

The Larger Ethical Issue: Is It Right?

The National Institute of Justice report (1985, 70) has described this as "The most fundamental issue in the political debate." The key question is whether we can shift responsibility for the ultimate sanction by which we define our normative behavior to those whose motive is profit. Regardless of the efficacy of the privatization effort, many are concerned about the symbolic statement being made. Ira Robbins (1986, 29) has asked:

> Does it weaken that [symbolic] authority, however-as well as the integrity of a system of justice-when an inmate looks at his keeper's uniform, and, instead of encountering an emblem that reads "Federal Bureau of Prisons" or "State Department of Corrections," he faces one that says "Acme Corrections Company"?

and at the larger social level:

> I cannot help but wonder what Dostoevsky—who wrote that "the degree of civilization in a society can be judged by entering its prisons"—would have thought about privatization of corrections. (Robbins 1986, 30)

Proponents of privatization point out that the government retains ultimate control, that by the provisions of the contract and a valid contract monitoring effort, the state is providing sufficient symbolic leadership.

A New Actor on the Scene: Political Influence

Public policy is not formed in a vacuum. Observers of the growth of government have pointed to an "iron triangle" of decision makers who influence policy and spending in a given arena. This group of actors is made up of legislators, a concerned public (a "public interest group"), and the bureaucrats who administer policy. The scenario is painted something like this: The public interest group throws its political support behind a program they are interested in. The legislator(s) responding to this pressure sponsors legislation establishing and maintaining this program. The bureaucrats administer the program, responding to the interest group, keeping in mind the financial and political importance of the program to them personally (See Woll 1982 and Kaufman 1976).

If this scenario is realistic, and most would concede that there is much truth to it, it clarifies why corrections is in financial trouble in most jurisdictions. For reasons stated earlier, the public is diffuse and removed from decisions related to corrections. There are few organized groups interested in correctional policy. Some exceptions include prisoners rights groups and victims rights groups, but these groups are not very powerful. Correctional bureaucrats must fight for influence and funding with no real public interest group behind them. They compete for resources with other law enforcement groups whose impact on the public is much more apparent and immediate (police, courts).

Privatization of corrections threatens to change this situation. By its very nature, the construction and management of correctional institutions is a large-scale activity. Thus, companies which became involved in private corrections are very likely to have many resources at their disposal, and much to lose if decisions in the area are unfavorable. One could predict that these companies will mount lobbying campaigns directly with legislatures and other elected officials. Additionally, in an area which is more volatile and potentially impactful, these companies could mobilize public opinion in a direction favorable to their position.

Proponents of privatization point out that this process of influencing decision makers would provide corrections with a long overdue source of political power (see National Institute of Justice 1985, 72). Others see the increased flexibility and potential gains in efficiency resulting from privatization as enhancers of justice. Private prisons would give the government the opportunity to respond to crime without the need to consider the largescale expansion of correctional resources (Logan and Rausch 1985, 315).

Opponents point to the potential abuse of this power. The fears of opponents of privatization are that private vendors can, by political and public influence, manipulate the highly undefined and sensitive goals of corrections to an interest in profits by these companies rather than the "social good": "private operators, whose growth depends upon an expanding prison population, will develop into a powerful lobby pushing for everharsher sentences. A lobby which given the public's unabating fear of crime, lawmakers will find very hard to resist" (Legislative Research Council 1986, 9). Opponents also point out that increased efficiency, and the opening up of more prisons more quickly may not be in the public's best interests, given the relatively high rate of incarceration in the U.S. and the notion that if we have prison bed space, we will surely fill it (Elvin 1984).

Clearly, if privatization is to be a benefit, the profit incentives of corrections vendors must be aligned with the goals of society. "This problem relates to the question of whether the private sector can achieve profit maximization in a manner that is consistent with the public interest in sound corrections policy." (Cikens 1986, 458). If these goals are not aligned, then we would rely on the enactment of strong conflict of interest laws to avoid pitfalls in this public policy arena. These laws, at their current level of enforcement, have done little to curb the abuse of government contractor personnel policies. What are the potential areas of influence?

Directly on the Privatization Decision

It is unclear whether jurisdictions can enter into contracts for private corrections under existing laws. Most jurisdictions will require enabling legislation. Critics have pointed to this need as the beginning of a long relationship:

> The importance of this relationship is exemplified by CCA's[Correctional Corporation of America] inclusion of the Speaker of the Tennessee House of Representatives as an early shareholder in that company's future. The highly flexible nature of the state's power here means that private providers will need to cultivate, carefully and continually, legislative and other political friends, a need history teaches to be fraught with perils. (Keating 1985, 40)

The same author has noted the fact that the president of CCA (Tom Beasley) is also a former Republican Party Chairman in Tennessee and a close personal friend of the Governor (Keating 1985, 11).

In Pennsylvania, legislators imposed a one-year moratorium on the construction of private prisons after learning that Buckingham Security Ltd. was planning to build a "regional" high security facility there (Hornblum 1985, 29). Buckingham is run by an ex-warden and a businessman. There is no indication of political contacts as with CCA and Tennessee. Perhaps the failure of the Pennsylvania group to develop such political ties contributed to their legislative failure.

Corrections as a Whole

Can political influence by the private sector affect the amount of funding allocated to corrections? This is a key question. From the policymaker's point of view, the ideal situation would be for private firms to handle more inmates with less money. Despite claims and counterclaims, early evidence indicates that private companies can only marginally outperform (at best) public corrections. This notion, coupled with predictions of ever-increasing inmate populations suggests that there will be an increasing need for resources. In jurisdictions where privatization is adopted, it will be interesting to observe and gauge the success of private providers to attract resources to handle the expanding workload.

Of course, the very nature of the contract relationship will help ensure adequate resources for private vendors. Private vendors who allowed contracts to be written which would accept increasing workload without a corresponding increase in resources, *as public managers have done*, would soon be bankrupt.

Raw amounts of funding for corrections as a whole are not the only issue. The distribution of funding in a system where some type(s) of institutions are handled privately and same publicly will also be important. If private corrections gains a significant share of the low security market, will this deepen the troubles of public corrections by making it responsible for only troublesome, expensive, or high-risk inmates?

Once again there is little evidence with regard to lobbying efforts and funding when it comes to mainline corrections. However, in an article written in *Corrections Magazine*, Philip Taft (1983), presents some clear indicators of possible future trends in discussing the arena of private halfway houses:

> In 1976, halfway house administrators quickly learned the rudiments of lobbying and pressure tactics when the federal Bureau of Prisons eliminated all of its funds for

community-based programs. The IHHA [International Halfway House Association] organized a task force, including representatives from the Salvation Army and Volunteers of America, whose members traveled to Washington for talks with BOP director Norman Carlson. But Carlson claimed that budget money earmarked for community programs, the U.S. Marshals, and fees to local jails had been eaten up. The IHHA then turned its attention to Capitol Hill and, through a vigorous letter-writing and telephone campaign succeeded in replacing the funds (but not before angering Carlson, who had asked that the IHHA not go to Congress). The IHHA's political mettle was tested again in 1981, when the bureau announced it was once more slashing its community programs budget, this time from $26 million to $11.7 million. Fearful that this move would spell doom for hundreds of members, the IHHA alerted its network of political contacts and orchestrated another intensive lobbying effort of mail and phone calls to Congress. Ultimately, $6 million of the proposed $15 million was restored. (Taft 1983, 9)

All this happened in an era when private halfway house vendors were comprised primarily of nonprofit oriented groups with more of a social agenda than one of profit. This aspect of private corrections is becoming increasingly comprised of private, profit-oriented companies. These companies are more likely to play political and financial "hard ball." As the director of the Bureau of Prisons pointed out in his testimony before Congress on the issue "We have experienced situations in our Community Treatment Center Program where private, for-profit correctional corporations have initially underbid traditional nonprofit organizations such as the Salvation Army and Volunteers of America, and increased the cost of the service after the competition has withdrawn from the market" (Hearings 1986, 143).

There are other issues made by policymakers that could be effected by privatization. One is good time laws. These laws regulate the amount of good time given to inmates as a result of good (or at least not bad) behavior. Good time is one of the few areas of discretion in which correctional administrators have some control over population flow through their systems. Debators of the privatization issue have addressed the potential abuse of good time by private vendors to increase profits. Such vendors could also influence the laws which regulate good time for similar purposes.

Criminal Justice as a Whole

While the influence of private vendors can be anticipated most specifically in the corrections area, it does not require too large a leap in the imagination to see that influence spreading to the larger arena of criminal justice as a whole.

One of the primary areas of concern would be sentencing. Many jurisdictions, increasingly concerned with the perceived abuse of sentencing discretion by the judiciary, have turned to sentencing commissions controlled by legislators. These commissions are mandated to design strict sentencing guidelines that will determine choices among sentencing alternatives (probation, prison) and length of sentence. A relatively minor change by one of these commissions could dramatically change the number of inmates in a correctional system.

Legislatures also have the authority to define acts as illegal, or conversely, to remove such a definition from an act. Once again these decisions have a potentially large impact on inmate populations.

Taft (1983) also detected this legislative influence in his discussion of the Salvation Army's effort in Florida to handle the misdemeanant probation program. "In 1981, Rothbart [a Salvation Army manager] helped craft the state's new, stiff drunk-driving law. With that law, all first offenders will pay a $250 fine and perform 50 hours of community service. Implicit in the act is the Army's participation in administering the punishment" (Taft 1983, 40).

The decisions of the executive branch through enforcement priorities are also major determinants of numbers and characteristics of inmate populations. The Reagan administration's decision to emphasize relatively plentiful and easy to enforce drug cases over difficult to enforce white collar type cases has undoubtedly impacted the Federal Prison inmate population's 75 percent increase in inmates since 1981. Decisions regarding enforcement priorities also affect the type of inmate. Returning to the drug enforcement example, white collar criminals are more likely to be lower security level (cheaper, less problematic) than drug dealer/user criminals.

Finally, what drives the criminal justice system more than the reality of crime is the "fear of crime." This fear seems to be very unstable and at times is very different than the reality of crime, at least as measured through crime statistics. Other than politicians at election time looking for a plank of a political platform, there has been little vested interest in manipulating the fear of crime. The privatization of a major component of the criminal justice system raises this possibility.

Summary

Corrections, as a whole, is in crisis in the U.S. Expanding inmate populations and diminishing governmental resources have encouraged policymakers to look into the area of privatization as a way of handling the problem. The primary focus of this look to the private sector has been on substantive issues: can the private sector do it better and/or cheaper? At this point in time there is no clear cut answer to these questions. There are also some key legal questions which need to be addressed.

What has not been acknowledged to a large degree in the privatization debate is the symbolic and public policy impacts of the privatization of corrections. We must account for the fact that corrections rests in a system (criminal justice) in which symbolism plays a major role. The introduction of a new incentive (profit) to this system has the potential to profoundly alter the nature of decisions in corrections, and in criminal justice. This is especially true given the popular beliefs regarding the way public decisions are made and enforced in this country.

This shift in emphasis need not be bad. As long as the social good can be aligned with the profit incentives of the private sector, this movement may benefit corrections, which has been somewhat of a poor stepchild in the criminal justice system. However, if what is good for private vendors becomes misaligned with the public good, there is a high potential for abuse because of the uncertain and unstable nature of public perceptions of crime.

Beyond the symbolic question of private companies taking aver the management of entire correctional facilities, there are many areas where private vendors could effect public policy by influencing legislators or other public administrators. These areas include enabling legislation, corrections decisions, such as funding amounts or distribution, sentencing decisions, decisions regarding the criminalization or decriminalization of an activity, and the public's overall fear of crime.

It is no coincidence that privatization has become popular at a time when public corrections, for a variety of reasons, has been unable to meet the demands of the system. For now, profit incentives are in line with the perceived public need. The issues addressed here will become more salient if privatization is adopted on a large scale, and crime and incarceration rates begin to dip, as many demographic forecasters predict by the early 1990s. At that point, corrections vendors will be under pressure to align social goals with their profit motive.

References

Bennet, J.T. and M. Johnson. (1981) *Better Government at Half the Price: Private Production of Public Services*. Ottowa, IL: Caroline House Publishers.

Camp, G. and C. Camp. (1986) *The Corrections Yearbook: 1986*. South Salem, NY: The Criminal Justice Institute.

Cikins, W.I. (1986) "Privatization of the American prison System: An Idea Whose Time Has Come?" *Notre Dame Journal of Law, Ethics and Public Policy* 2, 2: 445-64.

Dilulio, J. (1986) "Prisons, Profits and the Public Good: The Privatization of Corrections." *Research Bulletin* 21. Sam Houston State University Criminal Justice Center.

Durkheim, E. (1975) "The Normal and the Pathological." In R. Farrell and V.L. Swigert (eds.), *Social Deviance*. New York: J.B. Lippincott.

Elvin, J. (1985) "A Civil Liberties View of Private Prisons." *The Prison Journal*, Pennsylvania Prison Society, 65, 2 (Autumn-Winter): 48-52.

Gruber, L. (1986) "Private Sector Involvement in the Financing and Management of Correctional Facilities: Policy Issues in Perspective," unpublished draft.

Hanrahan, J. (1983) *Government by Contract*. New York: W.W.Norton.

Hearings. (1986) *Hearings before the Subcommittee on Courts, Civil Liberties and Administration of Justice of the Committee on the Judiciary*, U. S. House of Representatives, 99th Congress, 1st and 2nd Sessions on Privatization of Corrections, Serial No. 40, U.S.Government Printing Office (13 November 1985 and 18 March 1986).

Hornblum, A. (1985) "Are We Ready for the Privatization of America's Prisons." *The Privatization Review*, Fall: 25-29.

Kaufman, H. (1976) *Are Government Organizations Immortal?* The Brookings Institution, Washington, DC.

Keating, J.M. Jr. (1985) *Seeking Profit in Punishment: The Private Management of Correctional Institutions*. Washington, DC: American Federation of State, County, and Municipal Employees.

Lee, J. R. and L. Wollan, Jr. (1985) "The Libertarian Prison: Principles of Laissez Faire Incarceration." *The Prison Journal*, Pennsylvania Prison Society, 65, 2, (Autumn-Winter): 108-21.

Legislative Research Council. (1986) *Report Relative to Prisons for Profit*. Commonwealth of Massachusetts, House bill number 6225.

Logan, C.H. and S.P. Rausch. (1985) "Punish and Profit: The Emergence of Private Enterprise Prisons." *Justice Quarterly* 2, 3, (September): 303-318.

National Institute of Corrections. (1985) *Private Sector Operation of a Correctional Institution*. Washington, DC: National Institute of Corrections.

National Institute of Justice. (1985) *The Privatization of Corrections*. Washington, DC: National Institute of Justice.

Packer, H. (1968) *The Limits of Criminal Sanction*. Stanford, CA: Stanford University Press.

Robbins, I.P. (1986) "Privatization of Corrections: Defining the Issues." *Federal Probation* 50, 3: 24-30.

Roberts, A.R. and G.T. Powers. (1985) "The Privatization of Corrections: Methodological Issues and Dilemmas Involved in Evaluative Research." *The Prison Journal*, Pennsylvania Prison Society, 65, 2, (Autumn-Winter): 95-107.

Savas, E.S. (1982) *Privatizing the Public Sector*. Chatham, NJ: Chatham House Publishers.

Taft, P.B. Jr. (1983) "Private Vendors: Part II Survival of the Fittest." *Corrections Magazine* 9, 1: 36-43.

Woll, P. (1982) *Constitutional Democracy: Policies and Politics*. Boston: Little, Brown, and Co.

7

Federal Government Involvement in Private Sector Partnerships with Prison Industries

Barbara Auerbach

The federal government has strongly encouraged private sector involvement in prison industries for more than a decade. Federal legislation intended to allow widespread innovation by the states was enacted by Congress under the guidance of Senator Charles Percy of Illinois. Chief Justice Burger's much publicized "factories within fences" campaign has been widely viewed as a surprising and unprecedented display of judicial support for a corrections program. But the most important federal support has been that of the U.S. Department of Justice which over the years has spent several million dollars on research, technical assistance, and state aid to foster public/private partnerships in prison industries.[1] This paper looks at the nature of federal support, describes some problems associated with federal involvement in the development of partnerships in prison industries, and sets forth suggestions for future federal actions.

Innovation in corrections often begins in the states and spreads to the federal level, and there is ample evidence of state creativity in developing private sector involvement in prison industries. In Minnesota and Nevada, for example, state efforts predate federal involvement by several years. Nonetheless, dominant federal leadership in promoting such involvement began early and has been remarkably consistent.

Surveys in 1985, 1987, and 1989 show that the while the number of partnerships is growing slowly, the number of prisoners involved remains very small at approximately 5,000 nationwide (Criminal Justice Associates 1985, 1987, and 1989). Whether this is a typical rate of growth for joint ventures or should be seen as an indication that growth is ceasing, is not yet clear. In either case, the future actions of the federal government will be crucial in determining the future of such partnerships.

Description of Federal Involvement

The Department of Justice's support for research and technical assistance broadening and strengthening the role of state prison industries began in the early 1970s and continues to the present date.[2] From the beginning, the rationale for change was two-pronged: (1) private sector methods, attitudes, and involvement were necessary if common state prison industry problems of limited markets, unskilled staff and workers, undercapitalized plants and equipment, and an atmosphere more akin to a sheltered workshop than a factory, were to be overcome; and (2) wages for prisoners based on productivity were a necessary ingredient for the protection of both prisoner workers and free world labor and industry.[3] In addition, the research is strongly colored by belief in the potential power of private sector prison industries to normalize the lives of prisoner workers and the institutions in which they live.

Once the identification of the private sector as a vehicle for change had been made, the logical next step was the development of a model that could be tested and modified by the states (Econ, Inc. 1978).[4] The Free Venture model was implemented first in Connecticut, and subsequently in six other states.[5]

At this stage, "hands-on" private sector involvement was not a major focus of the model; instead, the adoption of private sector methods and techniques by state prison industries was emphasized. By 1980, however, federal legislation authorizing actual partnerships in prison industries between the public and private sectors was in place. The payment of prevailing wages and normal worker benefits was required as a condition of participation in the Prison Industries Enhancement (PIE) program, which the new legislation had established under the Department of Justice's program arm, the Law Enforcement Assistance Administration (later the Bureau of Justice Assistance [BJA].[6]

Regulations for the PIE Program required: (1) statutory authority to administer prison industry programs; (2) contributions to victim compensation or victim assistance programs at not less than 5 percent nor more than 20 percent of gross wages; (3) consultation with organized labor; (4) consultation with local private industry; (5) payment of prevailing wages; (6) assurances that the program would not result in the displacement of employed workers; (7) assurances that inmate participation was voluntary; (8) provision of inmate worker compensation for injuries; and (9) substantial involvement of the private sector (BJA "PIE Program Application Kit," 1987).

Why was such significant federal involvement necessary? The interstate transport of prison-made goods had been legislatively prohibited in the 1930s and 1940s under pressure from business and labor groups, thus making it impossible—even for states that authorized the open market sale of prison-made goods within their own borders—to move those goods across state lines. If modern corporations, which generally market their goods on a nationwide (or at least regional) basis, were now to be the partners of prison industries, the prohibitive legislation had to be removed. Senator Percy's bill (See note 6) did remove most of the major restrictions preventing experimentation with joint ventures in prison industries for a small number of pilot projects. The legislation was amended in 1984 to include twenty such pilot projects, and simultaneously BJA effected an administrative change in the definition of project, such that "project" could be equated with state or county. Finally, the law again amended in late 1990 to allow up to fifty pilot programs to participate. Thus, in theory, all of the prison products of as many as fifty states or counties may now legally enter the stream of interstate commerce.[7] As of 1990, more than twenty certifications had been awarded by BJA.[8]

There are legitimate "noncertified" projects as well, since legal restrictions apply only to goods; projects involving services need not seek certification. In addition, partnerships that do not wish to expand their markets beyond state boundaries do not need federal approval. There are also some noncertified projects which place products in interstate commerce but for some reason have not been certified and are therefore operating in apparent violation of the interstate commerce prohibition. As of January 1990 there were twenty-nine noncertified projects in operation. (Criminal Justice Associates, 1991).[9]

Federal judicial involvement has been limited to the out-of-court advocacy of former chief justice Warren Burger. (There have been no significant cases encouraging private sector prison industries per se, though a number of cases have moved the status of inmates who work for private companies increasingly closer to that of full employees.[10]) Under his auspices, two major conferences of corrections, business, and labor leaders were held to further the concept of joining the public and the private sectors in a united effort to create "factories within fences."[11] The Chief Justice, who normally fervently avoided press coverage during his years on the bench, allowed himself to be interviewed on national television and encouraged coverage of major speeches in which he advocated the creation of partnerships in prison industries.

In large part because of his strong interest, the National Center for Innovation in Corrections was established at the George Washington University, in order that a permanent base might exist for the furthering of these partnerships. The Center was partially funded by the National Institute of Corrections and the National Institute of Justice. Center staff explored possibilities for the development of new ideas for public and private sector efforts to establish the factories envisioned by Chief Justice Burger until 1988 when funding was discontinued.

For more than ten years, then, through the Carter, Reagan, and now the Bush administrations, and with the blessing of political figures from the left and the right,[12] support from the federal government has been remarkably consistent. There is little doubt that without federal support, the destructive effect of overcrowding on all prison programs could have eclipsed joint ventures in prison industries.

The following section attempts to describe the two broad areas of federal involvement in the development and operation of partnerships which may require new and different responses in the future—the regulation of partnerships and the provision of incentives.

Partnership Problems and the Role of the Federal Government

In addition to its role in encouraging and assisting states and counties to join with the private sector in creating prison industry partnerships, the federal government is also responsible for regulating partnerships to avoid exploitation of prisoner workers or the creation of unfair competitive practices harmful to manufacturers or workers in the community. This dual role of leadership and regulation has led to muddled regulatory practices at best.

The major area of regulatory concern centers around the payment of prevailing wages to inmates, as required by the Percy legislation. The importance of maintaining wage levels comparable to those found in similar community operations lies in the need to avoid unfair competition as much as in the need to protect prisoner workers. State prison officials, unaccustomed to prisoner wages above a few dollars per day in most cases, tend to be uneasy about the effect of the relatively large sums of money that must be paid to prisoners who work for the private sector. Private sector entrepreneurs operating in a correctional context are eager to pare wages as much as possible, given the additional costs of doing business in a prison.[13] Prisoners tend to focus on the sharp increase in wages over traditional prison industries jobs that such programs provide, not on the relationship between the wages they are being paid and those paid to workers in similar occupations on the outside. It was foreseen by Congress that prison administrators would hesitate to pay prisoners high wages and that the general public would also object, particularly in times of high unemployment. Provisions therefore were made within the Percy legislation to allow deductions from a worker's wages for family support, restitution, taxes, and payment of part of the cost of incarceration. As a result, some citizen and political support for partnerships has been generated by publicizing the amounts raised through the deduction process (Fedo 1981).

But if the use of deductions has helped to quell opposition, it has not changed correctional administrators into firm advocates of wage equality for prisoners. Rather, the dramatic increase in the number of prisoners and the resultant pressure to adjust limited program opportunities to involve as many prisoners as possible have prevented the development of any real support for the concept of a normalized work place within the prison. Partnerships do not fit well into an overcrowded prison. In fact, they generally provide quality programming for a relatively small number of prisoners and take a significant amount of planning and administrative resources to establish and maintain.

In a large number of cases it appears that departments of corrections do not have the resources to attempt to recreate the real world of work inside the prison. Instead, they often choose to employ as many prisoners as possible with the least possible fiscal outlay, sacrificing the development of inmate skills in an attempt to avoid the violence they fear widespread idleness will produce. In such an atmosphere, little chance exists for any real support for the prevailing wage concept.

As the administrative agency responsible for the implementation of the PIE program, the Bureau of Justice Assistance of the Department of

Justice is responsible for oversight of the PIE projects through its "certification" mechanism. No project is certified until the appropriate state Department of Labor (which has the power to set the prevailing wage by occupation and geographic area) has notified BJA in writing that the proposed project wage range falls within the prevailing wage range. For certified projects, then, it appears that at the entry level, the prevailing wage is being paid to inmate workers. But projects which are not certified may be paying wages at less than the prevailing rate.[14] Noncertified projects have tended to peg their wage scales lower than certified projects.[15]

Adding to the pressure to eliminate the prevailing wage requirement, the suggestion has been put forth from the prison industries community that prisoner workers might best be thought of as Third World workers for purposes of wages. By paying prisoners say, $1.00 per hour (a sum considerably above the current rate of pay for most state prisoner workers but considerably below the federal minimum wage), labor intensive manufacturing work could be kept in the United States, where it would contribute to the gross national product, and at the same time allow for the training and employment of the nation's prisoners. Because so much of this kind of work has already been relocated "off shore," the assumption is that anything which can be done to prevent further flight should be seriously considered. It is argued that the use of prisoners at Third World wage levels would be a considerable improvement over the current situation, and is much more likely to appeal to prison administrators than programs which require the payment of the prevailing wage.

The problem in terms of wage regulation in partnerships is that there is essentially no enforcement, other than the initial setting of the wage for certification purposes.[16] It is an important issue because it reveals the deep-seated resentment and fears about prisoners and the confusion as to goals, both penological and industrial, that continue to plague the development of sound policies for private sector prison industries. BJA's role of encouraging the development of partnerships may have clouded its ability to carefully monitor wage policies for certified projects, but the major problem lies outside the certification program where enforcement has been almost totally nonexistent.

Private sector employment of prisoners in the past was marred by extreme exploitation—prisoners were essentially "sold" to private entrepreneurs who worked them to their graves in many cases—and as a result, federal legislation preventing the use of prison labor was passed at the behest of labor, industry, and prison reformers (Conley 1980). The theory of the Percy legislation was that exploitation could be avoided by requiring the payment of the prevailing wage. Twelve years into the program, it has become clear that legislation alone is not enough. Lax enforcement has led to a situation in which very few prisoners earn wages above the federal minimum wage (Criminal Justice Associates 1991).

The second major area in which the federal role needs reassessment is in the provision of incentives for private sector involvement. Contrary to expectations, few private sector firms have come forward to participate in partnerships, even though the program has been well publicized.[17]

Why should this be so? The president of Zephyr Products, the sheet metal company that operates a partnership with the Kansas Department of Corrections, has suggested that an all-inmate work force creates a number of problems for the entrepreneur. He believes that such a work force has strong group cohesion (due to institutional living conditions) that can influence production levels more than would be the case in the normal factory—mood swings of individuals tend to be more dramatic and group emotional volatility is commonplace. Moreover, according to Zephyr's president, common incentives (e.g., the hope for advancement to middle management positions) are not available to prisoner employees, and the traditional fear of being fired is less effective than in the free world since certain basic needs of the worker will be met by the prison whether or not he is employed. Finally, he notes that the inmate work force is often more manipulative than a free world work force, as a result of which free world staff often become overly involved in the problems of inmate workers to the detriment of their job performance (conversation with the author, 1986).

Certain characteristics of the prison itself pose other problems for the private sector. Hidden business costs, inherent in the prison setting, often necessitate more supervisory time and effort than comparable operations outside the prison. These characteristics often include high inmate turnover rates; high inmate training costs; prison procedures and policies that inhibit the movement of workers, staff, and materials; and a general misunderstanding of the profit motive on the part of prison staff that can hamper private sector performance. Finally, the fear of government red tape, concerns over potential accusations of exploitation, and fear of the prison setting also contribute to private sector reluctance to become involved with the prison unless some attractive incentives can be offered to offset the disadvantages.

States that have formed successful partnerships typically have offered incentives to the private sector. Those incentives have included reduced rent and utility costs and reduced employee benefit costs due to the prison's preexisting obligation to provide health care to all inmates. The federal Targeted Jobs Tax Credit is not available to partnerships since it applies only to ex-offenders and not to those currently serving sentences. The federal Job Training Partnership Act, which provides federal funds through the state Office of Economic Development for vocational training for certain categories of disadvantaged citizens including inmates, has been used by some partnerships.

Some companies have found that inmate workers are more productive than outside workers under some circumstances.[18] In general, however, the private sector has not found that the potential benefits of partnerships with the prison necessarily outweigh the potential drawbacks, and there is a clear-cut need for reassessment of federal policies as to the desirability of various approaches that might enhance the opportunities for the private sector. This is a particularly difficult issue since government also must not create an artificially attractive environment—incentives must make economic sense in the long run.

Future Approaches

Given the important role that work plays in the lives of all Americans, both as a source of dignity and as a means for economic survival, one of the most destructive effects of imprisonment is the removal of the prisoner from access to the work place. The lack of skills and training which typify most prisoners further underscores the need to provide access to work for those who wish to work while serving their sentences. Realistic work experience is one of the few nonintrusive, rehabilitative programs which the prison can reasonably provide without major expenditure, if it can create effective partnerships with the private sector. Experience to date has shown that the public generally supports work programs, that a small but growing number of states and counties have created effective partnerships that neither disrupt the prison nor exploit the prisoner workers, and that organized labor and manufacturers can and will accept partnerships that make a serious effort to compete fairly.

But none of the benefits of partnerships between the prison and the private business sector can take place unless wages for prisoners are held at least to the federal minimum wage. And, of course, the Percy legislation requires payments of the local prevailing wage.

Secondly, the federal government must play a more creative role in establishing policies which encourage the development of jobs for that segment of our population which suffers the highest unemployment rate—prisoners. If prison work programs can be a meaningful part of a national industrial policy that recognizes the benefits of jobs in the prison, there may be some hope for real change in the status of workers in the nation's prisons. And there is strong (albeit dated) precedent for the inclusion of prisoner workers in nation's industrial policy. During the Second World War, prisoners made a significant contribution to the war effort:

> The value of total state prison industrial production before Pearl Harbor averaged $15.5 million per year. The exact extent of the increase in production which followed the federal government initiative (the War Production Board set up a Prison Industries ranch to assist the federal government in procuring from prisons any goods it needed for the war effort) is not clear, but in the first half of 1944 state prisons produced nearly $18 million worth of industrial products for war use alone. The record in relation to agricultural production is equally striking. (Hawkins 1981, 91)

As a starting point, the Third World model has appeal as long as the minimum wage is held. Given the costs of transportation involved in the movement of goods from the Far East, for example, there may be offsetting benefits to performing labor-intensive manufacturing tasks within U.S. boundaries, allowing a reasonable profit to be made with wages set at the federal minimum or above. Given the potential for political turmoil in Third World nations, perhaps the prison can be a more stable alternative. In any event, the possibilities should be examined.

The federal government also must play a stronger role in protecting the various elements involved in and affected by partnerships. Work benefits controlled by federal policy have been haphazardly applied to prisoners. In some states, for example, FICA deductions are taken from prisoner workers and employers, while in others federal regulations have been interpreted as prohibiting prisoner involvement in the Social Security Program. Workers' Compensation payments, which are specifically required by the Percy legislation (but which must be paid after release) are available in some states but not in others. Federal tax deductions vary considerably from state to state and no uniform federal policy has been developed.

Arguments as to the need for federal enforcement of wage policy have been set forth above. The importance of such enforcement in protecting all parties is difficult to overestimate. The Departments of Labor and

Justice should develop joint regulatory and enforcement mechanisms which govern employees and employers involved in partnerships.

In the interest of protecting both free world and prisoner workers, unions might be brought into the partnership process. Their presence would assure that free world labor was not being harmed by the partnership and also would allow partnership workers to organize if they so chose. The federal government could take a strong leadership role in bringing the unions and the prisons together, given deeply embedded concerns expressed by correctional administrators who fear that organizing prisoners will lead to a loss of control.[19]

As to incentives for the private sector, there are a number of actions which the federal government could take. One very pressing need for small businesses interested in partnerships is start-up capital. Low cost loans or grants could be made available, perhaps through the federal Small Business Administration or some other similar organization. In 1981 Senator Robert Dole (of Kansas) introduced legislation creating a nonprofit Corporation for Prison Industries which would have made funding available to businesses interested in forming partnerships.[20] That legislation did not emerge from committee, but might be reintroduced or redesigned to improve its chances of passage.

The Job Training Partnership Act should be continued and expanded, and the Targeted Jobs Tax Credit should be amended to cover current offenders involved in partnerships. Some form of federal purchasing preference, similar to the Small Business Administration's minority business set-aside program, could be created.

In sum, though the federal contribution to date has been extremely valuable, it is clear that legitimate industrial and penological goals could be furthered through more creative and effective federal policies for private sector prison industries. What is needed now is clear recognition on the part of federal leaders that partnerships represent a rare opportunity to generate meaningful benefits for the state, the private sector, and for prisoners.

Notes

1. "Partnership" will be used in this paper as a generic term for a variety of relationships between the public and private sectors. Two broad models exist: the "customer" model, in which prisoners work for the department of corrections which has contracted to provide goods or services for a private sector firm; and the "employer" model, in which the prisoners work directly for a private sector firm.

2. The first modern federal study of note, known as the "Iowa" study, was followed by seventeen other studies conducted by the federal government. For a full listing, see the attached bibliography under "reports" (Stratton and West).
3. For a thorough discussion of the history of prison industries and the need for this kind of change, Gordon Hawkins has written a fine review and analysis (Hawkins 1983).
4. Econ, Inc. created the Free Venture model as part of this in-depth study of the problems and potentials of prison industries. Ultimately, the model included the following elements: (1) a full workday for prisoners; (2) a wage based on production, with the base wage significantly higher than typical payments to prison industry workers; (3) productivity standards comparable to free-world industry; (4) final responsibility for hiring and firing industry workers resting with industrial management; (5) self-sufficient to profitable shop operations within a reasonable period of time after start-up; and (6) industrial coordination with appropriate correctional and other agencies assigned the task of placing released prisoners in jobs.
5. Colorado, Illinois, Iowa, Minnesota, South Carolina, and Washington. The Law Enforcement Assistance Administration funded the Free Venture program and strongly encouraged state participation. Direct awards to the seven states, totaling more than $2 million, were made to assist in implementing industrial and administrative improvements.
6. As part of the Justice System Improvement Act of 1979, Congress passed an amendment sponsored by Senator Charles Percy of Illinois (later codified as subsection (c) of Section 1761 of the U.S. Code), which authorized the Law Enforcement Assistance Administration to establish seven Prison Industry Enhancement pilot projects. The legislation authorized goods produced by the projects to be placed in interstate commerce and sold to the federal government if: (1) the inmates working in the projects were paid at a rate not less than that paid for work of a similar nature in the relevant locality; (2) prior to the initiation of the project local union organizations were consulted; and (3) the employment of inmates would not result in the displacement of employed workers, be applied in occupations where there was a surplus of available labor in the locality, or impair existing contracts for services.

    The law also authorized deductions of up to 80 percent of a participating inmate's gross wages for taxes, room and board, family support, and contributions to the state's victim compensation fund. Inmates were also to be entitled to receive normal state and federal employment benefits, such as workers' compensation.

    No direct subsidies to states were made under the PIE program, on the assumption that access to new and wider markets was sufficient incentive for involvement and because financial aid to upgrade prison factories was not perceived as necessary to implement the program concept.
7. The legal issues involved in the movement of prison-made goods are complex. Two separate laws, the Hawes-Cooper Act of 1935 and the Ashurst-Sumners Act of 1940, are involved. Hawes-Cooper authorized the states to pass legislation prohibiting the entrance of such goods produced in other states, while Ashurst-Sumners makes it a federal offense to move prison-made goods across state boundaries, irrespective of individual state laws. Section 1761 negates Ashurst-Sumners for the twenty pilot projects, but Hawes-Cooper remains in effect, despite efforts to remove it. Thus, in theory, even certified projects may be in violation of state law in some cases. For a more thorough discussion of the legal issues involved in private sector prison industries, see CJA 1987, 71-80.
8. Major PIE projects have included a partnership between the Control Data Corporation and Minnesota Correctional Industries in which as many as 140 maximum security male prisoners assembled computer disk drives and wire harnesses; a joint

venture between Zephyr Products, Inc. of Lansing, Kansas in which up to forty medium and minimum security men and women produce metal products in a factory located near the prison; the production and sale of sign and printing products by Utah Correctional Industries to a number of private companies in the Northwest; the production of water beds by approximately 100 male prisoners at the Northern Nevada Correctional Center in Carson City for the Vinyl Products Corporation; a telephone answering service staffed by wards of the California Youth Authority for Trans World Airlines; and a sewing operation staffed by CYA wards for the Olga company; two garment manufacturing operations at the Purdy Treatment Center for Women and the Men's Reformatory at Monroe as part of a joint venture between the Washington State Department of Corrections and BRB Inc., a Seattle women's outer wear manufacturer; and a number of garment and telemarketing operations owned and operated by a variety of private sector companies in conjunction with the Nebraska Department of Corrections and employing several hundred male and female inmates.

9. Noteworthy noncertified projects involving services have included a telephone answering operation staffed by women of the Arizona State Prison in Phoenix for the Best Western Corporation and a telephone answering service staffed by Oklahoma prisoners for the Howard Johnson's Corporation.

The assembly of sprinkler units by Mississippi prisoners for Cool Mist, Inc., a Mississippi corporation, is an example of a project which operated in apparent violation of the Percy Amendment. The project ceased to operate in 1981.

10. See, for example, *Wentworth v. Solem*, 548 F.2nd 773 (8th Cir. 1977); *Worsley v. Lash*, 421 F.Supp. 556 (N.D. Ind. 1976); and *Alexander v. Sara*, 559 F.Supp. 42 (M.D.La. 1983).

11. For a summary of conference results, see The National Center for Innovation in Corrections (1986), *National Conference on Prison Industries: Discussions and Recommendations*. The George Washington University: Washington, DC.

12. For example, the Percy legislation was supported by both Senator Strom Thurmond of South Carolina, a staunch conservative, and Senator Edward Kennedy of Massachusetts, generally thought of as a friend of organized labor.

13. In a study required by the Kansas Legislature (Arthur Young 1981), Arthur Young found that because of high turnover, low skills, and interruptive prison procedures, Zephyr Products, Inc. (which was employing a prison work force) had no competitive advantage, and that in fact it was suffering from a competitive disadvantage compared to similar Kansas companies with a nonprison work force.

14. This is not necessarily the case, since workers in similar occupations are not always paid the prevailing wage in the community either. Wages are a function of market forces and union activities, and many American workers are paid at the federal minimum wage, for example, which may or may not be the prevailing wage in a given industrial area.

15. For example, in Mississippi no wages were paid to prisoners working under a partnership with the Cool Mist Corporation. The 1987 survey by CJA showed that when prisoners in private industry partnerships worked directly for the private company, wages were considerably higher than when they worked for the department of corrections which then subcontracted with a private sector company.

16. Organized labor, particularly the AFL/CIO and the Teamsters, has made isolated attempts to intervene in wage discussions, but in general they have had minimal impact on the setting of project wages. The BJA has no enforcement role as a program agency of the DOJ, and the DOL is not involved and so does not normally become aware of wage problems experienced by prisoners in private sector prison industries.

17. The Bureau of Justice Assistance and the National Institute of Justice report that departments of corrections have found it extremely difficult to identify and convince a private sector company to locate within a prison.
18. The Control Data Corporation found that its productivity rates inside Minnesota's Stillwater prison were higher than in any of their similar free world plants (Berthothy, 1983).
19. Chief Justice Burger has encouraged consideration of the need for union involvement in partnerships (*National Conference on Prison Industries, Discussions and Recommendations*, 6).
20. S. 1597 would have enabled the "Corporation" to award financial assistance by grant, contract, cooperative agreement, or loan to any correctional system proposing a project which met the requirements of the Percy legislation.

References

Reports

Abt Associates, Inc. (1985) *Corrections and the Private Sector*. U.S. Department of Justice, National Institute of Justice. Cambridge, MA: 11-28.

Arthur Young and Company. (1981) *Cost Impact of Using Inmate Labor in a Manufacturing Environment.* Leavenworth, KS.

Canadian Criminal Justice Association. (1986) "New Partnerships: Corrections and Private Enterprise." *Proceedings* of the Canadian Criminal Justice Association Conference. Ottawa, Ontario.

Criminal Justice Associates. (1985) *Private Sector Involvement in Prison-Based Businesses*. U.S. Department of Justice, National Institute of Justice. Lafayette Hill, PA.

_____.(1985) *Research in Brief: The Private Sector and Prison Industries*. U.S. Department of Justice, National Institute of Justice. Lafayette Hills, PA.

_____.(1987) *Work in American Prisons*. U.S. Department of Justice, National Institute of Justice. Philadelphia.

_____.(1991) *Developing Private Sector Prison Industries*. U.S. Department of Justice, National Institute of Justice, Philadelphia.

Econ, Inc. (1978) *Study of the Economics and Rehabilitative Aspects of Prison Industry*. U.S. Department of Justice, Law Enforcement Assistance Administration. Vols. 1-7. Princeton.

Georgetown University Law Center, Institute of Criminal Law and Procedures. (1974) *Prison Industries Planning Study: The Role of Prison Industries Now and in the Future*. U.S. Department of Labor. Washington, DC.

Institute for Economic and Policy Studies, Inc. (1980) *Assets and Liabilities of Correctional Industries*. U.S. Department of Justice, Law Enforcement Assistance Administration. Alexandria, VA.

_____.(1985) *Development of Jail Industries*. U.S. Department of Justice, National Institute of Corrections. Alexandria, VA.

National Center for Innovation in Corrections. (1986) *National Conference on Prison Industries: Discussion and Recommendations*. The George Washington University, Washington, DC.

Stratton, J.R. and J.P. West. (1971) *The Role of Correctional Industries*. U.S. Department of Justice, Law Enforcement Assistance Administration. University of Iowa. Iowa City.

U.S. General Accounting Office. (1982) *Report to the Attorney General: Improved Prison Work Programs Will Benefit Correctional Institutions and Inmates*. Washington, DC.

University City Science Center. (1981) *Impact of Free Venture Prison Industries Upon Correctional Institutions.* U.S. Department of Justice, Law Enforcement Assistance Administration. Philadelphia, PA.

Articles

Adamson, C. (1984) "Toward a Marxian Penology: Captive Criminal Populations as Economic Threats and Resources." *Social Problems* 31, 4: 435-58.

Berthothy, R. (1983) "Prison Industries: Seven Pilot Projects Paving Way for More Private Involvement." *Corrections Digest* 14, 10 (May 4): 10-11; and 14, 11 (May 18): 4-6.

Burger, W.E. (1982) "More Warehouses, or Factories with Fences?" *New England Journal of Prison Law* 8, 1, (Winter): 111-20.

Cannon. M.W. (1984) "Our Irrational Corrections System: Two Proposals for Making it Sane." *Judges Journal* 23, 3: 8-13, 44-45.

Cikins, W.I. (1986) "Privatization of the American Prison System: An Idea Whose Time has Come?" *Notre Dame Journal of Law, Ethics, and Public Policy* 2, 2: 445-464.

Clark, L.D. (1975) "Labor Law Problems of the Prisoner." *Rutgers Law Review* 28, 4 (Spring): 840-60.

Conley, J.A. (1980) "Prisons, Production, and Profit: Reconsidering the Importance of Prison Industries." *Journal of Social History* 14, 2: 257-75.

_____. (1982) "Economics and the Social Reality of Prisons." *Journal of Criminal Justice* 10, 1: 25-35.

Cullen, F.T. and L.F. Travis III. (1984) "Work as an Avenue of Prison Reform." *New England Journal on Criminal and Civil Confinement* 10, 1 (Winter): 45-64.

Demos, N. and L.S. Lucas. (1986) "Industries Initiative—PIE: Inmates Work Free World Style." *Corrections Today* 48, 7 (October): 62-65, 73.

Fedo, M. (1981) "Free Enterprise Goes to Prison." *Corrections Magazine* 7, 2 (April): 5-13.

Funke, G.S. et al. (1982) "The Future of Correctional Industries." *The Prison Journal* 62, 2: 37-51.

Goodman, S. (1982) "Prisoners as Entrepreneurs: Developing a Model for Prisoner-Run Industry." *Boston University Law Review* 62, 5 (November): 1163-95.

Haller, D.M. (1986) "Prison Industries: A Case for Partial Privatization." *Notre Dame Journal of Law, Ethics, and Public Policy* 2, 2: 479-501.

Hawkins, G. (1983) "Prison Labor and Prison Industries." *Crime and Justice, An Annual Review of Research.* Edited by M. Tonry and N. Morris, Vol. 5. University of Chicago Press, Chicago: 85-127.

Lightman, E.S. (1982) "The Private Employer and the Prison Industry." *British Journal of Criminology* 22, 1: 6-22.

McConville, S. and E.H. Williams. (1985) "Crime and Punishment: A Radical Rethink." *The Tawney Society*, London: 33-37.

Miller, N. (1980) "Inmate Labor Compensation Issues." *Legal Rights of Prisoners.* Edited by Geoffrey P. Alpert, 217-242.

Potuto, J.R. (1980) "An Operational Plan for Realistic Prison Employment." *Wisconsin Law Review* 1980, 2: 291-333.

Schaller, J. (1981) "Normalizing the Prison Work Environment." *Justice as Fairness: Perspectives on the Justice Model.* Edited by David Fogel and Joe Hudson. Cincinnati: 219-34.

Singer, N.M. (1973) "Incentives and the Use of Prison Labor." *Crime and Delinquency* 19: 200-11.

Vito, G.F. (1985) "Putting Prisoners to Work: Policies and Problems." *Journal of Offender Counselling, Services, and Rehabilitation* 9, 3: 21-34.

8

PRIDE of Florida: A Working Model For Inmates

Judith Schloegel

In the 1980s one of the most significant developments in corrections was a change in the operation of prison industries. Whereas corrections historically has operated and managed prison industries. more recently the private sector has become involved in the operation and management of these industries.

The centerpiece of this development was the advocacy of retired Chief Justice Warren E. Burger for "factories with fences." Due in large part to his efforts the National Center for Innovation in Corrections was established in 1984 at The George Washington University in Washington, D.C. The Center's purpose was twofold: (1) to foster the increase of prison industries nationwide and (2) to develop a model at the state level by which legislatures, corrections, local businesses, the media, and the community at large could work cooperatively to establish private sector prison-based businesses. At the end of its three-year tenure the Center published a report that summarized its work and offered recommendations for the ongoing development of this effort.

The key ingredient in the future success of prison industries will be the involvement of the private sector and the use of business principles.

This means that the company managing the industry provides the necessary training, job opportunities, and work incentives.

How this works out in practice may be seen, not hypothetically, but actually, by examining the experience of a Florida-based company, PRIDE—Prison Rehabilitative Industries and Diversified Enterprises.

History of PRIDE

In 1981 the Florida legislature authorized PRIDE, a nonprofit private sector company, to manage the industries in the state's correctional institutions. The mandate of the legislature stressed training for marketable job skills, employment, and help with post-release job placement. This approach has been successful.

In 1988-89, 4,470 inmate workers moved through 2,600 work stations located in PRIDE's diversified industries within twenty-two correctional institutions. Over 2,000 on-the-job training certificates were awarded to inmate workers.

Since 1 July 1988, PRIDE's job placement program has placed approximately 900 ex-offenders in jobs. Monies generated by PRIDE fund all of its facility development and expansion without the aid of state appropriations.

PRIDE'S Industry Environment

The experience of inmates who work in a PRIDE industry provides them with two valuable ways of preparing to work in society. One is the work environment itself; the other is the work ethic instilled by industry supervisors and managers.

Work Environment

By creating a work environment in the prison comparable to that in the free world, PRIDE helps to prepare inmate workers for their return to society. This may be seen in several ways.

First, the types of industries PRIDE manages and initiates are similar to those found in the free world. For example, furniture refurbishing, printing, optical and dental services, vehicle renovation, tire remanufacturing, agricultural production, and computer drafting. In these industries state-of-the-art equipment is used and inmates participate in on-the-job training. By acquiring marketable job skills they develop the self-image of an "employee," and for those with no prior work experience this is the first step to post-release employment and subsequent job retention.

Second, the work environment of PRIDE inmates is comparable to that of free workers. They must get to the job, be ready to work, and perform acceptably. While the schedule of the correctional institution dictates referral and attendance, the inmate workers, like free workers, must follow the direction of the supervisor, perform job duties according to their abilities, recognize their responsibilities to the industry as a whole, and relate positively to management and co-workers.

Third, the supervisors and managers of PRIDE industries come with experience in private sector business. They oversee the inmate workforce as they would any other. Because they operate a business, they train inmate workers in how to respond to the supervisor's demands, how to handle differences, and how to value the structure and authority needed to meet production and budget goals. In addition, supervisors introduce inmate workers to key industry values of safety and quality—values they will need to incorporate into any job outside the prison.

Fourth, co-workers give PRIDE inmate workers a realistic feel for on-the-job cooperation and communication. Co-workers are the same individuals sharing the prison environment, attending count, passing through guarded hallways, and conforming to the rules of a correctional institution. But from the moment they enter the industry site until they exit, inmate workers interrelate with their co-workers in a world-of-work environment. Personality differences, competition, and frustrations must for them, as for free-world workers, be sublimated in order that the demands of the industry be met.

Work Ethic

A realistic work experience is not always enough to help an inmate make a successful transition to society. Those who work with the inmates know this. The supervisors, managers, and other PRIDE staff often go out of their way to provide specific direction in meeting the job-related needs of the inmate worker population. As a result inmate workers acquire a work ethic.

Converting Potential to Reality

The underlying principle of PRIDE is to make maximum use of the work experience just described and to draw on the inmates' familiarity with it. The attitudes and skills reinforced by supervisors are the same attitudes and skills needed by inmates to work successfully in the free world. This may be seen in the following ways:

1. Inmate workers live in a prison setting in which conformity and subjection are mandated. In the work environment inmates are expected to make contributions and take initiative. The PRIDE program rewards workers through an established Suggestion Program. Workers who submit recommendations to an industry manager that result in a more productive industry may receive financial compensation. It is the role of a skillful supervisor to help inmates keep the different expectations of the prison and work environments in balance.

2. Inmate workers are challenged to do "more than time". They are encouraged to take advantage of an educational opportunity offered by PRIDE—Career Education Assistance. PRIDE funds up to $300 toward a correspondence course related to the inmate's work in the industry.

By participating in the industry's on-the-job training programs, the inmates move through modules that break down the individual tasks required for the successful attainment of a marketable job skill. They are awarded two types of certificates: (1) for modules accomplished and (2) for skills achieved. It is the responsibility of the supervisor to direct this training. By motivating inmates to perform according to their potential and by helping them to acquire positive work habits, supervisors reinforce workers in that most important element, the work ethic.

The list that follows exemplifies the type of supervision PRIDE inmate workers receive. These activities initiated by supervisors attest to the quality of the training they provide, their commitment to preparing workers for jobs upon release, and the successful businesses they operate. As a result, inmate workers are motivated to improve production in the industry.

- Seminars conducted for workers by outside vendors to enhance the industry training. For example, in agricultural industries guest veterinarians advise inmate workers on animal care treatment and reproduction.

PRIDE of Florida: A Working Model for Inmates

- Meetings called by supervisors on quality improvement. For example, training sessions on goal setting, speaking with confidence, dealing with customer complaints, and plant safety.

- Additional certification. For example, certification at the state or national levels in welding, electrical work, and paint/seals.

- Job search training. For example, a twenty-three hour course on how to find and keep a job, conducted by a supervisor after work hours.

- Assistance with job readiness. For example, a supervisor assists inmate workers in formulating a resume, preparing for a job interview in which the issue of a conviction must be discussed, and providing letters of reference regarding the worker's job performance and attitude.

- Post-release employment. For example, supervisors make contacts with other business representatives to hire responsible workers for their companies. These supervisors continue to show support by calling workers hired after release, offering them encouragement and advice.

PRIDE's TIES Model Program

PRIDE solidifies the efforts of its supervisors and managers by operating a Department of Inmate Programs and Out Placement Assistance. This department integrates training, industry, education, and support as a holistic approach to running a business with an inmate workforce. The accompanying chart outlines six levels by which inmate workers participate in the TIES Program.

Levels three through six point directly to the importance PRIDE places on the integration of industry work with postrelease employment of inmate workers. In other words, the provision of job assistance is not merely tacked on to the inmate's experience in PRIDE as an isolated activity; rather this "support" component is contingent upon the inmate's on-the-job training. Briefly the model is as follows.

Transition Planning

Four months before release an inmate will be given a PRIDE Release Plan by the supervisor assessing the inmate worker's need for a job, a place to live, and a community support contact. Within three weeks an action plan developed by PRIDE department staff is returned to the worker. Ongoing correspondence with the inmate regarding the plan occurs through a postage-free mailer.

The initiative and self-determination fostered in industry training have prepared the inmates to claim responsibility for their plans in returning to the community.

Prerelease Employment Training

Eight weeks before release the inmate will participate in a job readiness program focusing on employment and personal adjustment.

A review of the inmate's performance in the industry serves as the basis of this orientation. Their training in a world-of-work environment gives credibility and meaning to video material, work books, and related discussions used in the orientation.

Postrelease Assistance and One Year Follow Up

The plan developed by the inmate worker in cooperation with the supervisor and department staff is activated immediately upon the inmate's release. Ongoing support and monitoring in the community are provided for one year.

Because the postrelease plan was developed in an environment emphasizing training, industry work, and education, the ex-PRIDE worker experiences the transition to the community in continuity rather than as a disjunct, awkward re-entry process. The direction and assistance they have known from their supervisor in the industry and the help of a willing employer and support contact in the community create a relational binding in the inmate's return to society.

Conclusion

Having trained, supervised, and educated the inmate worker, PRIDE provides the ongoing support necessary for the fulfillment of its mission: the operation of a successful business with trained inmate workers, who will return to society as employable, self-reliant, contributing women and men.

PRIDE TIES Program

Level 6	**One Year Follow-Up** Regular Communication With Ex-Offender, Employer and Community Contact
Level 5	**Postrelease Assistance** (At Time of Release) Job; Housing/Support Services; Community Contact
Level 4	**Prerelease Employment Training** (8 Weeks Before Release) Job Readiness Program
Level 3	**Transition Planning** (4 Months Before Release) Inmate's Plan for Employment, Housing/Support Services and a Community Contact
Level 2	**Training/Work** (1 Month to Indefinite Period) Inmate Programs 6 Months Into PRIDE: - Victim Restitution - Career Education Assistance - Suggestion Program On-The-Job Training Certification
Level 1	**Intake** (At Hiring)

9

The Public-Private Partnership: A Challenge and an Opportunity for Corrections

Norman R. Cox, Jr.
William E. Osterhoff

Contemporary policies and practices in law enforcement and criminal justice, such as the "War on Drugs", mandatory sentencing requirements, and more stringent bail/bond practices, have contributed to unprecedented crowding in the nation's prisons and jails. As a result, correctional management faces new challenges, but more importantly, new opportunities are emerging that may significantly change the way government has traditionally managed correctional institutions, programs, and services.

Institutional crowding is of monumental proportions. A record average daily population of more than 770,000 inmates were incarcerated in the nation's prisons as of 31 December 1990. The rate of incarceration of 293 sentenced prisoners per 100,000 residents also was a new record. (Bureau of Justice Statistics, 1991c). There also were more than 405,000 inmates being held in local detention facilities as of 30 June 1990 (Bureau of Justice Statistics 1991a). During the past year, there were nearly 20 million jail admissions and releases (Bureau of Justice Statistics 1991a).

The United States has entered the 1990 decade with combined average daily prison and jail populations well in excess of 1 million inmates. In addition, approximately 3 million adult offenders currently are under probation or parole supervision (Bureau of Justice Statistics 1991b). Increases in juvenile corrections populations also are occurring.

Since 1980, the nation's prison and jail populations have more than doubled. To keep pace with the current growth in the incarcerated offender population, prison and jail capacities would need to be increased by approximately 1,500 additional beds each week (Bureau of Justice Statistics 1991a, 1991c). An even greater increase in additional capacity is required to relieve the overcrowded conditions that exist in many of the nation's prison and jail facilities. A National Institute of Justice study (Mullen, Chabotar, and Carrow 1985) indicated that more than 77,000 beds were added by state prison systems from 1980 to 1985. Currently over 100,000 additional beds are being constructed each year. Annual operating costs for corrections have increased from $1 billion in 1965 to more than $19 billion in 1990 (American Correctional Association 1991).

The dramatic increase in the nation's correctional population may be attributed to a number of factors. Among these factors are increased crime rates, heightened fears of being victimized, increased arrests for drug and alcohol related offenses, a shift from an emphasis on rehabilitation and reintegration to a renewed emphasis on punishment, tougher criminal codes, mandatory sentences, and strict federal court guidelines that prohibit conditions constituting "cruel and unusual" punishment. Significant reversals of these conditions are not anticipated in the immediate future. It is too early to determine the impact on prison and jail populations of the use of intermediate punishments. Compounding the problem is a public that is less than enthusiastic about increased taxes to pay for the corrections facilities that are required, and a public that is changing its attitudes about the capability and the desirability of having the public sector being solely responsible for the solution to society's correctional problems.

To meet the challenge presented by these developments, good correctional management practice require's that new solutions be explored and evaluated for implementation. Correctional managers and political decision makers must be prepared to examine alternative approaches to traditional institutional program and service delivery. One of the most promising alternatives brings together the public and the private sectors to resolve the problems associated with explosive growth by developing more effective and efficient responses than can be provided by the public sector alone.

Public-private ventures have been utilized to help resolve society's problems in fields as diverse a public health, mass transit, wastewater treatment, and aerospace. In addition, all levels of government have contracted for professional services to augment public resources in architectural, engineering, and construction projects. Contracting with the private sector also has occurred in planning, management, and legal areas. The use of private services in corrections currently is practiced to some degree in the majority of states. These services include medical and mental health care, food service, architectural services, community-based facilities, prison industries, correctional facility financing, and correctional facility management.

History of Privatization in Corrections

The practice of contracting with private sector firms and individuals for the provision of products or services traditionally supplied by the public sector, has a long history in this country, such contracting actually predates the U.S. Constitution (National Academy of Public Administration 1989). Privatization also is not new to corrections. Unfortunately, the experience has not always been positive or progressive.

One of the earliest examples of fee for service involved American jails, where fees were collected from inmates or their families to provide for the salaries of the sheriff and jailer. Additional fees were paid to the jailer for better food, improved accommodations, visiting rights, and other marginal conveniences that are today considered basic essentials. Since there was a general lack of concern or sympathy for the plight of the prisoner by the general public, facilities were often inadequate in areas of sanitation, vermin control, temperature, and ventilation. Classification was often non-existent and supervision was poor resulting in mixed housing of prisoners charged with all types of crimes. Men, women, and even children were sometimes housed together with victimization frequently occurring.

Other forms of private sector involvement in corrections included the participation of private industry, generally in the forms of leased labor, contract labor, and public account systems (Sexton, Farrow, and Auerbach 1985). The use of contract or leased inmate labor temporarily reduced inmates idleness and overcrowding while resulting in additional income to operate the jails and prisons or for the private gain of corrections officials. Because industry's primary concern was on maximizing profits, exploitation of adult and juvenile offenders was not uncommon. Under the contract or leased labor systems, the inmates generally received no compensation while working long hours under poor conditions. Under the public account system, similar conditions prevailed, except that prison industries were operated by the correctional agencies, which sold products on the open market in direct competition with private industry.

Opposition to the contract labor, leased labor, and public account systems developed rapidly. By 1900, a number of states had passed legislation that restricted the use of inmate labor by private firms as well as the sale of prison-made goods on the open market through "state use" laws. Legislation also was passed by the federal government that restricted interstate commerce of prison-made products and the use of inmate labor on federally funded projects. As a result, private sector involvement in correctional industry was substantially reduced. Recently, however, there has been a renewed interest by the private sector in prison industry programs (Sexton, Farrow, and Auerbach 1985).

Private enterprise also has played a significant role in the development of community-based corrections. Concerned citizens and religious groups established the first halfway houses and group homes for adult offenders. Other significant community corrections programs, including probation, were started in the same manner. As the focus of corrections shifted from a rehabilitation philosophy to an emphasis on reintegration during the late 1960s and 1970s, numerous community-based correctional programs were developed. Many of these programs were implemented through contracts with private profit and non-profit agencies, the Law Enforcement Assistance Administration (LEAA), and other governmental agencies. Cooperation between private sector community-based corrections programs and public sector agencies has been generally favorable, although evaluation data indicate mixed results when costs and effectiveness of private and public sector programs are compared.

The juvenile justice field also is heavily indebted to the early efforts of individuals and private organizations whose concern for the welfare of delinquents, status offenders, and dependent and neglected youth contributed to the development of the juvenile justice system. Unfortunately, as in adult corrections, there were examples of abuse, neglect, and exploitation of youth at both private and public levels. While the focus in adult corrections was changing from rehabilitation in prison to reintegration into the community, a movement to de-institutionalize troubled youth was gaining momentum. Massachusetts led the movement by closing its juvenile institutions and by allocating 60 percent of the 1983 budget for the Division of Youth Services for purchase of services from private, non-profit organizations (Mullen, Chabotar, and Carrow 1985).

Financing and construction of public institutions by the private sector also played an important role in frontier America. Many public buildings, including courthouses and jails, were financed and constructed by the railroads to encourage settlers to locate near rail depots. The Pauley Jail Building and Manufacturing Company of St. Louis, Missouri privately financed many of the jails it built around the turn of the century. Today, major investment banking firms compete aggressively to help government finance the massive prison and jail construction and contracting activities associated with the explosive growth of the corrections population.

Contemporary Practice

Institutional Services and Programs

While the use of privately contracted correctional services and programs varies considerably from state to state, forty-one states were using at least one privately contracted service in 1985 (Mullen, Chabotar, and Carrow 1985). The area in which privatization has made the strongest impact is the provision of medical and mental health services, areas that have been the focus of considerable litigation during the past decade. In 1985, almost two-thirds of the states were using private contracting for at least one medical or mental health service (Mullen, Chabotar, and Carrow 1985). This trend has continued because of general satisfaction with contracted medical and mental health services and because reduced litigation has resulted.

Provision of food services was the second most frequently contracted areas in corrections. Approximately 40 percent of the states currently were using or were planning to use private vendors for at least part of their food service needs. Competition among private food service providers has resulted in a number of firms from which correctional administrators can select a variety of options tailored specifically to their individual requirements. In 1985, private contracting for maintenance or transportation services was reported in approximately 25 percent of the states. Private contracting was used least (less than 9 percent) in the areas of security (Mullen, Chabotar, and Carrow 1985). The minimal use of private contracting for security services was consistent with the high priority that correctional administrators placed on security and the potential requirement for the use of force to maintain control over the inmate population to prevent disturbances, assaults, and escapes. Recently, however, private corrections companies are entering into contracts with government for the provision of total facility management, operations, and security. It is likely that this trend will continue.

Community-Based Services

Privatization of various forms of community-based corrections services has long been established through the use of private contracts from public agencies to operate various forms of programs and services, including halfway houses, work release programs, prerelease centers, group homes, and treatment centers for alcohol and drug offenders. In general, private contracting for community-based facilities and programs has presented more advantages to local, state, and federal correctional agencies than disadvantages. Evaluation data show mixed results when costs and performance are compared with the public agencies. In some jurisdictions, however, contracting with private agencies for specific programs on an annual or fee basis is the only viable option available. Acceptance of privatization by public sector employees and professional organizations has been generally favorable.

Probation and parole agencies also are increasing the use of private contracting to provide specific services and programs to offenders under probation and parole supervision. Probation and parole staff are increasingly becoming community resource managers instead of the traditional direct service providers. Many of the programs and services that probationers and parolees require can be contracted for and more effectively provided by private resources in the community. These services also can be contracted on an "as needed" basis, thereby providing greater flexibility in service provision.

Increased use of privately operated community-based correctional facilities and programs can be anticipated as local, state, and federal correctional agencies continue to struggle with increased offender populations. Additional opportunities for private contracting of innovative community-based correctional services will result from intermediate punishment plans that are being implemented throughout the nation to increase the range of sentencing options.

Prison Industries and the Private Sector

During the past decade, there has been a renewed interest in prison industries and vocational training programs. Former Chief Justice Warren Burger's advocacy and conceptualization of prisons as "factories with fences" suggests new opportunities for cooperation between private industry and corrections. Prison industry programs expose inmates to job skills, reduce idleness, provide a source of income to the inmates and the institution, and provide productive services to the state or community.

At present, all fifty states have some types of prison or jail industry programs. While prison industry programs in most states are operated by the state corrections departments, private sector interest and involvement in prison industry programs is slowly increasing. In 1987, there were thirty-eight private sector prison industries in operation in twenty-six institutions in fourteen state correctional systems and two county jails (Auerbach, Sexton, Farrow, and Lawson 1988). In a few states, private firms operated industrial programs in facilities they had built or leased on prison grounds. In other states, private firms simply contracted for inmate labor and supplied materials while the corrections departments provided the facilities and inmate supervision (Mullen, Chabotar, and Carrow 1985).

Further developments in private sector involvement in prison industries are clouded by a number of political and legal issues (Sexton, Farrow, and Auerbach 1985). A survey of private sector involvement in prison services and operations (Camp and Camp 1984) reflected both an interest and a reluctance on the part of correctional authorities for additional involvement with private enterprise in prison industries in the near future. That ambivalence is still not completely resolved. With burgeoning prison and jail populations, opportunities for the private sector to establish and operate institutional industry programs have never been greater. Future growth will require the support of both the public and private sectors, with the primary energy coming from the private sector since resources for prison and jail industries are limited. The entrepreneurial and development skills necessary for significant expansion of meaningful industry programs also are most likely to be found in the private sector. Where private sector involvement in prison or jail industries has occurred public sector acceptance has been cooperative and enthusiastic (Auerbach, Sexton, Farrow, and Lawson 1988). Resulting benefits to inmates, correctional administrators, and the public should be substantial.

Financing of Correctional Facilities

The explosion in prison and jail populations has fostered a building boom in corrections. In 1989, 108,000 new prison beds and 37,500 new jail beds were constructed for a combined total expenditure of $6.0 billion. In 1990, 128,000 new prison beds and 55,000 new jail beds were built at a cost of $8.9 billion.

The building boom, coupled with the inability of state and local government to finance the needed new construction through traditional methods such as general obligation bond issues or higher taxes, has encouraged the entry of private investment firms into the area of correctional facility financing. Prestigious Wall Street investment banking firms were attracted by the growing investment opportunities in the corrections field while simultaneously seeking new areas to expand their services in an increasing competitive and aggressive financial marketplace.

While the lease-purchase of buildings and other large cost items by state and local government is not new, only recently has the lease-purchase concept become an important option in the field of corrections. It is likely that state and local government will use the lease-purchase option more frequently as current indebtedness approaches legal limits and as the public becomes less willing to pass additional bond issues, thereby transferring current obligations on to future generations. Resentment expressed by the public toward tax increases and passage of tax limitation legislation also have made lease/purchase arrangements increasingly more attractive and acceptable to government officials.

Institutional Facility Management and Operation

In 1981, the U.S. Attorney General's Task Force on Violent Crime recommended that federal and state governments explore the private operation of prisons. Shortly thereafter, a number of private corporations organized along the lines of private hospital corporations emerged to finance, build, and operate private prisons. Many of the firms attempted to market their services as "cheaper and better" than government can provide. The President's Commission on Privatization (1988) recommended that contracting should be regarded as an effective and appropriate form for the administration of prisons and jails at the federal, state, and local levels.

Since 1981, several firms have been incorporated specifically for institutional facility management and operations. Yet, it is this area where the greatest resistance to private sector involvement in corrections has been exhibited. Early resistance was expressed by public employee unions, professional organizations, corrections administrators, sheriffs, legislators, and prisoner advocate organizations.

Concerns expressed by correctional employees have centered around anticipated loss of jobs, job security, and benefits. Correctional administrators and sheriffs have expressed reservations about questions of liability and about the potential loss of control over their corrections facilities, staff, and inmate populations. Professional associations, including the National Sheriffs Association and the American Jail Association have officially expressed opposition to the privatization of corrections for similar reasons. The American Correctional Association, on the other hand, has endorsed the concept.

Public officials also have become aware of the potential leverage that will be gained by the private sector as its involvement increases in functions and responsibilities that traditionally have been under public control. In addition, the issues of liability, inmate classification, security, and the use of force (particularly deadly force), remain of primary concern to elected and appointed officials. These concerns also have been expressed by the American Bar Association. The American Civil Liberties Union and other prisoner advocate organizations fear that cost and profit motives will ultimately outweigh considerations of inmate welfare and public safety, as has occurred in the past. Presently, the American Bar Association has called for jurisdictions to postpone privatization until the constitutional, statutory, and contractual issues are resolved (Robbins 1988).

Despite this initial resistance private management of adult institutions has continued to grow over the past decade. By 1991, the private corrections industry was a $200 million industry with approximately 15,000 beds under supervision. This represents only 1 percent of the total corrections market (public and private). At the current rate of growth, private corrections is expected to capture 3-4 percent of the total market by 1995.

In the 1984 Camp and Camp survey, only 22 percent of the adult correctional agencies indicated willingness to contract with the private sector for the management of an entire facility. By 1991, there were twenty states with specific legislation authorizing private sector operations of correctional institutions with similar legislation introduced or pending in twelve additional states (Privatization Council 1990). The trend toward privatization has been accelerated by the contracting activities of such bellwether states as California, Florida, and Texas as well as the federal government. California led the trend in contracting community correctional services during the 1970s and during the 1980s moved toward larger minimum custody (return to custody) adult institutions. Florida moved toward adult facility management by the private sector with enabling legislation for counties in the 1980s and by 1990 had solicited proposals for the first 900-bed medium custody facility for state prisoners.

In 1987, Texas contracted for the design, construction, financing, and private operation of four 500-bed minimum custody state prerelease facilities, the largest single privatization effort at that time. Current legislation authorizes another 2,000 beds to be contracted to the private sector.

The Immigration and Naturalization Service (INS) of the U.S. Department of Justice, began contracting for detention facilities for illegal aliens in the 1980s, followed by the U.S. Marshals Service (USMS) in 1989, and the Federal Bureau of Prisons (FBOP) in 1991. The USMS solicited proposals for the design, construction, financing, and operation of two 440-bed maximum security detention facilities and the FBOP sought the same services for a 1,000 bed medium custody facility for joint use by the FBOP and the INS.

Although resistance persists, the movement toward contracting for higher custody facility management signals a growing acceptance of privatization in corrections. This trend is occurring at all levels of government.

The Public-Private Partnership Approach

In a study of prisons for profit, the Legislative Research Council of the Commonwealth of Massachusetts (1986) concluded that private sector firms have not demonstrated their ability to provide better services at lower costs. The study called for additional information and improved performance of private sector firms in providing correctional services. Other studies have shown similar results.

Privatization, when defined as the practice of contracting with private sector firms and individuals for the provision of products or services traditionally supplied by the public sector, does offer some advantages for government. As defined, however, privatization suggests supplanting public products or services with private products or services. Because of the magnitude and complexity of the problems faced by corrections, the emerging concept of a public-private partnership may hold more promise for corrections than the concept of privatization. Instead of supplanting public products or services by the private sector, the concept of a public-private partnership suggests supplementing the provision of public products or services by the private sector.

The concept of a public-private partnership has been articulated by the Research and Policy Committee a nonprofit organization of 200 business and professional leaders, educators, and public officials. It is the Committee's position that it is in the best interest of both the public and the private sectors to form a cooperative relationship to solve the increasingly complex problems of state and local government (Research and Policy Committee 1982).

The public sector and the private sector are both integral components of a modern economy. Government policies and activities affect the welfare of its citizens through its public service functions and through its laws, regulations, taxes, and fiscal policies, all of which effect private sector activity. The private sector, which is composed of a rich mosaic of profit and nonprofit organizations engaged in a wide variety of enterprises with diverse objectives, likewise has an important public dimension. As corporate citizens of the community, private organizations have a stake in the well-being and the future of the community, just as individuals do in their capacity as citizens (Research and Policy Committee 1982).

A public-private partnership implies cooperation among individuals and organizations in the public and private sectors for the purpose of mutual benefit. The objective of a public-private partnership is to pursue mutual goals in such a way that the participants contribute to the benefit of the broader community while pursuing their own organizational goals and objectives (Research and Policy Committee 1982). The basic premise upon which the public-private partnership concept is formulated includes the assumption that economic success, survival, and health of the private sector, in the long run, depend on the well being of the communities in which corporations operate and on the endurance and well-being of the society in which they exist. Since the private sector mutually benefits from and affects society, corporations should take a leadership role in the public sector's response to social issues and problems. Traditional public administration principles are not sufficient to guide the implementation of privatized services. Rather, new concepts and approaches are needed (National Academy of Public Administration 1989). Utilization of relevant expertise in politics, government, economic development, and community action can reduce the hazards of private involvement and increase the likelihood of success in solving society's problems (Research and Policy Committee 1982).

Historical developments and contemporary trends in corrections suggest that neither the public sector nor the private sector, when acting alone, have the capacity or the resources to solve the present crisis in corrections. Fear of crime, reported crimes, victimization data, and recidivism rates clearly indicate that government has not been able to provide the protection from criminal activity that citizens have the right to expect. Protection of life and property is not exclusively a government concern or responsibility (Research and Policy Committee 1982). The criminal justice system is dependent on private citizens for reporting crime, for assisting in the prosecution of offenders, for assisting in the reintegration of offenders into the community, and for public funding of local, state, and federal criminal justice system agencies. The interdependence of the public and private sectors also was acknowledged by the American Correctional Association (1984 and 1991) which urged the need for mutual cooperation to solve current corrections problems.

The concept of a public-private partnership can be visualized as a continuum with exclusively public sector responsibilities at one end of the continuum and exclusively private sector involvement at the other end. Other responsibilities fall along the continuum depending upon their respective public and private sector involvement. At the end of the continuum where private sector involvement is more acceptable are correctional services and programs, including medical and mental health care, food service, and alcohol and drug treatment programs. At the end of the continuum where public control is more acceptable are correctional systems management, institutional operations, and facility ownership. Toward the center of the continuum are community-based correctional facilities and programs, prison industries, and selected special purpose facilities and programs that can be operated jointly by the public and private sectors.

Benefits of Private Sector Involvement

There are situations where private sector involvement has distinct advantages over the public sector. Mullen (1985) suggested that private sector participation may be particularly advantageous for corrections when rapid mobilization, experimentation, decentralization, specialization, and regionalization are desired. It may be advantageous to contract for the provision of needed facilities and services when there is a need for rapid mobilization of additional facilities and staff. Because of the flexibility and capability to rapidly construct, renovate, or acquire additional facilities and to hire additional staff, private sector contracting may facilitate the accommodation of short-term population shifts resulting from court-ordered compliance deadlines or changes in legislation. Planning for permanent facility expansion can then proceed on a more carefully planned basis.

Private sector contracting also may allow for experimentation with innovative programs and new methods of service delivery without making permanent commitments to staffing until adequate evaluations have been completed. Considerable program flexibility can be achieved by governmental agencies if traditional bureaucratic constraints to innovation can be minimized (Mullen 1985).

Decentralization of correctional facilities and services to provide greater geographic and programmatic diversity may also be possible by contracting with the private sector. Contracts with local contractors who employ community residents and have the confidence of local public officials may circumvent opposition to programs and services that are under the direct control of a centralized agency (Mullen 1985).

Another potential advantage of private sector involvement includes the ability to achieve greater specialization of correctional institutions and programs. Offenders with special needs are difficult to manage in the best of systems. Contracting with the private sector for specialized institutions and programs for special needs offenders may offer significant benefits over generalized housing of all inmates (Mullen, 1985). Examples include specialized facilities and programs for the criminally insane, sex offenders, offenders with alcohol and drug related problems, geriatric and infirmed offenders, and DUI offenders. Work release and prerelease centers also could be financed, constructed, and operated by the private sector.

For many years, regionalization of correctional facilities and programs has been advocated by correctional professionals and by state and national advisory committees. The potential of regionalization has been largely untapped, however, because of the political and jurisdictional disputes that emerge when regional planning activities begin. The private sector, not being bound by jurisdictional politics, may be better able to foster the development of shared facilities among states or among counties within a state (Mullen 1985).

Each of these suggested areas of private sector involvement are concerned with supplemental services required by government. Private sector firms willing to assume a supplemental role can successfully market their specialized services to government without the adversarial relationship that has dominated early privatization attempts. Successful examples may be found in the use of mass transit authorities in public transportation, private rural/metro fire department services for fire and rescue services, and the National Aeronautics and Space Administration in space exploration (Research and Policy Committee 1982).

Realities of Privatization

In reality, few of the areas where private sector involvement may be particularly advantageous to government have been explored. Instead, private corrections companies have simply sought to replace government as managers of correctional institutions. Rather than exploring the opportunity for specialization or experimentation as a means of supplementing and supporting public sector management, private corrections companies have contributed to polarization and mistrust by:

- marketing their services as "cheaper and better";

- attempting to orchestrate the takeover of an entire state correctional system;

- bidding below cost to capture market share;

- building speculative facilities which were poorly planned and badly executed, leaving government and investors with serious losses; and

- using high pressure lobbying efforts with local governments which often result in alienation rather than persuade.

Likewise, government has contributed to the poor performance of private corrections by rigidly requiring that bids from private companies be 10 percent below equivalent government costs. This requirement coupled with government's inability to accurately define its own costs, oversimplifies a complex issue and suggests that cheaper is always better. Clearly, the cheapest correctional institution to operate is one that is old, understaffed, overcrowded, and underbudgeted (Reinhardt 1991).

This is not to say, however, that private sector involvement in institutional corrections does not work. On the contrary, despite the poor performance of some private corrections companies, others have brought improvements to the institutional environment. A 1988 study sponsored by the National Institute of Corrections evaluated comparable public and private adult minimum security institutions in Kentucky, and comparable public and private juvenile institutions for difficult youthful offenders in Massachusetts. The results indicate that the costs were similar, but a majority of the performance indicators showed that the privately operated facilities had an advantage. In the private institutions, services and programs were rated higher; there were fewer escapes and disturbances;

and, staff and inmates were more comfortable in the environments of those institutions (See Hatry et al. chap. 15). Therefore, in some areas, the private sector can bring improvement to institutional corrections. To meet its full potential, however, private corrections requires a new approach—a public-private partnership approach.

Conclusion

A review of historical and contemporary private sector involvement in corrections reveals five key factors that are pertinent to any discussion of privatization in corrections. It can be concluded that:

1. Historically, private sector involvement has produced both significant advances in corrections, as well as flagrant abuses.

2. Traditionally, government has been and currently continues to be resistant to privatization of institutional corrections while accepting private sector provision of specialized and community-based correctional facilities and services.

3. Contemporary approaches to privatization have contributed to polarization and mistrust.

4. Performance of the pioneer companies has been less dramatic than promised but privatization is gradually gaining broader acceptance.

5. Research has demonstrated that the private sector can improve institutional corrections.

Privatization, as traditionally defined, requires government to surrender a traditional service to the private sector; therefore, confrontation is inherent in the process. Such an adversarial climate militates against the open and rational discussion necessary to explore and refine the concept of private sector involvement in corrections. Private sector involvement in corrections should be viewed as a continuum with opportunities for public-private cooperation and mutual benefit at various points along that continuum. Corrections, like other societal responsibilities, must deal with problems that are too complex to be solved by either the public or the private sector alone. For the public and private sectors to be more effective in creating solutions to the current crisis in corrections, a new climate of cooperation must be created. A new focus must emerge with less of an emphasis on traditional privatization concepts and more of an emphasis on the public-private partnership approach. Such a focus combines the strengths and proficiencies of each sector to create viable solutions to those complex problems facing corrections today.

References

American Correctional Association. (1984) *Policy Statements and Resolutions*. College Park, MD.

_____ .(1991) *Directory*. College Park, MD.

Attorney General's Task Force on Violent Crime. (1981) *Final Report*. Washington, DC: U.S. Department of Justice.

Auerbach, B.J., G. E. Sexton, F. C. Farrow, and R. H. Lawson. (1988) *Work in American Prisons: The Private Sector Gets Involved*. Washington, DC: U.S. Department of Justice.

Bureau of Justice Statistics. (1991a) *Jail Inmates, 1990*. Washington, DC: U.S. Department of Justice.

_____ .(1991b) *National Update*. Washington, DC: U.S. Department of Justice.

_____ .(1991c) *Prisoners in 1990*. Washington, DC: U.S. Department of Justice.

Camp, C.G. and G.M. Camp. (1984) *Private Sector Involvement in Prison Servies and Operations*. Washington, DC: U.S. Department of Justice.

Commonwealth of Massachusetts. (1986) Legislative Research Council.

Mullen, J. (1985) *Corrections and the Private Sector*. Washington, DC: U.S. Department of Justice.

Mullen, J., K.J. Chabotar. and D.M. Carrow. (1985) *The Privatization of Corrections*. National Institute of Justice Issues and Practices. Washington, DC: U.S. Department of Justice.

National Academy of Public Administration, Panel in The Management of Privatization. (1989) *Privatization: The Challenge to Public Management*. Washington, DC.

President's Commission on Privatization. (1988) *Privatization: Toward More Effective Government*. Washington, DC: U.S. Government Printing Office.

Privatization Council. (1990) *Compendium of State Privatization Laws, 1990 Supplement*. The Privatization Council, Inc., Washington, DC.

Reinhardt, W.G. (1991) "Private Prisons." *Public Works Financing*. June.

Research and Policy Committee. (1982) *Public-Private Partnership, An Opportunity for Urban Communities*. New York: Committee for Economic Development.

Robbins, Ira P. (1988) *The Legal Dimensions of Private Incarceration*. Washington, DC: American Bar Association.

Sexton, G.E., F.C. Farrow, and B.J. Auerbach. (1985) *The Private Sector and Prison Industries*. Washington DC: U.S. Department of Justice.

10

Minimizing Liability with Private Management of Correctional Facilities

Linda G. Cooper

With the ever-increasing population in prisons and jails today, governments are looking for alternatives to traditional facility construction and management. Beds need to be added quickly and efficiently and still meet all constitutional requirements. One alternative, privately built and managed correctional facilities, is moving out of its infancy into a solid, reasonable alternative to the many problems facing today's correctional administrators.[1]

Initially, there was much concern about the issues of liability with utilization of a private contractor. As with any new concept, resolution of issues that could ultimately have an impact upon the economics of such a venture must be resolved. As the concept takes hold and operations are actually in place, many of the issues are resolved through the day-to-day actions of all parties. Others are resolved as the law surrounding the issues develops.

Initial liability issues in privatization dealt with the ability of a government to contract essential governmental functions such as management of correctional facilities. When Corrections Corporation of America first began marketing, the question asked by counties and states was whether it was legal to contract with a private corporation for operation of the jail or prison. Implied in this question was the issue of government's liability if it delegated functions to the private contractor. Although the courts have not addressed the specific delegation of correctional functions, delegation of various governmental functions has not been overturned by the Supreme Court or lower courts in the last half century.[2]

The United States Constitution and federal law do not prohibit a private company from managing correctional facilities. Many states have broad grants of authority to contract in general, while others have enacted specific statutes authorizing private prison contracts.[3] There is nothing inherently wrong with delegation of correctional facilities, although overall the ability to delegate depends largely upon specific state statutes or lack thereof.[4]

Even the issue of the ability to sue a private contractor for violations of constitutional rights of incarcerated people has been resolved.[5] As the government is held accountable for constitutional violations, so is the private contractor. Just as a government is responsible for day-to-day functions and operations, so is a private contractor. Any violation of a right guaranteed by federal, state, or local legislation is the responsibility of the private contractor. Resolution of this issue alleviated many of the concerns of prison rights advocates, as well as government.

Much energy was devoted to whether delegating and contracting with the private sector could be done. This issue so overshadowed the concept that in 1986 the American Bar Association (ABA) House of Delegates passed a resolution calling for a moratorium on privatization until the complex constitutional, statutory, and contractual issues were developed and resolved.

As states and counties resolved this issue to their satisfaction and moved to privatize jails and prisons, the issues of delegation and liability arising thereunder took a back seat. The focus then became the resultant liability from the ordinary day-to-day operations and contractual agreement. Even the ABA is moving from the academic question of whether you can delegate to when you do delegate, take proper precautions as you would with any contractual agreement.[6]

The government can not sit back, take it easy, and forget liability once functions are delegated to a private contractor. There is no absolute ability to delegate all functions and to totally divest of liability. However, by taking steps to minimize liability (including use of a seasoned, experienced contractor) the government has not only found an economic solution to today's problems, it has found one which increases control over operations.

Minimizing governmental liability in the private contracting area should be addressed through a properly drafted contract. The groundwork for an effective contract is laid at the time the decision is made to privatize. The formulation of a bid proposal or a request for proposal should take into consideration requirements and clauses that will be implemented into a standard working agreement. Expectations on the part of the government toward the private contractor, as well as the powers and parameters of the contractor, are to be clearly established.

The very structure of the relationship between the governmental entity and the private contractor can have an impact on the overall liability of the governmental entity. Establishing the relationship, private contractors as independent contractors or agents of government, is a seemingly useless exercise but could result in enormous liability issues.

Typically, the private contractor is considered an independent contractor of the government, performing functions in the stead of the government. An independent contractor is one who provides a service and has control of the manner of service delivery. The government, in contracting with an independent contractor, prescribes the job but does not set out the details of "how the job is to be performed." Negligent action of the independent contractor does not create liability with the government, except where (1) the injury is caused by the government's own negligence; (2) the government knew or could have ascertained that the contractor was not qualified to do work; (3) the government provides unsafe premises; (4) there is negligent exercise of control when the government retains some control over the work or interferes with the work; (5) the work of the independent contractor violates statutes and the government has notice and does not object.[7] Most pertinent in the private contracting situation is liability on the part of the government when proper investigation and caution is not taken in choosing a contractor. Obviously, a detailed background search as to the private contractor's past history and ability must be ascertained. If a cursory review of qualifications takes place resulting in a private contractor with a history of problems or less than satisfactory performance, responsibility for negligent acts of the contractor can be passed to the government.

Potential for governmental liability increases if the private contractor is considered an agent to the government. If the government details the way in which the private contractor is to perform the services and is involved in the day-to-day operations, an agency relationship can be created. If the actual directions of how to implement certain functions come from the government, such a relationship is created and the government can be held liable for actual constitutional and tort violations on the part of the private contractor.

Therefore, it is very important for the government to reduce the potential for liability and to carefully structure its relationship between the private contractor and the governmental entity. This is not to say that the government should have a strictly hands-off relationship in dealing with the private contractor. Rather, the private contractor should be given the overall parameters of the job to perform and should be responsible for working out the details as to how the actual task will be accomplished. The government will then monitor the private contractor's polices and procedures as to implementation of the task. Monitoring by the government would not be considered day-to-day involvement in carrying out the actual job duties.

The contractor is required to carry insurance to cover all types of possible violations, including those for civil rights or constitutional violations, and to indemnify the government for all costs and judgments associated with claims against the government. This is one further reason for choosing a financially stable, experienced private contractor. An indemnification plan will not assist in reducing liability if the company is not financially stable and able to back up the indemnification requirement.

The contract must spell out the expectations of both parties and establish an avenue for unexpected occurrences. In addition to establishing the relationship of the parties, which as indicated above has a great impact on minimizing liability, other areas must be addressed that could eventually affect liability.

Just as in a government-managed detention facility, health care is a litigation-generating area. The responsibility of both the government and the contractor for provision of health care must be clearly delineated. Establishing clear lines of responsibility will resolve future conflicts as to liability if care is not properly given. The government has a duty to monitor and ensure that care is provided. The real issue in this area, according to experience, is a conflict over who pays, rather than the adequacy of the care. However, clearly establishing responsibility to resolve this issue is of the utmost importance in a good working relationship.

The contract also should address the use of force. Government can delegate the use of force necessary to operate a facility. Appropriate training, policies and, where applicable, licensing of correctional officers will further reduce questions of liability. Generally, escapes or necessity to use force outside the facility is not an issue since the private contractor utilizes local law enforcement in the same manner as the government.

Obviously, the government has a responsibility to monitor the provider of services. If it is demonstrated through the monitoring process that the contractor is not providing adequate services or is following policies that violate the constitutional rights of the inmate, it is possible that the government, as well as the private contractor, can be held liable.[8] This stresses the importance of a reliable experienced contractor and appropriate monitoring on the part of the government.

The contract is the one document that solidifies the intentions of both parties. Special detailed attention should be given to it. Setting out expectations on the part of the government with respect to operational standards (such as meeting American Correctional Association Standards, applicable court orders and constitutional requirements) establishes the parameters under which the private vendor must operate. Thus, if the private vendor does not operate according to these standards, the governmental entity has a breach of contract remedy. Many of the pitfalls touted by the opponents of privatization can be eliminated by a clearly drafted contract.

In drafting the contract clauses, both parties must be very careful to clearly outline the services to be provided without establishing new rights on the part of the inmate. Certain contractual language can be held to bind a state or contractor even though the Constitution or state law does not require the parties to provide the services. For example, it can be set out in the contract that the private vendor is to provide rehabilitative services and to utilize specific programs. If, for some reason, the state and private contractor decide to eliminate these programs, the inmate may have the ability to sue both the state and the private contractor for the denial of a contractually provided interest. Liability is thus created solely because of contractual language.

No one contemplates totally divesting the governmental entity of all functions through the use of private management. The line between completely divesting all responsibility versus allowing for day-to-day operation must be maintained. Areas which have an impact on the liberty and freedom of the inmate (including calculation of good time and sentence dates or transfers to more secure facilities) should be left to the governmental decision maker, thereby avoiding claims of excess and unconstitutional delegation.

As privatization develops, it becomes quite clear that issues of liability become a function of a contractual relationship. Those of us from the government side moving into the private sector must refocus on the importance of a contract and contract interpretation. It seems easy to say that liability for all parties can be minimized by a simple document. Failure to perform or inadequate performance becomes a breach of the contract and remedies and liability evolve from the contractual language. Simple, though it may and should be, this one document governs the future of the government and private contractor's relationship.

Notes

1. Although many "mom and pop" operations existed for management of detention facilities, it was not until 1984, when Corrections Corporation of America was formed, that "privatization" or private operation and management of governmental detention facilities moved into the forefront as a viable large scale alternative.
2. This is according to Ira Robbins, renowned critic of privatization.
3. States with specific legislation allowing privatization include Arkansas, Colorado, Florida, Louisiana, Massachusetts, New Mexico, Oklahoma, Oregon, South Carolina, Texas, and Utah.
   Some states, such as Kentucky, allow privatization even though specific legislation has not been enacted.
4. See Logan 1987.
5. West v. Atkins, 815 F. 2d 993 (4th Cir. 1987). For a more detailed discussion of Section 1983 Liability, see Thomas 1987.
6. The ABA Criminal Justice Section has passed a resolution setting out general guidelines for contractual agreements with private entities for prison management.
7. Restatement of the Law Second Torts and Agency 2d, as adopted and promulgated by The American Law Institute.
8. Crooks v. Nicks, 872 F. 2d. 800 (8th Cir. 1989).

References

Logan, C. (1987) "Privatizing Prisons: The Moral Case." *Enlightenment.* Adam Smith Institute, November.

Thomas, C. (1987) "Evaluating the Liability Risks of Privatization, The Role of 42 U.S.C. Section 1983." *American Society of Criminology*, November 14.

11

Privatization of Corrections: A Threat to Prisoners' Rights

Harold J. Sullivan

The movement for privatization of a wide range of government activities is a response to fiscal pressures on the state and to an ideologically founded distrust of the public sector encouraged by the Reagan and Bush administrations. Although few activities would seem to be more quintessentially public responsibilities than the punishment of criminals, even corrections has become a major target for privatization (See Brakel 1988a; Camp and Camp 1984; Mullen et al. 1985; Savas 1987; Wollan 1986; Wooley 1985; Emory Law Journal 1987).

In weighing the advisability of private correctional facilities we must first understand that public and private criminal justice institutions are not just competing service providers. They differ in ways that are more significant than their concern for profitability. The measures of their relative worth must include concerns beyond unit cost and economic efficiency. Awareness of the legal distinctions between public and private institutions must inform the debate over privatization in the criminal justice system in general and in corrections in particular.

Under the American system the state is subject to constitutional restraints that simply do not apply to the private sector. A question that must concern all who consider reliance on privatized corrections is whether when it comes to the preservation of constitutional protections, there is any substitute for direct governmental responsibility.

Persons who have been convicted of crime do not give up all rights. Subjected to limitations necessitated by the overarching concern for security within correctional facilities, prisoners retain, for example, some of their fundamental First Amendment rights of freedom of speech and of religion. Of perhaps even more direct concern in the correctional context are the Eighth Amendment prohibition against "cruel and unusual punishment" and Fifth and Fourteenth Amendment prohibitions on the imposition of punishment "without due process of law." Certainly if privatization could be used to evade or escape constitutional protections of prisoners' rights, then the debate over privatization of corrections might engage the interests of more than state budget officials looking for ways to cope with rising deficit projections, or public employees unions concerned about public sector jobs or private entrepreneurs seeking ways to make profits at tax payer expense. This article seeks to stimulate further debate on the implications of privatization for the rights of prisoners.[1]

Public vs. Private: The Constitutional Difference

The Constitution of the United States restrains state power not private conduct. The liberties protected by the Bill of Rights and the Fourteenth Amendment are protected from only infringement attributable to government action. The basis for the different treatment of government and private infringements on "liberty" can be found in the words of the Fourteenth Amendment's command that "*[n]o state* shall deprive any person of life, liberty or property without due process of law" (emphasis added). According to a long line of Supreme Court decisions dating back to the Civil Rights Cases of 1883 before one can challenge an alleged denial of due process rights, he or she must first show that the deprivation results from "state action."

In large part because it is the state which decides who will be incarcerated, many who have discussed the issues surrounding privatization of corrections have assumed that the activities of "private" prisons, which have contracted with the state to provide correctional "services," will be considered state action, and therefore that constitutional protections for prisoners must be observed (Johnson 1986; Kay 1987; Mayer 1986; Robbins 1986; Robbins 1987; Thomas & Calvert Hanson 1989; Wooley 1985; Emory Law Journal 1987). Because the Supreme Court has not yet had the opportunity to rule on any case arising out of a private prison, it is not yet at all certain how the Court might apply the State Action doctrine to privately owned and operated correctional facilities. The Court has, however, decided a number of cases that raise issues that must be considered by anyone who is interested in understanding the extent to which constitutional restraints will apply to the actions of private correctional facilities. There can be little doubt that private correctional facilities will be largely funded by the state, regulated by the state and that they will fulfill functions which otherwise would have to be provided directly by the state. The question then is whether they, for constitutional purposes, will be treated as if they were the state.

Identifying State Action

There is nothing new about private institutions, both profit making and not-for-profit, providing services paid for by government. This fact has forced the courts to determine the circumstances under which the actions of such private service providers will be treated for constitutional purposes as if they were actions of the state itself. If public funding and regulation were sufficient to transform the actions of private service providers into the constitutional equivalent of actions of the state itself, then a vast array of "private" institutions in America would be subject to constitutional restraints.

In recent years the U.S. Supreme Court has made it increasingly clear, however, that state funding and/or regulation of a private agency is insufficient to establish the necessary state action to trigger constitutional protections. Generally, only those specific private actions that are directly "ordered" or "initiated" by the state or in which state officials have directly participated are subject to constitutional restraint (*Moose Lodge No. 107 v. Irvis* 1972; *Jackson v. Metropolitan Edison* 1974; *Blum v. Yaretsky* 1982; *Rendell-Baker v. Kohn* 1982.)

Two 1982 Supreme Court decisions, *Rendell-Baker v. Kohn* and *Blum v. Yaretsky* in particular raised issues similar to some that could arise in litigation concerning privatized corrections. The cases involved constitutional challenges to actions of privately owned facilities, one a school for "maladjusted" students and the other a nursing home. Both institutions received virtually all of their funding from state governments. Both were subject to extensive and detailed state regulation. Because both institutions were so heavily reliant on government funding, it is fair to say they owed their existence to government programs, the first to a Massachusetts program requiring the state to provide education for "special needs" students (*Rendell-Baker* 1982) and the second to Medicaid coverage for nursing home expenses of indigents (*Blum* 1982).

In these cases the Supreme Court identified the very limited circumstances under which constitutional guidelines would apply to actions of governmentally funded and extensively regulated private institutions. In effect the Court ruled that the level of funding or the degree of overall regulation does not determine the applicability of constitutional restraints to actions of privately owned and operated institutions. In *Blum*, for example, although the Court recognized that the decision to transfer categories of patients to lower levels of nursing home care was mandated by detailed regulation, if the determination concerning which specific patients would be transferred were left in private hands, the state could not be held accountable for such decisions nor would the private decision makers be required to follow Fifth and Fourteenth Amendment Due Process guidelines in making those decisions (Phillips 1984, 715).

In *Rendell-Baker v. Kohn* the Court ruled that employees of a privately owned school for "maladjusted" students may be summarily dismissed without the due process protections that would apply in a publicly owned facility. The Court found that the state action requirement had not been satisfied despite the fact that virtually all of the students at the school were referred to it in fulfillment of the State's obligation under Massachusetts law to provide education for "special needs" children. Despite the fact that the school was heavily regulated, received from 90 to 99 percent of its funding from the State, and issued diplomas certified by a local public school committee (*Rendell-Baker* 1982, 832-33), the Court decided that the specific decision to dismiss employees was not subject to constitutional challenge.

From these and other recent cases (see *Flagg Bros., Inc.* 1978 and *Lugar* 1982) it has become clear that unless government compels a private actor to make a specific decision in an individual case, only direct official participation in the implementation of a policy or in determining individual eligibility for some government mandated sanction or benefit will trigger constitutional restraints applicable to government action.

The so-called "public functions" doctrine, which has been identified as "the most persuasive means of finding that conduct of a private corrections firm constitutes state action," (Thomas & Hanson 1989, 942), provides an exception to these state "compulsion" or "participation" requirements. When the state turns over to a private institution a function that has traditionally been performed "exclusively" by the state (*Jackson* 1974, 352-53) the private institution in question is held to the same constitutional standards as if it were the state. To date the Court has only recognized two such traditional and exclusive public functions: the conduct of elections that determine "'the uncontested choice of public officials'" and a company town that "has taken on *all* the attributes of a town" (*Flagg* 1978, 158). Although Justice Rehnquist in *Flagg* mentioned such "functions as education, fire and police protection, and tax collection" for possible inclusion in the exclusively public functions category, he explicitly withheld judgment concerning whether government "might be free to delegate to private parties the performance of such functions and thereby avoid the strictures of the Fourteenth Amendment" (*Flagg* 1978, 163-64). In weighing whether the Court might recognize these and other areas as exclusively governmental functions, one commentator has observed, "[a]s of late, the Supreme Court has demonstrated little inclination toward characterizing any function as traditionally the exclusive prerogative of the State" (Ayoub 1984, 915). As Justice Rehnquist, himself, stated in *Flagg*, "[w]hile many functions have been traditionally performed by government, very few have been "'exclusively reserved to the State'" (1978, 158).

In essence in the public functions area the Court asks whether the activity in question is one that the state has exercised alone or if it is one for which the private sector has shared responsibility. This requirement of state "exclusivity," however, is not purely a question to be determined through historical research. In *Flagg Bros. v. Brooks* (1978, 160), the Court opened the door for a private agency to exercise, free of constitutional restraints, what had been historically an exclusive public function as long as the state continues to provide *some* potential alternative channels for redress to those adversely affected by the private party's action.

The issue in *Flagg* was whether Fourteenth Amendment due process requirements applied to "a warehouseman's proposed sale of goods entrusted to him for storage, as permitted by the New York Uniform Commercial Code" (1978, 151). The U.S. Supreme Court rejected the finding of the U.S. Court of Appeals that "New York not only had delegated to the warehouseman a portion of its sovereign monopoly power over binding conflict resolution . . . but also let him, by selling the stored goods, execute a lien and thus perform a function which had traditionally been that of the sheriff" (1978, 155).

Although Justice Rehnquist argued that "the settlement of disputes between debtors and creditors is not an exclusive public function" (1978, 161), he placed greatest emphasis on the fact that within the law there were options available to block the proposed sale. It was the availability of such options that appeared to dictate the Court's conclusion that the warehouseman in question had not been delegated an exclusive public function. He had, in effect, not been delegated "exclusive" control over this alleged governmental power. The state still retained some role. As the warehouseman exercised his "private" role, he would be free from constitutional restraint. Only the state would be subject to the Fourteenth Amendment when, and if, it were called upon to intervene.

In their dissenting opinions in *Flagg* Justices Marshall and Stevens challenged the majority's "exclusivity" standard on a number of grounds. According to Justice Stevens the Court's position was based "on some vague, and highly inappropriate, notion that the respondents should not complain about this state statute if the State offers them a glimmer of hope of redeeming their possessions . . . through some other state action" (1978, 172, n.8). As Justice Marshall emphasized, the alternative available to one damaged by the private use of state power may in reality prove so burdensome to the party seeking redress as practically to leave them at the mercy of the private party arguably clothed with the authority of the state (1978, 166-67). In the instant case Justice Marshall pointed out that the only legal remedy available to Flagg would have required her to put up money potentially greater than the value of the goods in dispute. While the remedy in question, "replevin," was technically available, "it is also true that, given adequate funds, respondent could have paid her rent and remained in her apartment, thereby avoiding . . . [the] eviction [which later led to] the seizure of her household goods by the warehouseman" (1978, 167).

Privatization: A Threat to Prisoners' Rights

Following *Flagg* the question for those attempting to establish that a private agency is exercising a "traditional" public function becomes whether the state completely abdicated its power to a private entity. If yes, and if the activity in question has been "traditionally" and "exclusively" a governmental prerogative, the private party now exercising state power is bound by the constitution as if it were the state. If, however, the state retains *some* continued role in the exercise of the power in question, the private party may be free from constitutional restraints as it exercises its share of what had been a governmental power. The state in turn may also be free of constitutional responsibility and legal liability for the actions of the private agency to which it has delegated some portion of what had been traditionally an exclusive public function.

Privatized Corrections: The Litigation to Date

No case concerning a privately owned correctional facility has as yet been heard by the U.S. Supreme Court. Some who have argued that the actions of private correctional facilities will be considered "state action" have sought support for their position in the Supreme Court's decision in *West v. Atkins* 1988 (Thomas and Calvert Hanson 1989).

In a 42 USC section 1983 action West alleged that Atkins," [a private] physician under contract to provide medical care" (1988, 2252) to inmates at North Carolina's Odam Correctional Center, acted "under color of law" when he failed to provide adequate medical treatment (1988, 2253). According to the Court, the state had a constitutional obligation under the Eighth Amendment to provide adequate medical care to those whom it incarcerates and denies the opportunity to seek alternative care for themselves. (1988, 2258-59) When Atkins contracted with the State to provide medical care to state prisoners, he in effect assumed that State obligation himself. He became a state actor.

Although Thomas and Calvert Hanson (1989) view this decision as virtually settling the question of whether the actions of private correctional agencies, which have contracted with the state to provide correctional services, will be subject to legal liability for failures to fulfill constitutional obligations, this decision can be interpreted as having far narrower significance.

According to the decision of Justice Blackmun, the terms of Atkins contract with the state made him virtually indistinguishable from a state employee, and a long line of Supreme Court decisions has held "that a public employee acts under color of state law while acting in his official capacity or while exercising his responsibilities pursuant to state law" (1988, 2256). In this case the services Atkins provided "as a physician employed by North Carolina to provide medical services" (1988, 2258) to inmates were provided to them within a state owned and operated prison.

To conclude that the actions of those who provide correctional services in *private* facilities under contract with the state will be treated for constitutional purposes as state action would be contrary to the Supreme Court decisions in such cases as *Blum* (1982) and *Rendell-Baker* (1982). In both of those cases contracts between the states and the private institutions in question did not transform the actions of the private institutions into state action. *West* concerned the actions of an individual whose contract with the state made him the equivalent of a state employee. Employees of private institutions that contract to provide services to the state have not to date been considered, themselves, the equivalent of state employees (*Rendell-Baker* 1982). Since in *West* the Court did not assert that corrections is traditionally an "exclusive" public function, the constitutional status of privately owned correctional facilities and of the actions of employees of such facilities remains in doubt.

Even before the Supreme Court's decision in *West*, commentators who have argued that privatized corrections facilities will be subject to the same constitutional restraints as those operated by the state have looked for support for their position to the lower federal courts. *Medina v. O'Neill*, (1984) the only court decision that has directly addressed issues involving private correctional facilities (Wooley 1985, 328), does indeed generally support the continued applicability of constitutional protections. *Medina* concerned the detention of stowaways in a private facility pursuant to an Immigration and Naturalization Service order. Plaintiffs challenged the failure of the INS to oversee their detention, contending that the conditions within the facilities within which they were detained amounted to "punishment" in violation of their Fifth Amendment Due Process rights (*Medina* 1984, 1032).

The *Medina* Court found in favor of the detainees because, in the words of the Court, "detention is a power reserved to government, and is an exclusive prerogative of the state" (1984, 1038). Because Congress delegated its authority over immigration to the INS and because the

Congress authorized the INS to designate places of detention for excludable aliens, the Court concluded that both the INS and the private facilities in which it ordered the plaintiffs detained were bound by the Fifth Amendment Due Process standards.

The question for anyone considering this case is whether its findings decide the issues of the constitutional status of private corrections. Because this decision was vacated in part on appeal and because the Court of Appeals never reached the state action question, the answer is, in the technical sense, plainly no (Thomas and Hanson 1989, 943, n.68). Even the implications of the District Court's decision standing on its own, however, are unclear.

In finding that detention was an exclusive public function, the District Court failed to cite any relevant U.S. Supreme Court precedent.[2] As the Supreme Court's recent precedents make clear, before applying the public function doctrine a court must find that the activity in question has traditionally been performed exclusively by the state. Yet in concluding that detention is such a public function, the *Medina* Court failed to even explore the issue of whether there was historic precedent for private detention facilities.

If, on the other hand, the decision is based at least in part on the Court's conclusion that the statutes demonstrate that "Congress intended the agency to furnish suitable facilities which comply with minimum due process standards," (*Medina* 1984, 1040) then the evident failure of the INS and the private parties detaining the plaintiffs would amount to a failure to meet statutorily imposed legal obligations. The application of constitutional standards would then hinge on the specific statutorily imposed tripartite relationship between the INS, the private shipping concern and the detainees. This could leave open the question of whether in instances in which statutory requirements were less clear, treatment of detainees in a private facility would be regulated by constitutional standards.

In *Milonas v. Williams* (1982), another decision relied on by those who contend that private correctional facilities will come under the State Action Doctrine, the Court of Appeals for the Tenth Circuit focused on the degree and nature of the interactions between government and private institutions. The Court's decision upheld a Section 1983 Civil Rights judgment against a private school for violating the rights of youths who were assigned to it by the state because of behavioral problems. The

Court did not find explicitly that the school performed a "public function," rather it found against the school because some students " [had] been involuntarily placed in the school by state officials who were aware of, and approved of, certain of the practices which the district court has enjoined" (*Milonas* 1982, 940). The Court's decision, however, does not make clear whether the state placement of the youths alone would trigger constitutional protections or whether the state's "approval" of the challenged practices was the determining factor in finding state action. If the state's approval of the practices was the determining factor, then the result might be different were a state to decide to follow a less pervasive regulatory policy toward private institutions in which prisoners or detainees are confined.

Both Paul B. Johnson and Ira Robbins have argued that the *Milonas* decision provides a basis for concluding that constitutional restraints will be applied to private correctional facilities even in the absence of a court finding that private correctional institutions perform exclusively public functions. They base their conclusion on such factors as "the involuntary nature of confinement, the detailed nature of contracts between the government and the private entities, the level of government funding, and the extent of state regulation of policies and programs" (Robbins 1986, 328-29; Johnson 1986, 4).

In support of their conclusion that funding and regulation would trigger a finding of "state action," the authors cite the U.S. Supreme Court decisions in *Blum v. Yaretsky* (1982) and *Rendell-Baker v. Kohn* (1982). Their reliance on these cases is, however, puzzling in the extreme. In both cases the Supreme Court found that state action was *not* present despite the almost complete reliance on government funding of the institutions in question. On the issue of regulation state action was also found to be absent in both cases cited because the government regulation did not dictate the specific decisions under challenge.[3]

Together the sometimes ambiguous decisions in *West* (1988), *Medina* (1984) and *Milonas* (1982) have provided the principle supports for the conclusions of many commentators that privatization cannot be used to evade constitutional protections of prisoners. Some commentators have gone on to warn states that, if they are, themselves, to avoid legal liability for possible abuses of constitutional rights which might follow from the practices of private correctional facilities, they must carefully regulate and supervise private correctional facilities (see, e.g., Mayer 1986, 321;

Wooley 1985, 327-30). These warnings combined with the reasoning supporting them, however, border on the tautological. On the one hand we are told that the Courts will find state action, and thus both the state and the private prison contractors liable for constitutional violations, *because the state so heavily and comprehensively regulates* private agencies that provide correctional services. On the other hand, we are warned that because the states will be held liable, the *states ought comprehensively to regulate* private correctional facilities in order to assure they will not have to pay for abuses not of their own making. Because they are so certain that constitutional restraints will govern private correctional facilities, many commentators on "privatization" of corrections generally ignore the very real possibility that the state can avoid liability and shield private contractors from liability precisely by limiting the state's role in the management of private corrections agencies.[4]

Privatized Corrections and the State Action Doctrine: The Unsettled Issues

Constitutional litigation in the corrections area generally has involved Eighth Amendment challenges to prison conditions that impose "cruel and unusual punishment," First Amendment issues relating to free expression and religious rights and Fifth and Fourteenth Amendment challenges to the imposition of discipline without due process. Although the Supreme Court's decision in *West v. Atkins* (1988) did not directly address the constitutional status of privately owned correctional facilities, it nonetheless appears to indicate that the state cannot evade its responsibility for assuring that those whom it incarcerates are free from "cruel and unusual punishment." Because the state, under virtually any conceivable privatization scheme, would certainly retain responsibility for conviction and sentencing, it would appear improbable that the state could evade the commands of the Eighth Amendment.

While the continued application of the Eighth Amendment would likely assure inmates some minimal governmental protection for their physical well-being, the status of issues relating to "classification," security, the use of force, and procedures for enforcing discipline and crediting or withholding "good time" (Mayer 1986, 316-17; Wooley 1985, 320-23) might well depend on the nature of the contracts entered into by the state and private prison operators. On such questions, it is far from certain that privatization could not lead to the diminution of governmental responsibility and of constitutional rights.

It is certainly true that in some of its recent decisions the United States Supreme Court may well have seriously eroded prisoner rights even within government operated correctional facilities (see Cohen 1988). The issue for us, however, is not the precise nature or adequacy of constitutional requirements as interpreted by the court, rather it is when the rights to Due Process, which continue to exist, apply in privatized correctional facilities.

Supreme Court decisions applying the State Action doctrine leave the status of constitutional protections within privatized correctional facilities dependent on two factors: first, on the precise nature of the contractual relationships between the state or federal governments on the one hand and private corrections agencies on the other; and second, on whether or not all aspects of corrections will be deemed traditionally and exclusively governmental functions.

Even if a state's contract with operators of private prisons specified in detail the conditions of incarceration, including, for example, specific procedures to be followed in administering discipline and/or providing security, there are reasons to doubt that the U.S. Supreme Court would find that the requirements of the State Action doctrine had been met. The lesson of cases such as *Blum v. Yaretsky* (1982) is that even the most extensive state regulation is not enough to attribute the actions of privately owned institutions to the state or to require that those private institutions, themselves, adhere to constitutional requirements.

When, however, state officials or employees participate directly in disciplinary proceedings or in maintaining security within "private" correctional institutions, such participation would trigger constitutional restraints. When public and private officials or employees act in concert, the actions of both are considered by the Court to be subject to constitutional limitations. (See, e.g., *Lugar* 1982, 937). If, on the other hand, private actors, such as private security personnel, act independently of the state, the Supreme Court will not likely view their actions as controlled by constitutional restraints (see, e.g., *Hurt* 1986).

How might privatization be used to escape constitutional restraints and both state and private prison operators' liability? If the requirements of the State Action doctrine are triggered by extensive government

Privatization: A Threat to Prisoners' Rights

regulation of, and direct participation in, specific decisions of private institutions, then the greater the discretion left to such institutions, the less the chance that they or governments will be held to constitutional standards. Were governments to leave significant discretion in the hands of private prison operators over security and disciplinary matters and, more importantly, leave implementation of such policies to private prison employees, then the continued applicability of constitutional restraints would likely depend on, first, whether the courts determine that the activity in question is traditionally an exclusive public function, and second, whether there is a continuing government role in the exercise of the public function.

Although decisions concerning what constitutes a criminal offense and who may be subject to a criminal sanction are clearly both traditionally and exclusively governmental functions (Mayer 1986, 320), there is considerable historical precedent for privately owned and operated jails and places of detention. According to Brakel (1988b, 176), "imprisonment in this country began as a 'private' enterprise—if one can justify the public-private distinction at a time in history when government was rudimentary and social responsibilities were small-scale—and persisted as such well into the 19th century and (with modifications) in some locales into the 20th." Indeed, Travis et al (1985) argue that the development of publicly run institutions was a response to the record of abuses in private facilities.[5]

Today, even before the current drive for privatized corrections gained momentum, there was extensive private involvement in providing juvenile facilities, halfway houses, drug and alcohol rehabilitation centers (see Camp and Camp 1984; and Mullen 1985, McCrie 1990).

For the courts to conclude that corrections traditionally has been an "exclusive" public function, therefore, they will have to disregard both historical precedent and current practice. The fact of private corrections in the past means simply that corrections cannot be viewed as a function that has been traditionally "exclusively" performed by the state. In addition the *Flagg* (1982) decision appears to permit private actors participating in the execution of even a traditional and exclusive public function to disregard constitutional restraints as long as the state provides those adversely affected by the private action some possible alternative governmental channels for protecting their interests.

Even if the Courts ultimately decide to disregard the traditional role of private agencies in corrections and determine that corrections is an "exclusive" public function, it might still be possible for private correctional institutions and the state to evade constitutional protections available to prisoners in purely public corrections facilities. If, for example, the state provided guidelines for private correctional officials in applying discipline and crediting "good time," but left actual implementation to the private prison operators, the private agents could avoid the procedural Due Process requirements demanded of public prisons as long as the state, itself, provided prisoners some means of appeal or some alternative channels to challenge abuse of the state guidelines. As both Justices Marshall and Stevens made clear in their *Flagg* (1982) dissents, however, alternative channels might well prove burdensome to those who must rely on them—so burdensome as to make their routine use impractical. Under such conditions the initial decisions of the private prison operators on matters of discipline and security might stand unchallenged even though those decisions were arrived at without Due Process.

Finally, no matter how the Court finally resolves the question of whether corrections is for state action purposes the exclusive prerogative of the state, the state might be able to avoid the application of constitutional protections of prisoners' rights simply by making placement in a "private" correctional facility, instead of a public prison, a matter left to a prisoner's discretion. If the state were to provide for both public and private correctional facilities, prisoners could be given a choice. If the state were attempting to influence prisoners to in effect waive their constitutional rights, it might offer such inducements as possible early release or more rehabilitation options to "persuade" prisoners to elect the private facilities. Under such circumstances even if the Court determines that corrections is an exclusive public function, because the state has not completely abandoned the corrections field to private contractors, both the contractors and the state might be freed from liability for any alleged denial of constitutional rights within private correctional facilities.

Conclusion

Although our recent very limited experience with privatized corrections facilities provides little immediate cause for alarm (see, e.g., Brakel 1988b), the possibility remains very real that privatized corrections may threaten prisoners' rights. At a time when the Supreme Court has shown decreasing solicitude for the rights of prisoners (and indeed for all citizens), it should surprise no one that the specter of privatization, itself, has not been the cause of much particular general concern. At the same time as recent Court decisions may have eroded rights in general, the Court's approach to the State Action doctrine has increasingly raised the threshold of state involvement that is required before *any* constitutional restraints apply to what is ostensibly private conduct. There is no reason to expect that this inclination to insulate action of private institutions, which provide services to the state or in the place of the state, from constitutional constraints will not continue. There is little basis for any confidence that this trend will not extend to private correctional facilities as well.

Is there any way to continue to protect the rights of prisoners in the face of privatization? Certainly the possibility exists that state contracts with private corrections providers could contain even more safeguards for prisoners than the Constitution would require of the state itself. The most direct solution, however, for assuring the continued rights of prisoners in private correctional facilities would be for the state to retain for itself authority to make all decisions that directly implicate prisoners rights. If state officers continued to make all decisions concerning such questions as discipline, classification, and "good time" credits, then there would be no significant diminution of constitutional protections. If those state officials responsible for such decisions were to maintain independence from the private prison operators, then they might make such important decisions in a neutral fashion after truly adversarial proceedings between prisoners and private prison operators. Such proceedings might provide even greater protections for prisoners than those that exist today in the publicly run prisons.

While those who have argued for privatization of corrections have claimed that privatization would not threaten prisoners' rights, few could seriously argue that a driving force behind the movement for privatized corrections has been a concern for prisoners' rights. In assessing the prospects for prisoners rights in private corrections facilities, we must recognize, therefore, that the best safeguard for constitutional rights is continuing state responsibility for, and control and operation of, corrections facilities.

Notes

1. This article updates and revises arguments which first appeared in Sullivan (1989).
2. Contrary to the argument of the District Court the decision cited by the District Court, *Flagg Brothers* (1982, 157) citing *Fuentes* (1972, 84) provides no support for the conclusion that "detention is a power reserved to government." On the contrary, the decision argues that only deprivation of property and, by implication, liberty *by the state "or private persons whose action 'may be fairly treated as that of the State itself"* may be subject to constitutional challenge. The circumstances under which actions of private detention facilities, or persons employed by them "may fairly be treated as that of the state itself" is *not* addressed by the decision.
3. Recognizing the apparent conflict between its decision and that of the U.S. Supreme Court in *Rendell-Baker* (1982), the *Milonas* Court argued that the cases can be distinguished. Although both cases concerned institutions in which the state had place "special needs" youth, the precise issue in *Rendell-Baker* concerned the discharge of employees at the school while *Milonas* concerned the treatment of students at the school. "The [U.S. Supreme] Court recognized that 'in contrast to the extensive regulation of the school generally, the various regulators showed relatively little interest in the school's personnel matters.'" 102 S.Ct.2764, cited at 940.
4. Although Kay has recognized that by limiting its supervisory role over the details of prison administration, the state might "effectively ... shield the private contractor from civil liability," she argues in so doing the state" might increase its own liability on the theory that it did not comply sufficiently with its responsibility to assure proper care of prisoners placed in its custody" (Kay 1987, 872-74). As Kay, herself, acknowledges, however, no such state liability has as yet "been addressed by any court" (Kay 1987, 873)
5. For additional discussion of the role of the private sector in the nineteen th century, see generally Cody (1987) and McCrie (1990); also see Mayer (1986, 311); Savas (1987, 898); Emory Law Journal (1987, 253-54). None of these authors, however, discuss the implications of the historical role of private corrections under the Supreme Court's "public functions" doctrine.

References

Ayoub, H. (1984) "The State Action Doctrine in State and Federal Courts." *Florida State University Law Review* 11 (Winter):893-920.
Brakel, S. (l988a) "Privatization in Corrections: Radical Prison Chic or Mainstream American?" *New England Journal of Civil and Criminal Confinement* 14 (Winter): 1-39.
_____ .(1988b) "Prison Management, Private Enterprise Style: The Inmates Evaluation." *New England Journal of Civil and Criminal Confinement* 14 (Summer): 175-244.
Camp, C. and Camp, G. (l984) *Private Sector Involvment in Prison Services and Operations.* Washington, DC: U.S. Department of Justice, National Institute of Corrections.
Cody, W. (l987) "The Privatization of Correctional Institutions: The Tennessee Experience." *Vanderbilt Law Review* 40 (May): 829-49.

Cohen, F. (1988) "The Law of Prisoners' Rights: An Overview." *Criminal Law Bulletin* 24 (July/Aug): 321-49.
Emory Law Journal (1987) "Private Prisons." 36 (Winter): 253-283.
Johnson, P. (1986) "What are the Legal Problems in Privatization of State/Local Corrections?" *Corrections Digest* 17 (April): 1-10.
Kay, S. (1987) "The Implications of Prison Privatization on the Conduct of Prisoner Litigation Under 42 U.S.C. Section 1983." *Vanderbilt Law Review* 40 (May): 867-99.
Mayer, C. (1986) "Legal Issues Surrounding the Private Operation of Prisons." *Criminal Law Bulletin* (July/August): 309-25.
McCrie, R. (1990) "Three Centuries of Criminal Justice Privatization in the United States." A paper presented at the Western Regional Science Association Meeting, Molokai, Hawaii, Feb. 21-25, 1990.
Mullen, J. (1985) *The Privatization of Corrections*. Washington, DC: U.S. Department of Justice, National Institute of Justice, U.S. Government Printing Office No. 027-000-1226-4.
Robbins, I. (1986) "Privatization of Corrections: Defining the Issues." *Judicature* 69 (April/May): 325-331.
_____ .(1987) "Privatization of Corrections: Defining the Issues." *Vanderbilt Law Review* 40 (May): 813-28.
Savas, E. S. (1987) "Privatization of Prisons." *Vanderbilt Law Review* 40 (May): 889-99.
Sullivan, H. (1989) "Privatization of Corrections and the Constitutional Rights of Prisoners." *Federal Probation* 53 (June): 36-42.
Thomas, C. and Calvert Hanson, L. (1989) "The Implications of 42 U.S.C. section 1983 for the Privatization of Prisons." *Florida State University Law Review* 16 (Spring): 933-962.
Travis, L., Latessa, J., and Vito, G. (1985) "Private Enterprise and Institutional Corrections: A Call for Caution." *Federal Probation* 11 (December): 11-16.
Wollan, L. (1986) "Prisons: The Privatization Phenomenon." *Public Administration Review* 46 (November/December): 678-81.
Wooley, M. (1985) "Prisons for Profit: Policy Considerations for Government Officials." *Dickinson Law Review* 90 (Winter): 307-32.

Court Cases

Blum v. Yaretsky (1982), 457 U.S. 991
Civil Rights Cases of 1883, 109 U.S. 3
Flagg Bros. Inc. v. Brooks (1978), 436 U.S. 149
Hurt v. G.C. Murphy Co. (1986) 624 F. Supp. 512, affirmed 800 F.2d.260
Jackson v. Metropolitan Edison (1974), 419 U.S. 345
Lugar v. Edmondson Oil Co. (1982), 457 U.S. 922
Medina v. O'Neill (1984), 589 F.Supp. 1028
Milonas v. Williams (1982), 691 F.2d 931, U.S. cert. den. 460 U.S. 1069
Moose Lodge No. 107 v. Irvis (1972), 407 U.S. 163
Rendell-Baker v. Kohn (1982), 457 U.S. 830
West v. Atkins (1988) 108 Sct 2250

12

Proving Privatization Works

H. Laws McCullough
Timothy S. Maguigan

Among the options available to authorities facing critical corrections issues is a partnership with a private sector company. Pricor is one of the major companies in the field.

As is true of the private firms in this field, providing humane and practical alternative solutions to the problems associated with correctional facilities has been a fundamental mission of Pricor since its founding in July of 1985. The publicly-held company is headquartered in Murfreesboro, Tennessee. The name Pricor stands for privatization corporation.

Pricor's goal is to offer a cost-effective and professional solution to the crises facing governmental agencies. The company's correctional services include juvenile and adult facility operation and management; management of facility design/ construction; nonresidential programs; and innovative financing approaches. Pricor can provide full-service facility operations including staffing and training of personnel, as well as medical and food services. In addition, the company can indemnify a contracting agency by accepting the exposure for liability associated with the facilty's management, protecting the agency against the financial impact of litigation. The management of the design and construction of correctional facilities was one of the earliest services provided by Pricor and remains an important component of the comprehensive correctional services offered to governmental agencies. In the management of the design and construction of the Rutherford County, Tennessee Adult Detention Center, the company completed the project six months ahead of schedule and $40,000 under budget.

In the financing of detention, correction and community-based facilities, Pricor has been involved with financing proposals for governmental agencies that are designed to alleviate the overcrowding of correctional facilities without the need to burden the taxpayer.

As is the case of other private companies in this field, Pricor works closely with the contracting authority to provide exactly the services that are desired. An example of how Pricor works with government authorities to establish programs specific to a community's needs can be found in the management of the Tuscaloosa Metropolitan Minimum Security Detention Facility in Tuscaloosa, Alabama.

Prior to the construction of this facility, Tuscaloosa and communities in the surrounding county were forced to house their inmates in several facilities. Tuscaloosa County operated the County Jail, which held felons, county misdemeanants and females from all jurisdictions within the county. This jail was under court order and limited to seventy-six males and twenty-four females. The city of Tuscaloosa operated an eighteen-bed, male-only jail out of police headquarters. The nearby city of Northport also had a small holding area in the police headquarters. Due to the limited bed space, the cities were forced to house some inmates in other counties. Persons serving weekend sentences were routinely turned away and there were difficulties executing writs and collecting fines.

In 1984, construction began on the Tuscaloosa Metropolitan Minimum Security Detention Facility, a multijurisdictional facility for misdemeanants. The county and cities formed a Jail Advisory Committee to oversee operations and explore private management of the jail.

Pricor was awarded the contract for complete facility operation and management in the spring of 1986 and the facility opened in June of that year. It was the first and remains the only adult correctional facility operated by the private sector in the state of Alabama.

The facility has a capacity of 144 and houses all those charged with misdemeanors and felony property crimes. All persons arrested in the county are booked at the facility.

The Tuscaloosa Metropolitan Minimum Security Detention Facility has a full-time staff of twenty-nine, including twenty-five security staff and four administrative/support staff. The facility has been operating at or near capacity since 1989 and books approximately 9,000 persons each year. Since the facility opened, both Northport and the city of Tuscaloosa have been able to close their jail operations.

Prior to opening, staff members were provided with 160 hours of pre-service training. All staff members, with the exception of the administrator, were hired locally. Pricor provides all on-site medical services, recreation, security, classification, in-house work programs and staff training. Staffers work with volunteers and community agencies to provide religious programs and mental health services. As the average length of stay has increased, plans are under way to expand program areas to include education and drug abuse.

Facility operations are reviewed by the Contract Monitor and Jail Advisory Committee. The facility is regularly inspected by the State Department of Corrections as well as local regulatory agencies.

After four years of operation, response from the community is favorable. Facility staff works closely with law enforcement and the courts to coordinate local criminal justice activities. Governmental officials are pleased with Pricor's performance in managing all day-to-day operations. In May of 1989, in large part due to its performance in managing the jail, Pricor was awarded a contract to operate the new Tuscaloosa County Juvenile Detention Facility.

Tuscaloosa City Chief of Police Ken Swindle states, "We are very pleased with the way they [Pricor] have handled the jail. They have been very professional in their approach and they have established high standards for the staff they have hired. We have experienced no problems since operations began and the facility staff have been extremely cooperative with the City of Tuscaloosa." Hardy McCollum, chairman of the Tuscaloosa County Commission said, "Pricor has fulfilled the requirements set forth by the County and provided the services it offered in its original proposal. While we are still responsible for the jail operation, the County has been relieved of the day-to-day management. Pricor's management of the facility has been professional and cost efficient. This has proven to be an effective and beneficial partnership between government and the private sector."

Pricor also provides correctional services to governmental authorities charged with the responsibility of housing juveniles. The company currently operates two multijurisdictional juvenile detention centers. Like the Tuscaloosa Metropolitan Minimum Security Detention Facility, both juvenile correctional facilities are owned by the contracting authorities.

The Upper East Tennessee Regional Juvenile Detention Center in Johnson City, Tennessee was Pricor's first contract and dates back to October 1985. The facility, which serves seven counties and has a capacity of up to eleven males and females, was constructed as a result of legislation requiring that juveniles no longer be held in local adult jails.

Under the supervision of a government board, the facility suffered from a series of administrative difficulties in its first few months of operation. The members of the board then turned to Pricor.

Employees already working at the center were given the opportunity to remain and undergo extensive special training. Each employee completed 160 hours of training provided by Pricor's training staff. In addition to safety, security, and treatment procedures, the training addressed all areas required by American Correctional Association standards. As of this writing, two youth counselors from the facility have earned nationally recognized honors for their efforts with youth at the detention center.

Pricor began operation and management of the Tuscaloosa Regional Juvenile Detention Facility in September of 1989. The facility, which has the capacity for twenty-seven males and females, serves the juvenile courts and law enforcement agencies of Tuscaloosa and surrounding Alabama counties. Daily operations include security, supervision, support services, structured program activities, behavior management and individual, family, and group counselling. An extra wing connected to the facility was constructed to allow Tuscaloosa's juvenile court to be on-site at some point in the future.

Three nonresidential, correctionally oriented programs for youth are currently operated by Pricor. Two programs are designed to keep offending youth out of correctional institutions and in their home and community. Coordinated Alternatives in Richmond, Virginia is an intensive family preservation program that has been in operation since September of 1986. The program is operated under contract with the Virginia Departments of Corrections and Social Services. Rather than institutionalizing youth, this program brings together the offending youths and their parents, teachers and employers with Pricor counselors up to ninety times each month. Every effort is made to strengthen family ties and maintain appropriate behavior while keeping the youth in the community. The entire family is encouraged to accept responsibility for growth.

Teen Trax in Murfreesboro, Tennessee is operated by Pricor under contract with the Tennessee Department of Youth Development. The two-year-old program uses peer-influenced group counseling and adaptive skills training to help reduce commitments to state institutions. The program provides directional/goal planning for each youth and assists in networking all applicable services. Like Coordinated Alternatives, this nonresidential program lowers commitments to institutions thus lowering costs to the states.

Pricor's newest nonresidential program is a day treatment center located in Nashville, Tennessee for up to twenty youths who are in transition from institutional to community placement. The program components include computerized learning centers where each child can learn at his/her own pace. Vocational aptitude placements and a supportive employment program monitored by Pricor counselors serve to round out the program.

As is true of other private correctional service firms, Pricor offers the public sector an alternative solution to its correctional, educational and fiscal needs. Relationships with the agencies served are evaluated on a periodic basis to ensure that the company is providing effective solutions at a value. On occasion, it becomes apparent that privatization does not represent the best answer for a community. When that has happened, the contracting agency and Pricor have discontinued the relationship on amiable terms. Today, Pricor is responsible for the operation and management of thirty facilities and programs that serve, in total, more than three dozen public agencies in six states. The scope of these efforts proves that the privatization of correctional and educational services can have a meaningful impact on communities across the country and that public/private sector partnerships are working.

13

For Profit Jails: A Risky Business

Todd Mason

> *I don't want a committee report [on privatizing government operations]. I want action and results. Get the private sector in the driver's seat*
> —Reagan, 1982

Darrell Algernon Nelson had the driver's seat in mind 17 July 1990, as he stepped over a fence in Crystal City, Texas, and approached Eddie and Hortensia Trevino. Leveling a pistol at the couple relaxing in lawn chairs under a tree, the convicted armed robber from Washington, D.C. shouted, "Don't move. I want the keys to your car." The Trevinos survived the encounter, but their 1981 Lincoln didn't.

Now the residents here wonder if this impoverished outpost near the Mexican border will survive its brush with prison privatization. Mr. Nelson's unsuccessful escape was only one of the misadventures at the for-profit jails in Zavala County built with revenue bonds and rented out in 1989 to the District of Columbia.

In late 1990, alarmed by the vats of homemade wine bubbling in shower stalls and the fights by inmates wielding baseball bats, the District pulled out of the $46.50 per inmate per day arrangement. With its jails empty, the bonds in default and its general fund in the red, Zavala County is enduring layoffs rather than enjoying the hiring boom the private jail manager promised.

While Zavala County isn't representative of the private prison industry or of President Reagan's dreams, its example bears watching. It shows that the nascent industry bears the other unmistakable stamps of the Reagan years: rankly speculative ventures, sweetheart deals, and junk-bond financing.

In job-starved towns from West Virginia to Oregon, developers are selling for-profit jails and prisons as economic development projects. These promoters are holding out the prospect of a stable, growth industry with no pollution problems. Since the local government is pledging nothing to repay the bonds but the revenues generated at the facility, the pitch continues, it's also free of risk!

To the contrary, private prisons aren't sure deals or a clean and safe industry either. Communities with private prisons sweat out annual contract renewals, escapes, assaults, riots, fires and lawsuits. The credit ratings of these towns ride on the outcome. In short, there's ample reason for communities approached by prison developers to take up temporary residence in Missouri.

The private-prison industry itself deserves a measure of skepticism. For all of the explosive growth of prison populations during the 1980s, the prison crisis remains a creature of public policy. Some state legislatures are abandoning costly punishment strategies after a decade of tough-on-crime stances. For the 1990s, state budget deficits may well be the telling statistic. The private prison industry already is declining at its margin—the "rent-a-cell" market.

A Stunning Reversal in Texas

Consider the dramatic reversals for private prison operators in Texas. When the Zavala County jails opened in 1989, prison entrepreneurs were housing county, state, and federal inmates for profit, and were forging brand-new interstate markets as well. The District of Columbia, under court orders to ease overcrowding, was actually polling jailers by telephone prospecting for beds. Houston prison developer N-Group Securities, Inc., expressed the optimism of the day in a 1989 press release. "Counties and state and federal agencies with crisis overcrowding con-

For Profit Jails: A Risky Business

ditions will be lining up to pay for their prisoners to stay in these new facilities."

Two years later, only three of the six N-Group facilities are open and empty and the remainder have only short-term contracts to keep the wolf from the door. It wasn't obvious that any of the six counties would meet the first interest payment of $600,000 due in early 1992 on the revenue bonds sold in 1989 by Drexel Burnham Lambert, let alone their twenty-year schedules of payment.

What happened? First the prison promoters mistakenly assumed that the urgent interest in private facilities was an abiding one. Instead, the states and the District of Columbia used the private beds as a stopgap solution to overcrowding while they began construction programs.

What's more, rates of incarceration fell in client states like Oregon, Colorado, and the District of Columbia, partly because crime rates eased and partly because of changes in criminal justice policies. In Oregon, for example, the state legislature softened its mandatory sentencing guidelines as a response to overcrowding. The combination of slowing crime rates there and greater sentencing flexibility produced a turnaround so dramatic that Oregon itself was caught with surplus prison beds. The state tried to rent cells completed in mid-1991 but found no takers at $60 per prisoner per day.

Prison entrepreneurs also misjudged how quickly their ranks would multiply. Industry pioneer Corrections Corporation of America opened the first private facility in modern-day Texas in 1984, a detention center for the U.S. Immigration and Naturalization Service in Houston. Seven years later, Texas was home to twenty-four for-profit jails and prisons, half of them open and empty, plus fourteen oversized county jails also competing for prisoners (U.S. Government Accounting Office 1991).

Private prisons, or prison promotion to be precise, had become a growth industry. Depressed rural towns, some of which had bid unsuccessfully for public-sector prison projects, welcomed private prison operators with open arms. Inured by the speculative excesses of the 1980s, underwriters sold high-yield bonds, so-called "junk munis," to finance them, to be repaid from the prison's lease revenues.

The resulting stampede was an impressive demonstration of the power of profits. In Crystal City, Texas, the financial consultant, Diversified Municipal Services Inc., of Lebanon, Indiana, split off to compete with the promoter there, Detention Services, Inc. of Dallas. The project's alarm and electrical subcontractor, former Navarro County, Texas, sheriff Bobby Ross, began promoting prisons as Republic Detention Services, Inc.

Knowledge of the prison business was optional for promoters. Local officials in Hinton, Oklahoma, recruited Canam Construction Co. of Edmond, Oklahoma, to build a speculative 480-bed prison. Some months later, a Canam contractor, PEC Enterprises Inc., of Oklahoma City, turned up in tiny Hatch, New Mexico, citing the Hinton project as one of its accomplishments. How much of an accomplishment continues to be a matter of debate. Hinton city fathers insisted that PEC's limited role was to set type for its bond offering statement. PEC said it acted as a financial consultant. The modus operandi is clear in either version: have floppy disk, will travel.

In mid-1991, speculative prisons were completed, or about to be, in Texas, Oklahoma, Minnesota, and Georgia. Their total of 6,200 beds was nearly double the 3,500 beds built in 1989, the industry's best year in terms of growth and profits. The difference: the 1989 facilities were built the old fashioned way, by obtaining contracts to house prisoners first and then breaking ground.

Jail promotions underway in those states plus Colorado, Missouri, Mississippi, Alabama, Tennessee, Virginia, Indiana, Oregon and West Virginia, to name a partial list, would require the $275 million industry to double in size.

A Problem of Definition

Naturally, the members of this entrepreneurial fraternity attempted to define the problem out of existence. Houston-based N-Group maintained that its six facilities in Texas are not prisons, since they were built to jail standards instead, and not private either since the counties own them. The key, as Diversified Municipal Services saw it, was public-sector management because of the bureaucratic prejudice against private managers. Industry leaders saw the speculative developers as market "froth" that would dry up and blow away (hardly; Diversified Municipal Services, with prisons and jails under its belt, is courting at least seven other counties in four states).

The fact remains that these facilities compete for the same finite supply of prisoners and profits regardless of what stripes they wear. Not even financial failure reliably eliminates their challenge. When the builders of a juvenile facility in Brush, Colorado, turned it over to bondholders in lieu of foreclosure in 1987, for example, it was resold for the only use practicable. The new operator was a stronger competitor for juvenile detention contracts, thanks to the deeply discounted sale.

That's why CCA backed out of two speculative ventures and restated its 1990 revenues to reverse $1.1 million in proceeds from the sale of "development rights" conferring CCA's prison designs—and its imprimatur—to the promoters of facilities in Texas and West Virginia.

Though 1990 revenues climbed 50 percent to $55.5 million, net income for the year fell 87 percent, to $200,000, its first reversal since the company's inception in 1983. In its first quarter ended March 31, CCA reported a loss of $90,000 on revenues of $16.5 million, against a year-earlier net income of $250,000, on revenues of $11.7 million. It blamed that loss on new prisons in New Mexico and Tennessee that were oversized, if not truly speculative. Those projects, departing from CCA's norm, were financed with county revenue bonds.

A Trial-Basis Industry

Profits overall have been meager in the closely scrutinized industry, which suffers a unique credibility problem. It can't sell itself if it doesn't deliver cost savings over public-sector incarceration. But it can't cut its costs to the point that security and rehabilitation programs suffer because of the chorus of critics eager to prove that profits and prisons don't mix.

Many of the industry's gains have been explicit tests of its ability to deliver both quality services and discount prices. In Texas, for example, the state Department of Criminal Justice let two contracts each to CCA and to Wackenhut to house state inmates in the final months of their sentences. The four facilities were expressly a test of privatization.

Graphic evidence that the jury is still out on Wall Street, CCA's stock took a pounding in mid-1990 when Texas corrections officials issued a report critical of its operation of the prerelease facilities.

Cutting Corners in Crystal City

The results were even more distressing in Zavala County, Texas. The operators there counted on design innovations and low-wage scales to deliver profits and effective service. Instead, security and rehabilitation programs suffered, according to lawsuits and eyewitness accounts.

The design of the facility sought to reduce manpower needs by placing the guard station at the heart of four large dormitories. In practice the design made the facility largely unmanageable. After inmates hung blankets around their bunks for privacy, guards couldn't monitor the interior of the dorms. Nor did the facility have sufficient cells to segregate troublemakers.

More troublesome, the modestly paid guards at the facility appear to have been no match for the cons. In one case documented in arrest records, a guard signed out two prisoners for a work detail and delivered them instead to a brothel in Piedras Negras, Mexico, some fifty miles distant. The guard was arrested, not for aiding an escape, but for furnishing alcohol to inmates and those charges were dropped eventually. Authorities believe that many of the approximately eight escapes from the detention center and from the Zavala County Jail were aided by guards, although no charges were brought.

There's little comfort in the rebuttals of the operator, Detention Services, that local officials got too greedy. County officials required the firm to hire 80 percent of its guards from Zavala, for example, condemning the facility to a grossly inexperienced staff. The county demanded $4 per day per inmate rather than the $1 originally agreed upon, and withheld payments to the company when it failed to pay. As a result, the operator couldn't meet its payroll at times. The county and the company brought lawsuits and countersuits.

Meanwhile, prisoners began their own class action lawsuit in federal court alleging "systemic" violation of their rights. Plaintiff Ernest DeGraffin alleges he was assaulted there on 11 October 1989 by an inmate and subsequently denied medical services. The suit also alleges that inmates in Zavala did not have access to D.C. law books, or to education programs that provided "good time" credits to shorten prison terms.

Jonathan Smith, a staff attorney with the D.C. Prisoners' Legal Services Project, Inc., during a June 1990 visit, observed baseball bats in the dormitories, the attorney maintained. He saw a crude version of homemade wine called 'shoots' fermenting quite openly in the shower stalls. He learned that most of the inmates were unhappy being held in custody so far away from their families, and many were angered by what they perceived to be cultural insensitivities by the facility administration, fueled by such basic misunderstandings as serving pork chops to Muslims.

Zavala County took over management of the detention facility in late 1990, but the damage had been done. The District of Columbia declined to renew its contract that December and moved its prisoners to other facilities. Empty since last December, the detention center needs perhaps $1.8 million to add segregation cells and other security upgrades to be competitive today, estimates a county consultant. Zavala faces great difficulty raising the money with its credit rating in tatters and uncertain prospects even if it succeeds.

Belatedly, the county is concerned about what it bought in its "turnkey contract" for the financing, design, and construction of the facility. The work certainly was kept all in the family. Philip Packer, for example, was a vice president of Detention Services, and vice president also for the contractor, Hale-Mills Construction Co., a shopping center builder from Houston. He was a registered agent for the local arm of Diversified Municipal Services, which packaged the $4.4 million bond sale in 1988.

The financing works out to about $19,000 per bed. By contrast, CCA built its INS detention facility in Houston for $13,000 per bed in 1984 when construction costs in Texas were higher. (Mr. Packer notes that prepaid interest and other reserves accounted for $1.2 million in bond proceeds.) Significantly, it's CCA's money and reputation on the line in Houston, while the Zavala contractors have collected their fees and departed.

Long-Term Bonds, Short-Term Contracts

Zavala residents, in fact, made an extraordinarily risky bet on criminal justice policy in 1989. The detention facilities that were renting strongly in the 1980s were a drug on the market in the budget-minded 1990s. The first inclination in cost-conscious times was to release the low-risk inmates who would have be sent to detention facilities. Electronic home monitoring systems, boot camps, and work-release facilities, emerged as cost-effective alternatives and made the private-public debate moot. At the start of the 1990s, a medium-security prison was a minimum contender in the market for interstate transfers of adult felons.

But does that massive investment in concrete, sunk costs of perhaps $50,000 per bed, constitute a prudent investment? What happens if penology in the twenty-first century expands its repertoire of vocational and drug treatment programs and other community-based alternatives to prison adopting the model of Minnesota? If alternative sentencing eases prison overcrowding, who pays off $12.25 million in the Criminal Detention Center Mortgage Revenue Bonds in Fort Stockton, Texas, due 2009? Fort Stockton has very little influence over the political process that will determine criminal justice policies.

A Right to Prison Beds?

State legislatures have limited influence over sentencing decisions by local judges and prosecutors as well, however. In Texas, Harris County (metropolitan Houston) frustrated a prison compromise approved in the waning hours of the 1991 state legislature. To operate at 95 percent of capacity as required by federal court order, Texas routinely maroons recently sentenced prisoners in county jails until beds open up in the state penitentiary system. At the time, the state had 9,000 prisoners backed up in county jails, 3,700 of them in Houston, the law-and-order center of the state.

In the settlement, Texas offered to build 28,500 new prison beds by 1995, to pay a part of the cost of keeping state felons in county jails in the interim, and to affirm its duty to accept state prison inmates within sixty days of sentencing. For their part, the counties were to drop their lawsuits against the state and to accept alternative sentencing programs.

Houston preferred its chances before a federal judge who had already awarded it payments from the state of $40 per day for each state prisoner it places in rent-a-cell facilities. (The Harris County prisoners constituted a slender lifeline to some of the spec jails in the state.) The state, however, was a grudging rich uncle. Facing a $4.6 billion budget shortfall for its 1991-93 biennium, and an divisive battle over school funding, Texas legislators were left to consider the implied threat in its compromise proposal, that supplying unlimited prison beds wasn't a state obligation.

The frustration was evident in the numbers in California, another state beset by budget problems. Vying with Medicaid as the most out-of-control fund in the state budget, corrections expenditures increased sevenfold to $2.1 billion during the decade of the 1980s. The result was that the state prison system still was operating at 180 percent of capacity, and the recidivism rate within two years of release has doubled since 1967 to 64 percent. Privatization of adult prisons is a Bandaid solution to a hemorrhage of that magnitude. Community programs, however, "appear to have the potential to reduce state correctional costs and improve the treatment of certain offenders," in the view of California legislative analyst, Elizabeth G. Hill (California Legislative Analyst's Office 1991).

These aren't necessarily discouraging trends for privatization advocates. Historically, corrections bureaucrats have turned to private companies to operate vocational programs, drug rehabilitation, and youth offender facilities. It's reasonable to believe that private sector would find alternative sentencing programs an easier sell than adult, general-population prisons.

New directions won't compute for the promoters and investors who have loaded 1980s statistics into their personal computer spreadsheets and have drawn prison construction trend lines into infinity.

A Community Checklist

The risks deepen for the small-town targets of prison promoters. A track record will be even more important if corrections officials expect program operators to change criminal behavior. Some of the small towns with empty spec jails are too remote to succeed, and others lack adequate labor forces. Wisconsin is even attacking the raison d'etre of rural prisons: the Not In My Backyard syndrome. State officials there can override local zoning laws in siting halfway houses and other community-based facilities.

But small towns in desperate, rural America have great difficulty tempering their anticipation. Hatch, New Mexico has seen a steady drain of young people and families to the point that two of every three residents are age sixty-five or older. Many of them would move away if their homes would sell. They endorsed a private prison by an overwhelmingly vote in a local referendum in mid-1990.

The ranchers around Hatch, prosperous and not inclined to move, reacted differently. Tommy Bickle sued to stop the development, alleging, among other things, the developer exaggerated its experience and misrepresented its support in order to obtain zoning approval. The developer put the project on hold until the lawsuits were settled. Hatch residents ostracized Mr. Bickle, who lost his bid for reelection to the school board. "They feel I've killed Hatch's last chance," he says forlornly. "That's quite a burden" (Mason 1991).

Communities must not allow developers to exploit community divisions or to play on fears about economic decline, however acute. Nothing in these deliberations is quite as final as an empty, foreclosed prison to stand as a monument to local ineptitude. Communities must direct the debate to the essential questions.

Ask for References

The first of these is the experience and the reputation of the developer. Carl (Sonny) Emerson, vice president of Midland, Texas-based Private Prisons of America, Ltd. failed to tell citizens of Richwood, West Virginia about the failure of the youth facility he developed in Brush, Colorado. The town of 3,000 approved Private Prisons' plan to build a $50 million, 1,500-bed prison for a 2 percent fee, or $1 million, subject to obtaining financing and contracts to house prisoners.

Mr. Emerson described himself as a pioneer of private corrections. But he abruptly closed his halfway house in Denver in 1982, giving the federal government thirty days notice to remove Cuban juveniles who arrived in the Mariel boatlift. Mr. Emerson says he was pressured by state and city officials to get rid of the Marielitos, many of whom were criminals and mental patients.

The Brush facility failed, Mr. Emerson says, because his partners forced him out. His partners say he was ousted because his abrasive personality had offended potential customers.

Mr. Emerson grew angry during a public hearing in Richwood last November 15 when attorney Michael C. Farber, representing opponents of the prison, asked him where in his resume he had disclosed his personal bankruptcy filing in 1989 or his 1965 conviction in Colorado for receiving stolen property. (Mr. Emerson was pardoned in 1974.) Mr. Emerson replied that he didn't think it was appropriate, according to the hearing transcript. In fact, the contractor's reputation and contacts in the corrections community are key to obtaining contracts.

Still eager to believe, local officials ask, "But if it's built, won't someone use it?" Yes and no. In Eagle Pass, Texas, local officials have hired an attorney to pursue construction problems in a jail developed and built by the Zavala County team of Diversified Municipal Services and Hale-Mills. Completed in 1990, foundation problems have opened up cracks in its walls that admit daylight.

Define "Low Risk," Please

Foreclosure could take away a veto right that local authorities must hold over which prisoners become their neighbors. The anecdotal evidence here is full of rude surprises for communities. At a CCA jail in Santa Fe, New Mexico, a majority of the fifty-seven "low-risk" prisoners sent there by Oregon were convicted of murder or rape. CCA sent the inmates back after a local uproar. In Spokane, Washington, in 1989, the Sheriff's Department sent District of Columbia prisoners home after four, tense months.

Even bona fide low-risk prisoners cause problems. At the Eden (Texas) Detention Center, for example, illegal aliens with two years to serve or less have staged hunger strikes and started fires. They have filed five lawsuits and mounted eight escapes, one of them successful. The impact in the community so far is a single stolen bicycle, but the anxiety hasn't gone away six years later.

Communities need to ask this hypothetical question posed by Kansas City, Kansas prison consultant Robert Buchanan, a retired federal prison administrator: "Why would I be interested in sending my best inmates to another state" (Mason 1991)? A warden's short list of undesirable convicts includes some surprises: AIDS sufferers and transsexuals who defy normal gender classification.

No Help in Most States

Finally, communities must understand how much, or how little, protection they have under state laws. While many states have adopted comprehensive regulation of private prisons to settle issues such as where out-of-state prisoners are to be released, most states have not.

Regulation isn't necessary if city councils and county commissions heed this hoary investment rule: if it sounds too good to be true, it probably is.

References

California Legislative Analysts Office. (1991) *The 1991-92 Budget: Community Corrections.*

Mason, T. (1991) "Many For-Profit Jails Hold No Profits—Nor Even Any Inmates." *The Wall Street Journal* 87, 118: 1,4.

Reagan, R. (1982) " Remarks to the New York City Partnership." New York, January 14.

U.S. Government Accounting Office. (1991) *Private Prisons: Cost Savings and BOP's Statutory Authority Need to be Resolved.*

14

Low Cost, High Quality, Good Fit: Why Not Privatization?

Wayne H. Calabrese

As the privatization of corrections has taken root and grown, initial questions of propriety—"Should this be done?"—have given way to secondary questions of efficacy—"Does this work?" Perhaps inevitably in a time of dwindling public sector budgets and rising public service demands, those who seek a definitive answer to the question of privatization's value look to cost comparisons between public and private corrections. While the evidence thus far clearly establishes the economic advantages of privatized corrections, a careful analysis of the reasons for such advantages reveals a number of complex and subtle factors which contribute to cost savings. These factors are examined in the first section of this chapter.

Of course, the inquiry into the relative worth of privatized corrections does not end with a chart of purported cost savings. Indeed, those who are critical of privatized corrections often cite reluctantly admitted cost savings as direct evidence of failed service delivery. To these critics, a dollar saved is a service shorted. The record indicates otherwise. The quality of services delivered by privatized corrections has, in the main, been equal or superior to the quality of correctional services delivered by the public sector. The second part of this chapter explores the ways public sector administrators can ensure adherence to quality standards by private providers of correctional services.

Finally, the third part of this chapter addresses a proper role for privatization in our criminal justice system, a role which can complement existing prison systems without unduly threatening the continued central role of public sector corrections departments.

Cost Comparisons

Add to the list of life's great imponderables the question of how much we are paying for our prisons. Political and religious discourse appear deliberate and calm compared to the sparks raised by those who grind their axes on the stone of public/private corrections cost comparisons. The pitfalls are legion: aging public facilities compared to newly designed and constructed private facilities; security level, average length of stay, and offense category of compared incarcerated populations; required offender programming for public vs. private providers and degree of adherence to required standards; indirect and hidden public sector costs; to name only a few.

Indeed, the State of Florida paid a group of highly competent lawyers and accountants more than a quarter million dollars to determine the cost to Florida taxpayers of housing one inmate one day in a close custody (high security) facility and received a voluminous report which, in the opinion of many observers, raised more questions than it answered (Price Waterhouse 1990). This exercise demonstrated the nearly intractable Gordion knot facing those who seek a fair basis for comparison. Systemwide cost analysis, by definition, either must sacrifice distinguishing facility characteristics upon the altar of easily grasped, but often misleading, systemwide averages, or it must attempt to discern, list, impute, factor, delete, extrapolate, and otherwise massage all such site-specific factors into a committee-crafted, distilled unit cost which generally bears little or no resemblance to any single facility within the system.

Nevertheless, cost comparisons have been made that clearly indicate that privatization of correctional facilities leads to significant cost savings. In an article first published in the September/October 1989 issue of *NIJ Reports*, Charles Logan and Bill W. McGriff (1989) exhaustively examined the cost savings that Hamilton County, Tennessee realized through the privatization of its 350-bed Hamilton County Penal Farm. The authors state,

> Hamilton County found that contracting out prison management generated annual savings of at least 4 to 8 percent—and more likely in the range of 5 to 15 percent—compared to the estimated cost of direct county management. (Logan and McGriff 1989, 2)

In a report of the University of Florida at Gainesville, Center for Studies in Criminology and Law, Charles W. Thomas (1990) examined available data on forty-five privately managed correctional facilities. Of the ten facilities readily capable of cost comparison with a public counterpart, all ten evidenced cost savings ranging from 10.71 percent to 52.23 percent.

These two studies clearly indicate that while available data definitively substantiate the significant cost savings realized through the privatization of corrections, that same data reveal the difficulty inherent in such cost comparisons. Comparing "apples to apples" remains an elusive but important task.

Public policymakers require meaningful tools with which to craft sound policy decisions. Thus far, sound public policy has required private correction providers to demonstrate a cost savings to the taxpayers by delivering at least equivalent services at less cost. Private providers, in turn, have accepted and met this challenge. It is essential that our decision makers appreciate the story behind the numbers on the yardstick, if comparisons are to be fairly measured. The following analysis, or "story behind the numbers," is submitted in order to illustrate the reasons privatization, by its very nature, will almost always lead to lower costs without sacrificing service quality.

Construction Costs

While design-build and construction management models of new construction have made some inroads into public sector construction, the traditional three-party "pyramid" format, with the government/owner independently contracting with an architect-engineer firm to design the facility and with a general contractor to construct the facility, still prevails in most jurisdictions. The reasons for this continuing adherence to the traditional format include statutory/regulatory impediments or prohibitions, lack of public sector expertise or experience with relatively newer models, comfort with established methods, and so on.

The traditional public sector approach to constructing a new correctional facility has within its seemingly elegant three-sided design a built-in paradigm for cost overruns and missed schedules. First, the design phase must generally be completed before the construction begins. This lineal format adds months and consequential costs to the construction process. Second, the general contractor is generally selected through competitive bidding which requires an award to the "lowest and best bid." While the low bidder is not always selected, experienced contractors know that the "bottom line" receives significantly more scrutiny than the experience and credit-worthiness of the subcontractors contributing to the total. Accordingly, subcontractors are frequently selected for the wrong reason—low cost—without regard to the level of experience or expertise they may bring to the project.

Third, the contractor may intentionally underbid the project, relying upon anticipated change-orders to regain the temporarily lost profit margin. No construction contract yet devised can eliminate all "gray areas." The traditional public sector construction model requires the architect-engineer firm to approve and certify all change orders and then pays the architect-engineer firm a percentage of the cost of any such changes. This feature alone virtually guarantees cost overruns.

Perhaps as important as these obvious traditional public sector construction shortcomings is the less obvious drain upon the limited time and resources of the public administrator or department assigned to steward this triangular behemoth. Vast quantities of time and tax dollars are spent each year in a largely doomed effort to complete public works projects on a timely and budgeted basis. By contrast, private correctional providers, when called upon to design and construct a correctional facility, almost always proceed on a design-build basis with a guaranteed maximum price.

This system has many advantages. First, the design and construction processes are begun in coordinated tandem, saving months in the construction timetable. These time savings result in substantial cost savings based upon reduced project capitalized interest. Second, the general contractor is selected, as in turn are his subcontractors, based upon demonstrated expertise, experience and reliability. The experienced private provider is therefore confident that the general contractor's bottom

Low Cost, High Quality, Good Fit: Why Not Privatization? 179

line is not a bottomless well. A bond of trust in this essential relationship can develop due, in part, to the contractor's desire to become part of the private provider's established team for future projects.

This same relationship serves to reduce, if not eliminate, the proliferation of change orders. The private provider has given the public sector client a guaranteed maximum price for the project. This price has been bonded, and cannot be exceeded in the absence of client requested changes, without substantial direct loss to the private provider. The private provider's contract with the design build team passes this risk of loss to the general contractor/ architect-engineers insofar as possible. The desire to maintain a continuing and profitable relationship with the private provider impels the general contractor and his architect-engineers to resolve "gray area" disputes with the private provider in a creative give-and-take fashion without additional project cost.

Inasmuch as the project is delivered to the public sector client on a "turnkey" basis, the need for public sector participation in the day-to-day construction process is greatly reduced. Construction is monitored, rather than managed by the client. Only projects completed in accordance with project specifications and standards are accepted and paid for; incentive enough to generally guarantee completion of private design-build projects on time and within budget.

Operational Costs

Many of those who readily accept and agree with the premise that private providers can construct the same correctional facility in less time and at lower cost than the public sector, nevertheless have difficulty accepting the premise that the same private provider can manage and operate the facility at less cost with equivalent quality of service. Again, an examination of the factors contributing to operating costs reveals an almost inevitable cost advantage in privatizing corrections without any sacrifice of service quality.

Operational costs may be understood as consisting of three main categories: direct, indirect, and hidden. Direct costs, in turn, include costs associated with labor, supplies and services. Labor costs are comprised of wages and benefits. Private providers can, and generally will, pay wages equivalent to their public sector counterparts. Contrary to what some critics suggest, non-competitive wages result in disproportionately higher costs due to unacceptable levels of employee attrition. This results in increased employee training costs and other losses generally attributable to organizational upheaval.

The provision of employee benefits does, in fact, differ substantially between the public sector and the private provider. Public sector benefits include a retirement benefit known as a defined benefit plan which essentially guarantees the covered employee a specified benefit level upon retirement. This is generally expressed as a percentage of highest earnings formula. Private providers tend to either eliminate direct employer contribution retirement benefits, or if provided, the benefit is of the type known as a defined contribution plan. The defined contribution plan guarantees a level of contribution to a tax-deferred employee retirement account.

Quite often, the perceived advantages of the public sector retirement system are not realized by the public corrections employee. In order to qualify, the employee often must work for at least ten years before "vesting" in the system. This substantial waiting period in an employment sector that traditionally experiences relatively high attrition rates means that for a significant number of public correctional employees, no retirement benefits will accompany their years of service.

Private provider employees who participate in a defined contribution plan generally vest in five or fewer years and are able to withdraw their accumulated contributed benefit at any age upon termination of employment, subject to tax penalties under applicable IRS regulations. The tax-deferred growth of the account compared with its earlier vesting and greater accessibility make the defined contribution plan a better bargain for most employees.

It must be stressed that the decision whether or not to provide private provider employees with a retirement benefit rests not with the private provider, but with the public sector client. The cost of any such plan is passed through to the public sector client as a contract cost. While contracts mandating private providers to take over existing public correctional facilities and offer employment to existing public sector employees often require the continuation of an equivalent retirement benefit for the assumed employees, to this date, no new facility procurement has required such benefits for employees, relying instead upon social security contributions and expanded individual retirement account opportunities common to all private sector employees.

The savings resulting from this single benefit are enormous. Public employee retirement contributions currently hover between 20 percent to 25 percent of the employee's wages in most public sector systems. Privatization offers the public sector client the flexibility to eliminate or modify the cost of such benefits without demonstrably affecting the quality of provided service.

Private providers also save money with respect to the procurement of facility supplies. Bulk purchasing through established national accounts, together with less bureaucratic purchasing systems, reduce costs through competitive pricing and reduced administrative overhead. The procurement of facility services such as medical, food, program instructors, counselors, and so on also benefit from competitive private sector pricing and lower administrative overhead. In short, the direct costs of operating a facility will almost always be lower for the private provider than the public sector, for reasons inherent in the respective systems of each. To recognize this advantage of the private provider is not to indict the public sector employee as less capable or motivated; rather, it is a recognition that public sector protections and systemic redundancies are purchased at a cost and eliminated or modified at a savings.

Both the private providers and the public sector have indirect costs. The private provider recognizes these costs as corporate support or overhead; the public sector equivalent is known as "bureaucracy." In either case, these costs are difficult to quantify. They include allocated time of administrators/managers, payroll, accounting, purchasing, personnel, risk management and legal departments. An analysis of a typical county jail system is instructive. A true determination of the cost of incarcerating one inmate for one day in the county jail should include some allocation of the sheriff's salary and benefits, as well as any other line-item discretionary accounts that the sheriff may use to augment jail operations. The simplest personnel decision may well involve numerous individuals in the county's personnel, payroll, and legal departments. Any litigation arising from or related to the jail operation will require significant expenditures of time and money on numerous levels of the county government. It is readily apparent that any allocation of the indirect costs of a county jail system requires numerous subjective estimates that can vary widely from year to year, or facility to facility. Perhaps less apparent is the vested interest of public corrections officials charged with the task of determining their department's cost in underestimating such costs.

While neither the private provider nor the public sector is immune to the ravages of a "top-heavy" organization, pricing competition will tend to redraw the private provider's table of organization more quickly than the public sector's organizational chart. Additionally, as the privatization of corrections continues to mature and grow, the successful firms are able to allocate the overhead costs over an increasing number of contracts. This reduces the per inmate overhead allocation in a manner not available to the public sector.

No discussion of private/public cost comparisons would be complete without mention of the "hidden costs" of public sector corrections. These hidden costs are endemic to the public sector system. Private providers are sometimes criticized for operating on a for-profit basis, almost as though profitability is incompatible with the public good. The private providers have shareholder investors; the public sector has taxpayer investors. Both sets of investors expect a reasonable return on their investments. It is the means by which these expectations are measured that distinguish the private and public sectors from one another. The private sector marketplace regulates cost efficiency and quality of service by rewarding success and punishing failure. The public sector is not subject to the same rigors of the marketplace, and therefore is insulated in its "investor accountability." Public "profits" are seldom, if ever, returned to the investor. Budgets are exceeded and expanded, service quality suffers, and the hidden costs skyrocket until, as now, new and creative private market solutions are demanded by taxpayer investors in search of accountability.

Contracted Quality

The operating agreement between the government client and the private provider is the mortar in the relationship's foundation. A thorough and well-structured operating contract can serve to limit disputes and resolve those that do arise without protracted and costly delay. In order to guarantee that the operating contract will accomplish all essential objectives, the government client structures its competitive service procurement, most often known as the Request for Proposals, or RFP, so as

Low Cost, High Quality, Good Fit: Why Not Privatization? 183

to require prospective providers to submit comprehensive proposals that address all such objectives clearly and unambiguously.

Fortunately, a considerable number of RFPs have been issued by local, state and federal departments across the nation during the last five years. A certain consistency has developed among those RFPs by virtue of successive use and refinement so that those who wish to consider privatization of their corrections system need not reinvent the wheel.

The following contract areas should be carefully considered by the government client in the drafting of the RFP and Operating Agreement

Number of Facility Inmates

Not all facilities remain filled to capacity. Local jail populations may fluctuate widely based upon seasonal or other factors, such as large group arrests. State prison facility populations may vary in accordance with changing policy directives and court orders. It is essential that these population ranges be considered during the preparation of the RFP in order to ensure a firm basis for comparison of the proposers' respective per diem cost proposals. It be assumed that a given facility population will require full staffing by the provider. Any additional inmates will in all likelihood require only incremental operating cost increases to cover additional unit costs of food, medical services, utilities, etc. A properly drafted RFP and correlative operating contract can request and award pricing based upon such incremental populations in order to guarantee the government client the most precise pricing possible.

Standards

The RFP and operating contract should reference all performance standards that the client expects the provider to meet. Local and state standards, as well as national private board standards such as those promulgated by the American Correctional Association and The National Commission on Correctional Health Care, should be properly designated. Additionally, specific reference should be made to all court orders that will apply to the private provider. The client may also wish to consider requiring the provider to obtain appropriate classifications from the private entity that issues the subject standards within a prescribed time period (e.g., the provider must obtain applicable ACA certification within two years of the services commencement date). Such certifications will help to assure the client that the provider's operations are meeting at least the minimum comprehensive standards appropriate to the managed facility.

Staffing

The RFP should require the provider to submit a proposed facility staffing plan that sets forth all positions, assumed relief factor(s), wage scales, and intended subcontractors. The approved staffing plan can be attached to the contract as an incorporated item by specific reference. Any variation from the staffing plan should require prior express approval of the government client. The contract can provide that unfilled positions be filled within some reasonable period of time. All staff training requirements should be specified.

Proper staffing levels of fully trained and adequately compensated employees are the most essential assurance to the government client that the services provided by the private provider will be of consistently high quality. Careful attention to this area of the RFP and resulting contract will pay substantial dividends during the term of the operating contract.

Contract Monitoring

The operating contract will necessarily include provisions for monitoring of the provider's performance. Perhaps inevitably, a certain degree of competition exists between the provider and the government client's department of corrections. Established practice has been for the government client to designate a department employee as contract monitor, responsible for monitoring the performance of the private provider within the context of contract performance standards. Generally, the selected monitor is employed on a full-time basis at the contractor's facility.

Quite often the government corrections department has expressed some level of resistance to the concept of corrections privatization prior to the award of the contract. This resistance may have been overt and organized or it may have been behind the scene and unorganized. Either way, if a private operations contract is awarded, this lingering resistance can have a debilitating effect on the privatization effort. If a contract monitor perceives that his or her department superiors and peers are hostile to privatization, the monitor will inevitably be quick to find fault and slow to praise. As cost comparisons are generated favorable to privatization, pressures may increase to generate unfavorable quality of service reports.

Generally, contract monitors have performed well under difficult circumstances. Nevertheless, thoughtful voices are beginning to express the opinion that independent third-party contract monitors represent advantages to both private providers and their government clients.

In its March 1991 report to Texas Governor Ann Richards, The Texas Advisory Commission, chaired by Senator Gonzalo Barrientos, made the following finding:

> Finding 5: The TDCJ (Texas Department of Criminal Justice) should consider the use of third-party validation of all or parts of its monitoring process.
>
> Monitoring is an important aspect of any contracting effort. A well-structured monitoring process helps ensurethat the contracting body is getting the service it expects and pays for. It also ensures that the vendor is kept informed on a periodic basis as to how well it is providing the service and what adjustments are needed to keep its client satisfied.
>
> The importance of monitoring is recognized in the policies for contracted correctional facilities developed by the state. The statute requires contracts for correctional facilities to include provisions for monitoring the contracts by the Texas Department of Criminal Justice. The statute allows the department to establish the frequency of the monitoring visits, as well as the monitoring process to be used. The current contracts between the TDCJ and the two private vendors contain several monitoring provisions.
>
> The monitoring process set up by the TDCJ is a comprehensive one and includes the basic components generally recommended by the National Institute of Justice. The department has placed an on-site monitor in each facility to monitor all aspects of the contract and submit a quarterly report to the TDCJ. The quarterly report identifies areas where the private vendor is deficient in meeting the contract terms. The department also conducts annual audits of the facilities using teams of TDCJ auditors, who conduct similar audits of TDCJ-operated facilities.
>
> Monitoring service contracts is an inherently difficult process. Evaluation of performance is always a sensitive subject. Unless services can be easily quantified and subjective judgment eliminated, room for differences of opinion also exist. The monitoring process used by the TDCJ was examined to determine if additional methods exist to mitigate the difficult nature of the current monitoring efforts. The results of this review indicated the following:
>
> The difficulties inherent In a monitoring process are heightened by the competitive relationship set up in the statute between the TDCJ and the private vendors. This relationship results from the statutory provision that requires vendors to operate at a savings of at least ten percent when compared to an equivalent state-run program. The comparative efficiency and quality of the privately-operated programs in contrast to the state-run facilities establish a "fertile ground" for disagreements.

Differing philosophies involved in providing some services produce genuine disagreements from time to time between TDCJ management and the vendors as to TDCJ's monitoring assessments. As one example, the proper approach for assessing the adequacy of programming offered to inmates in the private facilities continues to be a topic of discussion between the TDCJ and the private providers. Neutral third parties can be useful in settling or avoiding disputes.

The state's $800 million Medicaid-funded nursing home program operated by the Texas Department of Human Services is monitored by a third party, the Texas Department of Health. One of the key purposes of the monitoring effort is to assess whether or not nursing home clients are receiving the care the state expects to be provided by the privately operated nursing homes.

In the delivery of correctional services by vendors on contract, the Criminal Justice Institute (CJI) recommends that in addition to having an effective monitoring process in place, periodic verification of monitoring results is desirable. The CJI publication, *Correctional Contracting: A Guide to Successful Experiences*, states: "It is a good practice, and especially when the contractor does not agree with the assessments of the Contract Manager, to call in an expert from the outside to conduct a formal evaluation."

A third-party evaluation effort can be tailored to meet the needs of the contractor. Basically, the scope of the third party's oversight can be selectively focused depending on the needs of the situation.

A third-party evaluation can be broad in scope and result in a complete review of all aspects of the contracted service and how it is being delivered.

Alternatively, a third-party evaluation can simply evaluate an existing monitoring system process and identify weaknesses that the contractor and the vendor can address cooperatively. The TDCJ currently uses third-party evaluations in other areas of its operations. For example, the department has third-party evaluators from the National Commission on Correctional Health Care assess health services in both its facilities and in the private facilities.

Conclusion

The TDCJ has instituted a thorough monitoring process. As in any monitoring process of a program of this size and importance, disputes may arise. This is particularly true in this case where the statute sets up a competitive relationship between the TDCJ and the vendors. The TDCJ has identified some areas where third-party evaluations are useful and have tailored those evaluations to meet their needs. The TDCJ should consider the use of an outside party in other areas to assist in the monitoring process as it deems appropriate to help alleviate misunderstandings that may arise. Various combinations of approaches to the use of a third part monitor could be considered to accomplish the desired goal—that services contracted for by the state are delivered properly and in a manner that provides both parties of the contract a reasonable way to identify and resolve disagreements. (Sunset Advisory Commission 1991, 25-27)

Possible third-party contract monitors include National Institute of Justice representatives, American Correctional Association representatives, university or community college professors of criminal justice, retired criminal justice officials, attorneys, and so on. The primary criteria by which a third-party contract monitor should be selected will necessarily include wide experience or knowledge of corrections practices and procedures, contract interpretation and application, and dispute resolution.

Contract Enforcement

While the goal of the government client and private provider is the elimination of contract disputes, disputes will nevertheless arise and require resolution. Currently, most operating agreements provide only for contract termination if alleged performance deficiencies are not remedied within a prescribed time period. Again, the Texas Sunset Commission thoughtfully evaluated the need for lesser, alternative contract sanctions in its March 1991 *Final Report:*

> Finding 6: The TDCJ should consider modifying its contracts for correctional facilities to include a range of sanctions for non-compliance.
>
> **Background**
>
> The Texas Department of Criminal Justice is responsible for the oversight and enforcement of the contracts for correctional facilities. The statute requires the contracts to specify that the state may terminate the contract for cause, which includes the failure of the private vendor or county commissioners court to meet statutory or contractual requirements. The TDCJ currently monitors its contracts with the CCA and Wackenhut through on-site monitors and annual audit teams. When the on-site monitors or auditors identify deficiencies, the private vendors are notified of the deficiencies.
>
> An effective enforcement program should provide a method to correct deficiencies in a timely fashion, discourage non-compliance with the statute and contract requirements, as well as penalize vendors for failure to implement corrective action and for chronic violations. Enforcement activities frequently incorporate a range of penalties that can be adjusted to conform to the seriousness of the deficiencies discovered. The review examined the approaches for enforcement of contract provisions set out in the statute and contracts. The results of the review indicated the following:
>
> The National Institute of Justice recommends that sanctions for non-compliance be incorporated into contracts for prison services. The contracts negotiated by the TDCJ meet this guideline. The contracts specify that contracts may be terminated for non-performance. Termination of the contract for non-performance is the only sanction written into the contracts. No alternatives to this single sanction are specified. Having a range of penalties would give additional enforcement flexibility to an agency contracting for ser-vices.
>
> Termination of contract is one of the most serious penalties that can be invoked by a contracting agency. The availability of only this enforcement action limits the ability of the enforcing agency to respond to differing situations. The department did consider including additional sanctions in its contracts; however, the contract negotiations

resulted in inclusion of only one sanction.

A range of penalties is often incorporated into statutes and contracts as an enforcement approach. It provides an enforcement body with a series of penalty options to meet varying levels of non compliance.

In addition to termination of contract for non-compliance, other enforcement sanctions have been written into state contracts for services. One agency with large contracting programs, the Texas Department of Human Services (DHS) uses this approach. Another agency, the State Purchasing and General Services Commission also uses intermediate sanctions.

The DHS contracts for the provision of services to the elderly and disabled. Many of its contracts contain provisions authorizing "vendor-hold" on contracted payments as well as "liquidated damages." These provisions are written into the contract without any associated statutory language authorizing their use. Vendor-hold provisions authorize the contracting agency to withhold payments to vendors until compliance with contract terms is satisfactory. The "liquidated damages" approach specifies in the contract the conditions under which money will be retained and the amount of money to be retained if services are not provided in full.

In contrast to the vendor-hold approach, money withheld for liquidated damages is not returned to the vendor. The State Purchasing and General Services Commission also employs sanctions of a similar nature in some of its contracts such as construction contracts.

The inclusion of a range of penalties in the contracts could enhance the department's enforcement of the contract. A range of penalties could be used to encourage the vendors to resolve less serious areas of non-compliance.

For example, contracts call for the vendor to make payments of money in lieu of taxes to local governments. Termination of contract would be too harsh a penalty for one-time non-compliance with this type of provision. An intermediate penalty would allow the TDCJ to reduce payments to a vendor by the amount owed.

As a second example, the TDCJ might determine that vendors were not complying with programming requirements for inmates. It would not be appropriate to terminate a contract for non-performance the first time this type of problem was uncovered unless it was of a very serious nature. Reduction in payment or with holding of payment until compliance occurred could be used more appropriately to match the actual level of non-performance.

Conclusion

The contracts with private vendors currently include one penalty for non-performance—termination of contract. This approach may have been necessary given the negotiations with vendors occurring during this first contracting experience. The department should consider negotiating a range of penalties in any future contracting effort. Other state agencies use this approach in their contract ing process which provides them with greater flexibility to match penalties with differing levels of non-compliance. (Sunset Advisory Commission 1991, 29-31)

As a result of the Sunset Commission's recommendation, The Texas Department of Criminal Justice Pardons and Paroles Division included an alternative lesser sanction in its most recently negotiated parole violation facility operating contracts with two private providers,

Wackenhut Corrections Corporation and Concepts, Inc., which allows the Division to withhold compensation from the provider until an alleged contract deficiency is remedied.

The prophylactic consequences of careful drafting of the RFP and operating contract provisions by the government client, combined with the effects of marketplace rewards and punishments upon private providers based upon relative levels of service performance, serve to guarantee a high quality of service delivery.

Resource Allocation

As discussed above, public sector corrections departments often perceive privatization as a threat or potential embarrassment. Yet, properly viewed, privatization can be presented as an integral part of a comprehensive correctional system with potential benefits to taxpayers and public sector departments alike.

Nearly every level of government responsible for incarcerating arrested or sentenced individuals is experiencing dramatic overcrowding and underfunding. Incarceration rates in the United States are at an all time high and continue to spiral upward in response to social pressures to remove offenders from our streets, neighborhoods and communities. From Willie Horton presidential politics to worried local elected officials scanning the morning headlines for news of heinous crimes committed by felons released after serving as little as one-fifth of their sentence, prisons and prison costs remain the number one domestic issue facing America today.

There are hardened criminals in our society who require hard time behind bars. Maximum security prison beds are expensive to build and costly to operate. Too often, however, these maximum security beds are home to medium and minimum security inmates, inmates who require neither the level of security nor the allocation of cost attendant to the level of security built into the design of their cells.

Rather than spend scarce tax dollars on the construction and operation of more maximum security prisons, the public sector should, whenever possible, reallocate its resources to the construction and operation of lower security diversionary or pre-release detention facilities designed to concentrate on the specific security, programmatic, and rehabilitative needs of the intended incarcerated population.

When viewed as a continuum, the correctional system offers many opportunities for maximizing limited public resources. First-time offenders, nonviolent offenders, parole violators, sentenced offenders within one or two years of release, geriatric offenders, offenders suffering from mental illness, and so on, all represent "niche" populations capable of being incarcerated in facilities that cost less to build, and operate than the maximum security prisons in which they are currently housed. Privatization is perfectly suited to meet the needs of such populations. Private providers can design, finance, build and operate efficient facilities dedicated to the specific correctional needs of a specified population group. Based upon consistent average-lengths-of-stay, type of offense, security level, and so on, appropriate programmatic and rehabilitative services can be tailored to meet the needs of the incarcerated population.

By removing and allocating minimum/medium security inmates from maximum security beds, at least two important goals are met. First, the number of available maximum security beds within a system is increased at a lower cost than through the construction of new high security prisons; and second, targeted offender populations can be dealt with in a manner consistent with their level of security and classification, hopefully with better rehabilitative results. Public sector corrections officials should therefore regard privatized corrections as less threatening to their continued core function as keeper of our most hardened cases.

This is not to say that private providers cannot effectively manage and operate maximum security facilities. Obviously, nothing in the nature of maximum security prisons, in and of itself, mitigates against the use of private providers. The suggestion to concentrate on the privatization of the many "niche" offender populations is merely a recognition of deeply felt institutional resistance and acknowledgment of a cost-effective, less threatening, direction for embracing privatization as a meaningful part of a larger whole.

Conclusion

While advocates and opponents continue to make their closing arguments with respect to the advantages and disadvantages of privatized corrections, the jury has returned its verdict: privatization saves money, provides quality services and fulfills a need. Money is saved because no one has yet developed a better pencil sharpener than free market competition. Quality services can be ensured through careful attention to sound drafting of competitive procurement solicitations and resulting operating contracts. When properly utilized, privatization can become a cost-effective tool for fashioning specific correctional solutions within the context of the larger correctional system continuum.

References

Logan, Charles H. and Bill McGriff. (1989) *Comparing Costs of Public and Private Prisons: A Case Study.* NIJ Reports (September/October).

Price-Waterhouse. (1990) *Estimation of the State's Cost of Building and Operating a Prototype Correctional Facility.* September 7.

Sunset Advisory Commission. (1991) *Final Report.* March. Chapter 4: "Information Report on Contracts for Correction Facilities and Services": 25-27.

Thomas, Charles W. (1990) *Private Corrections Adult Secure Facility Census.* Correction Studies in Criminology and Law. Gainesville, Florida: University of Florida, May.

15

Comparison of Privately and Publicly Operated Corrections Facilities in Kentucky and Massachusetts

Harry P. Hatry
Paul J. Brounstein
Robert B. Levinson

The cost and associated problems of incarcerating offenders is a major problem throughout the United States. The National Council of State Legislatures recently reported that appropriations for construction and maintenance of prisons grew faster than any other major program during the 1980s. The near doubling of the prison population during the decade and court orders against overcrowding have forced many states to boost spending for correctional facilities.

One of many options to alleviate this problem, one that has had major national attention, has been for states to contract to the private sector for the management and operation of correctional facilities. This chapter addresses the questions of cost and service quality/effectiveness. Most

---

This chapter has been adapted from the Executive Summary of the report "Comparison of Privately and Publicly Operated Corrections Facilities in Kentucky and Massachusetts," H.P. Hatry, P.J. Brounstein, R. Levinson, D.M. Altschuler, K. Chi, and P. Rosenberg, The Urban Institute, Washington, D.C., August 1989.

of the published discussion on these issues, thus far, has been conceptual. Very few studies have obtained empirical data to examine the cost and quality of private sector operation of correctional facilities and compare them to the cost of public facilities. Thus far, few such data have been forthcoming to aid states and local governments in making their choices.

Purpose of Chapter

This chapter presents the findings of a study undertaken during 1987-1988 to compare state government correctional facilities in two states (Massachusetts and Kentucky) that are managed and operated by private contractors to similar facilities managed and operated by public employees. The study's primary objective was to assess and identify any differences in cost, service quality, and effectiveness between the private and publicly operated institutions. A secondary objective was to identify reasons for any differences that were found. One set of comparisons such as provided here (even though it covers two separate states and a number of facilities) cannot provide definitive findings on comparative costs and service quality/effectiveness. In any case, such comparisons are never perfect. However, it seems highly desirable to begin to build a body of empirical information that, while far from perfect, nevertheless, provides relevant data on important measurable aspects. We hope that this work will stimulate others to undertake future cost-effectiveness comparisons and, later, meta-evaluations that examine a multitude of such studies to provide a more comprehensive picture.

Scope and Methodology

In Kentucky we examined the Marion Adjustment Center a privately operated minimum-security facility. At the time of the study it was the sole adult secure facility in the nation under contract by a state government. With the assistance of state corrections officials we selected a comparable, publicly operated adult minimum-security facility, the Blackburn Correctional Complex, operated by state employees. The Marion facility began operation under contract to the state in January 1986. Thus, it had been in operation for a little over two years as of the beginning of our data collection. We focused our data collection on operations in 1987 and the first part of 1988, excluding the private facility's first, start-up year.

In Massachusetts we worked with the Department of Youth Services to select two matched pairs of facilities, one of each pair being privately operated and the other publicly operated. All four facilities were juvenile secure treatment facilities containing the most difficult young offenders. We have some concern over the similarity of the inmate population in the matched paired facilities particularly in Kentucky. In Kentucky, the inmates assigned by the corrections agency to the private facility were those believed to be least likely to be a threat to the society if they escape. Our examination of the data on inmate characteristics for the private and public facilities, however, indicated that they were similar inmate populations, though, of course, not as equivalent as if inmates had been randomly assigned to each facility. (The public facility had more violent inmates and inmates with a longer average time before release, but it also had older inmates and a substantially larger proportion of white inmates. All these differences were statistically significantly at the 5 percent level.) In Massachusetts, assignments were approximately random to the facilities in each pair.

We used similar data collection procedures in both states. These procedures included the following:

- Extraction of data from agency records of such data elements as number of escapes and attempted escapes, returns to prison after release, results of facility inspections, and cost data;

- surveys of inmates and staff at each institution, using similar questionnaires at each institution in both states;

- interviews with officials involved in the operation or oversight of each facility, including wardens, program staff, central staff officials, and corporate executives; and

- a physical inspection by project staff of each facility using a visual inspection rating form that we designed for the inspections.

Thus, we sought information on performance from several sources: agency records, perspectives of public and private officials and staff, the offenders' perspectives, and our own observations.

We collected data for the period beginning in January 1987 through spring 1988, with some data elements covering periods into the summer of 1988. The bulk of our data collection and survey work was undertaken from January 1988 through September 1988. A team of two persons performed the data collection for each state.

Our review of the literature, while finding numerous discussions about the appropriateness and pros and cons of contracting, uncovered few empirical examinations of the actual costs and the effectiveness of private facilities, particularly analyses that compared public to private facilities.

Differences in Project Design between the Two States

There were some major differences between the comparisons in the two states that the reader needs to consider. They are as follows:

- In Kentucky we examined adult minimum security facilities. In Massachusetts we examined youth facilities, but those facilities housed the most difficult youth offenders

- The prisons in Kentucky housed over 200 inmates for the privately operated facility and 350 for the publicly operated facility. (The facilities had an average population of 206 and 353 respectively.) In Massachusetts the facilities were all quite small, each with 15-16 daily population.

- The contractor in Kentucky was a for-profit contractor selected after competitive bidding. The two private contractors in Massachusetts were non-profit organizations; the legislation in Massachusetts did not permit the use of for-profit organizations for these youth facilities.

- The building and land used by the Kentucky private facility was provided and owned by the contractor. In Massachusetts the programs each operated in facilities provided by the state; contractors were not responsible for facility maintenance costs nor for facility construction, rehabilitation, or most utility costs.

- Massachusetts Department of Youth Services had approximately twenty years of experience in contracting for secure care for juveniles. For Kentucky this was its first experience in contracting secure adult institutions.

Principal Findings

Below are the highlights of the findings on cost, service quality, effectiveness, and program content.

Cost Analysis Findings

The costs of privately and publicly operated facilities were quite similar for all three pairs (one in Kentucky and two in Massachusetts). For each pair, the costs for each facility were within plus or minus 10 percent of the other member of the pair on a cost per inmate-day basis. For all three public facilities, capital costs for the publicly operated facilities had already been expended and no capital costs were included in the public facility unit-costs.

In Kentucky, the private facility unit-cost was 10 percent higher than the public facility. This difference is likely to have occurred in part because of: (a) the inclusion of capital cost in the private organization price; (b) economies of scale achievable by the public facility with its inmate population being about 50 percent larger than the private facility. (The fixed costs of the facility can be spread over a large number of inmates to yield a lower unit cost.)

In Massachusetts, the publicly operated facility cost was approximately 1 percent lower than that of the privately operated facilities.

This similarity in cost in both states can be explained in part by three factors. First, a state is not likely to contract for a facility with a contractor whose price to the state significantly increases its existing unit-cost. Second, the contractors were all probably aware, before their final bids, of the existing unit costs for the public sector operations and recognized that their prices could approximate these public unit-costs. Finally, competition for these contracts, at least thus far, has not been sufficiently large to drive the cost significantly lower, if indeed lower costs are feasible. In Kentucky, the initial RFP elicited bids that were much higher than the unit cost budgeted by the state. The state then issued a revised RFP. Most bidders dropped out of the competition. The selected contractor substantially reduced its original bid. In the Massachusetts situation, the competition for contracts has been primarily limited to two or three principal contractors.

In Massachusetts, line employees of the public facilities, but not the private facilities, were unionized. In both states, salaries and fringe benefits were somewhat higher for public than for private employees. Higher public employee salaries in both states can be partly explained by longer years of public employee tenure; on average private sector employees were younger and had fewer years of experience.

For the Kentucky situation, we also estimated the additional capital construction cost had the state chosen to build its own facility and subsequently operate and manage it. This would have added considerably to the cost per inmate day. It would have made the publicly operated facility cost about 20 percent to 28 percent higher than the privately operated facility. This suggests that, in this instance, contracting has been less costly *if* the state's major alternative had been to contract a new facility for the 200-plus beds.

Service Quality and Effectiveness

Using survey information, physical observation, interviews, and agency record data, we examined a large number of service quality and effectiveness elements including physical condition, escape rates, information on security and control, information relating to physical and mental health of the inmates, adequacy of the facility's programs (e.g. education, counseling, training, recreational), particularly as perceived by inmates and staff, and indicators of rehabilitation such as reincarceration.

Tables 15A.1 through 15A.6 in the appendix to this chapter summarize the principal findings for each state. Tables 15A.1 through 15A.4 present data on the indicators that each of our two teams (one for Kentucky and one for Massachusetts) believe to be the most important indicators for the comparisons in that state (regardless of whether the particular indicators favored the public or private facilities). Tables 15A.5 and 15A.6 summarize the findings from all the performance indicators, without regard to their relative importance.

For a substantial majority of these performance indicators, the privately operated facilities had at least a small advantage. By and large, both staff and inmates gave better ratings to the services and programs at the privately operated facilities; escape rates were lower; there were fewer disturbances by inmates; and in general, staff and offenders felt more comfortable at the privately operated facilities.

Why is this so? Our data indicate that the privately operated facilities had younger and less experienced personnel, and staff who were compensated less (partly because of their lesser experience), than their counterparts in publicly operated facilities. Does additional experience and higher wages lead to higher quality performance? The data we examined do not indicate this to be the case. We conjecture that youthful enthusiasm may combat "job burnout" of longer tenured members.

While some differences in Kentucky could be due to differences in inmate characteristics between public and private facilities, the differences do not appear large enough to explain much of the difference in results. This is not an appropriate explanation for the differences found in Massachusetts. By and large, staff in the privately operated appeared to be more enthusiastic about their work, more involved in their work, and more interested in working with the inmates than their public counterparts. Management-wise, the privately-operated facilities appeared to be more flexible and less regimented, with staff subject to less stringent controls. These elements seem to have made life in the privately-operated correctional facilities more pleasant for both inmates and staff. Note, however, that the privately operated institutions in all cases were required to follow the same basic rules as the publicly operated facilities.

We suspect that at least some of the advantage of the privately operated facilities could be regained by the public sector in these corrections environments if management and organizational hindrances, such as rigid procedures, could be alleviated.

Conclusion

Based on this evidence, we conclude that use of privately operated correctional facilities for minimum security adult males and for difficult youth offenders is an appropriate option for state governments. It seems to be an important option, particularly if additional capacity is needed by the state. While these findings do not indicate that private operation should be substituted for existing public facilities, they do indicate that the use of the private sector, in appropriate situations, can be good for both inmates and the public.

Appendix

TABLE 15A.1
Massachusetts Performance Indicators[1]

Indicator	Public	Private	Statistical Probability
I. Conditions of Confinement			
A. Crowdedness: Percent of Capacity month mean capacity	99.9	99.3	NS
B. Mean Ratings of Room Conditions (index of 4 measures; 4=poor, 16= excellent)			
1. Staff ratings	11.8	<u>13.0</u>	<.05
2. Residents' ratings	10.7	<u>11.8</u>	<.10[2]
C. Mean Ratings of Facility Conditions (index of 4 measures: 4=poor, 16=excellent)			
1. Staff ratings	11.7	<u>13.1</u>	.05
2. Residents' ratings	9.1	9.4	NS
D. Physical Inspection of Conditions of Confinement by Research Team (Index of average ratings given on four subscales of visual inspection checklist, 1=poor, 7=excellent)			
Mean ratings	5.0	5.0	NS
E. Number of Areas of Noncompliance in Most Recent OFC Licensing Review	49	<u>21</u>	NA
F. Health Care			
1. Average number of Doctor Visits/month	<u>38.9</u>	71.7	<.05[2]
2. Average number of Doctors Visits because of injury or restraint/month	3.0	<u>1.0</u>	<.05
3. Resident health has changed since entry to the program (1=better, 3=worse)	1.9	1.8	NS
4. Average resident satisfaction with health care services (1=very satisfied, 5=very dissatisfied)	2.8	<u>2.0</u>	<.05[2]
5. Emotional Distress (9 item index: 9=more somatization, 36=No somatization)	25.6	25.3	NS
6. Average number of sick days for staff/month	.5	.5	NS

Indicator	Public	Private	Statistical Probability
G. Perceptions of Safety			
1. Ratings of program being safe for residents (1=strongly disagree, 4=strongly agree)			
a. Staff ratings	3.1	_3.6_	<.05
b. Residents ratings	2.9	2.7	NS
2. Ratings of program being safe for staff (1=strongly disagree, 4=strongly agree)			
a. Staff ratings	3.0	_3.4_	<.05
b. Resident ratings	2.9	2.8	NS
II. **Internal Security and Control**			
1. Number of escapes/attempts/awols in 15 months	13	_2_	<.05
2. Staff ratings of their ability to maintain control and safety (1=greater control, 4=no control)	1.4	_1.1_	$<.05^2$
3. Room confinements			
a. Percent of youth confined	73.1	_35.6_	<.05
b. Average length of confinement (in minutes)	383	_154_	$<.05^2$
4. Use of mechanical restraints			
a. Percent of youth restrained	_8.7_	17.8	$<.10^2$
5. Investigative reports filed over 15 months	12	_2_	NA
6. Residents' views on freedom of movement about the program (3 item index: 3= no freedom, 12=complete freedom)	4.5	_6.2_	<.05
7. Victimization and violence			
a. Average number of physical fights between staff and residents in last six months			
1. Staff estimates	3.0	_.4_	<.05
2. Residents' estimates	4.3	_1.3_	<.10
b. Staff use force to restrain youth (1=never, 4=very often)			
1. Staff ratings	2.4	_2.0_	<.05
2. Residents' ratings	2.4	_1.8_	<.05

Indicator	Public	Private	Statistical Probability
III. Social Adjustment and Rehabilitation			
A. Adequacy of personal counseling			
1. Percent of residents saying:			
a. They see a clinician as often as they want	50.0	48.3	NS
b. More counseling help is needed at the program	67.9	25.0	<.05
c. Resident ratings of personal counseling quality (1=very satisfied, 5=very dissatisfied)	2.7	2.2	NS
2. Staff provide necessary personal counseling (1=very much, 4=not at all)			
a. Staff ratings	1.8	1.2	<.05[2]
B. Vocational & Job Counseling			
1. Percent of residents receiving vocational education	54	43	NS
2. Percent of residents receiving work training	40	28	NS
3. Resident ratings of job/vocational education counseling (1=very satisfied, 5=very dissatisfied)	2.3	2.7	NS
4. Staff reporting they help residents find work and get reacclaimated after their release (2-item index: 2=very much, 8 not at all)	5.5	4.1	<.05
5. Percent of residents reporting they received help in making job contacts in the community	64.3	55.2	NS
6. Percent of residents reporting they had a job lined up after their release	25.9	34.5	NS
C. Education			
1. Percent in basic education track	65.2	65.5	NS
2. Percent in GED preparation	34.8	41.4	NS
3. Resident ratings of educational services quality (1=very satisfied, 5=very dissatisfied)	2.6	2.2	NS
4. Percent of residents saying they will continue their education after their release	21.4	48.1	<.05[2]
5. Staff ratings that program provides quality educational services (1=very much, 4=not at all)	1.7	1.1	<.05

	Indicator	Public	Private	Statistical Probability
6.	Staff reporting that they help residents get high school diplomas or GEDs (1=very much, 4=not at all)	1.8	1.0	<.05
D.	Residents' ratings of the variety of recreational activities (1=strongly disagree that there is a good variety, 4=strongly agree)	2.4	2.6	NS
E.	Percent of residents in drug program	33	50	NS
1.	Residents' rating of drug program (1=very satisfied, 5=very dissatisfied)	2.2	2.8	NS
F.	Percent of residents in alcohol program	36	53	<.10
2.	Residents' ratings of alcohol program (1=very satisfied, 5 very dissatisfied)	2.3	2.7	NS
G.	Staff Quality			
1.	Perceived staff competence (Index of three measures: 3=lower rated competence, 12= extremely positive rated competence)			
	a. Residents' ratings	6.9	7.6	NS
	b. Staff ratings	8.8	10.3	<.05
H.	Good time earned while in detention Average number of days	3.5	4.0	NS
I.	Percent of youth extended beyond maximum commitment	7.7	17.8	<.05[2]
J.	Percent of youth released early	7.7	1.4	<.05
K.	Recidivism of residents 1/1/87-3/31/88			
	1. Percent of youth recommitted to secure care over 15 months	12.7	7.1	NS
	2. Percent of youth revocated but not recommitted over 15 months	15.4	13.7	NS
L.	Percent of residents saying they will probably get into trouble with the law after their release	35.7	10.3	<.05
IV.	**Management Issues (Staff Ratings)**			
A.	Program management is adaptive and flexible (Index of 2 items: 2=inflexible, 8=very flexible)	5.7	6.8	<.05
B.	Job Satisfaction Index/Actualization (4 measures: 4=None, 16=Extreme satisfaction)	10.6	11.7	<.05[2]

Indicator	Public	Private	Statistical Probability
C. Resident ratings-staff do their job well (Index of 3 items: 3=poor performance, 12=excellent performance)	6.9	7.7	NS
D. Morale/Plans to leave job/corrections (3 measures: 3=poor morale, 12=great morale)	8.6	8.4	NS
E. Annual rate of turnover (total resignations and terminations/number of permanent lines)	33.8	44.3	NA
F. Average overtime/month (hours/staff person)	13.7	_8.2_	<.05
G. Average number of shifts/month covered by on-call staff	4.8	_.8_	<.05
H. Percent of Staff who have filed grievances against management	20.5	_0.0_	<.05
I. Percent of those not filing because they felt it was useless or were afraid of reprisals	20.0	12.5	NS
J. Percent of Residents who have filed grievances against staff	25.0	20.7	NS
V. Cost (in dollars)			
A. Average cost/bed/day	197	199	NA
B. Average cost/bed/year	71,956	72,493	NA
C. Average cost/15 bed program/year	1,079,347	1,087,390	NA

1. These are based on comparisons of two pairs of DYS secure treatment programs. One member of each pair is operated by the state, the other by private nonprofit organizations. Underlined numbers indicate advantage on the performance indicator (p<.10). "NS" is used to indicate no statistical advantage and "NA" to indicate that statistical analysis of the data element was not appropriate.

2. The difference observed obtains primarily from ratings in one of the two public private pairs, not both.

TABLE 15A.2
Key Performance Indicator Summary
Massachusetts

Performance Area	Total # Indicators	Number of Significant Differences favoring public	Number of Significant Differences favoring private	Non-Significant Differences
I. Conditions of Confinement				
A. Resident Surveys	7	0	2	5
B. Staff Surveys	4	0	4	0
C. Record Data	4	1	1	3
Total	16	1	7	8
II. Internal Security and Control				
A. Resident Surveys	3	0	3	0
B. Staff Surveys	3	0	3	0
C. Record Data	4	1	3	0
Total	10	1	9	0
III. Social Adjustment and Rehabilitation				
A. Resident Surveys	19	0	4	15
B. Staff Surveys	5	0	5	0
C. Record Data	5	2	0	3
Total	29	2	9	18
IV. Management and Staffing				
A. Resident Surveys	2	0	0	2
B. Staff Surveys	5	0	3	2
C. Record Data	2	0	2	2
Total	9	0	5	4
Totals	64	4	30	30
Percent	100.0	6.2	46.9	46.9

Percent of Indicators

Residents	31	0.0	29.0	71.0
Staff	17	0.0	88.2	11.8
Records	16	2.5	37.5	37.5

TABLE 15A.3
Kentucky Performance Indicators[1]

	Public	Private	Statistical Significance
A. Conditions of Confinement:			
Staff Replies			
1. Safe for staff	73 %	80 %	NS
2. Night staffing safe for staff	37 %	_79 %_	<.01
3. Facility is crowded	55 %	_4 %_	<.01
4. Inmate rooms are quiet	55 %	_82%_	<.10
Inmate Replies			
5. Night staffing safe for inmates	51 %	_67 %_	<.01
6. Food tastes good	_33 %_	10 %	<.01
7. Toilets/showers work	74 %	70 %	NS
8. Good place to spend time	52 %	_63 %_	<.05
9. Health worse now	21 %	34 %	NS
10. Dissatisfied with medical services	63 %	45 %	NS
11. Emotional distress index (9 items) (Never=3; Almost Always=0)	2.03	1.92	NS
Central Office Data			
12. Sick-call ratio	1:1.5	1:1.3	N/A*
13. Inmates hospitalized/quarter	1:50.4	1:38.2	N/A*

Subtally	Public	Private	?
Staff	0	3	1
Inmate	1	2	4
Central Office	0	0	2

[1.] Underlined numbers indicate advantage on the performance indicator (p< .10); "NS" is used to indicate no statistical advantage and "N/A" to indicate that statistical analysis of the data element was not appropriate.

Corrections Facilities in Kentucky and Massachusetts

		Public	Private	Statistical Significance
B.	**Internal Security & Control:**			
	Staff Replies			
	1. Avg. no. inmate/staff fights (6 mo. estimate)	1.4	<u>0.8</u>	<.01
	2. Avg. no. inmate/inmate fights (6 mo. estimate)	5.1	<u>2.5</u>	<.01
	3. Staff use of force (avg.) (6 mo. estimate)	2.1	<u>1.3</u>	<.01
	Inmate Replies			
	4. Avg. no. inmate/staff fights (6 mo. estimate)	1.7	<u>0.2</u>	<.05
	5. Avg. no. inmate/inmate fights (6 mo. estimate)	3.1	6.6	NS
	6. Use of force by staff (avg.) (6 mo. estimate)	1.7	<u>1.3</u>	<.10
	7. Inmates can choose daytime activities	30 %	<u>73 %</u>	<.01
	Central Office Data			
	8. Inmates with one or more disciplinary reports	<u>26 %</u>	41 %	<.08
	9. Escape & attempted escapes	1:19.6	1:51.6	N/A

Subtally	Public	Private	?
Staff	0	3	0
Inmate	0	3	1
Central Office	1	0	1

		Public	Private	Statistical Significance
C.	**Social Adjustment & Rehabilitation:**			
	Inmate Replies			
	1. Personal counseling (percent dissatisfied)	26 %	28 %	NS
	2. Drug abuse counseling (percent dissatisfied)	28 %	12 %	NS
	3. Alcohol abuse counseling (percent dissatisfied)	32 %	14 %	NS
	4. Good recreation variety	36 %	<u>58 %</u>	<.01
	5. Received vocational/job counseling	<u>68 %</u>	26 %	<.01
	6. Work training program (percent satisfied)	89 %	76 %	NS
	7. Staff helped inmate line-up release job	<u>74 %</u>	56 %	<.10
	8. Inmates report program helps you stay out of trouble	70 %	76 %	NS
	Central Office Data			
	10. GEDs earned ratio	1:9.0	1:5.3	N/A
	11. Completed vocational programs ratio	1:22.9	1:25.2	N/A

Subtally	Public	Private	?
Staff	0	0	0
Inmate	2	1	5
Central Office	0	0	2

		Public	Private	Statistical Significance
D.	**Management Issues:**			
	Staff Replies			
	1. Did NOT file grievance because useless/afraid	13 %	11.5 %	NS
	2. Of 14 items, no. favoring facility's work environment	2	<u>10</u>	<.06
	3. Worthwhile accomplishments at facility	54 %	<u>80 %</u>	<.05
	4. Of 12 items no. favoring facility's accomplishments	4	8	NS
	Inmate Replies			
	5. Grievances ratio	1:7.2	1:11.3	N/A
	6. Staff give conflicting information	<u>28 %</u>	50 %	<.05
	7. Staff do job well	58 %	57 %	NS
	Subtally	**Public**	**Private**	?
	Staff	0	2	2
	Inmate	1	0	2
	Central Office	0	0	0

E. **Cost:**
1. Unit cost/inmate/day — $26.97 $29.68
2. Unit cost/inmate/day (if state would have had to construct a new facility) — $37.97 $29.68

TABLE 15A.4
Key Performance Indicators

	Insignificant Differences Favoring Public Number	%	Insignificant Differences Favoring Private Number	%	Non-Significant Differences Number	%
Staff Replies	0	0 %	8	20 %	3	7 %
Inmate Replies	4	10 %	6	15 %	12	29 %
Central Office Data	1	2 %	0	0 %	7	17 %
Total	5	12 %	14	34 %	22	54 %

TABLE 15A.5
Overall Performance Indicator Summary
Massachusetts

Performance Area	Total # Differences	Number of Significant Differences favoring public	Number of Significant Differences favoring private	Non-significant Differences
I. Conditions of Confinement				
A. Resident Surveys	22	2	5	15
B. Staff Surveys	12	0	7	5
C. Record Data	6	0	2	4
Total	40	2	14	24
II. Intenal Security and Control				
A. Residents Survey	4	0	4	0
B. Staff Surveys	10	0	8	2
C. Record Data	5	1	3	1
Total	19	1	15	3
III. Social Adjustment and Rehabilitation				
A. Resident Surveys	27	0	4	23
B. Staff Surveys	12	0	6	6
C. Record Data	5	1	0	4
Total	44	1	10	33
IV. Management and Staffing				
A. Resident Surveys	5	0	2	3
B. Staff Surveys	16	1	6	9
C. Record Data	7	1	3	3
Total	28	2	11	15
Total	131	4.6	38.2	57.3

Percent of Indicators

Residents	58	3.4	25.9	70.7
Staff	50	2.0	54.0	44.0
Records	28	13.0	34.8	52.2

TABLE 15A.6
All Performance Indicators
Kentucky

		# Indicators	Number of Significant Differences Favoring Public #	%	Number of Significant Differences Favoring Private #	%	Non-Significant Differences #	%
A.	**Conditions of Confinement**							
	Staff Replies	20	2	4 %	8	15 %	10	19 %
	Inmate Replies	30	3	6 %	4	8 %	23	44 %
	Central Office Data	2	0	0 %	0	0 %	2	4 %
	Sub-total	52	5	10 %	12	23 %	35	67 %
B.	**Internal Security and Control**							
	Staff Replies	12	1	3 %	4	13 %	7	23 %
	Inmate Replies	14	4	13 %	6	19 %	4	13 %
	Central Office Data	5	0	0 %	2	6 %	3	10 %
	Sub-total	31	5	16 %	12	38 %	14	46 %
C.	**Social Adjustment and Rehabiliation**							
	Staff Replies	2	0	0 %	1	2 %	1	2 %
	Inmate Replies	38	4	9 %	5	11 %	29	64 %
	Central Office Data	5	0	0 %	0	0 %	5	11 %
	Sub-total	45	4	9 %	6	13 %	35	78 %
D.	**Management Issues**							
	Staff Replies	47	0	0 %	11	17 %	36	57 %
	Inmate Replies	14	2	3 %	1	2 %	11	17 %
	Central Office Data	2	0	0 %	0	0 %	2	3 %
	Sub-total	63	2	3 %	12	19 %	49	78
	Overall Totals							
	Staff Replies	81	3	2 %	24	13 %	54	28 %
	Inmate Replies	96	13	7 %	16	8 %	67	35 %
	Central Office Data	14	0	0 %	2	1 %	12	6 %
	Totals	191	16	8 %	42	22 %	133	70 %

16

The Development, Present Status, and Future Potential of Correctional Privatization in America

Charles W. Thomas
Charles H. Logan

The history of American corrections during the twentieth century is almost entirely a history of government correctional agencies pursuing such diverse and often contradictory purposes as deterrence, incapacitation, rehabilitation, and retribution. Although for-profit and nonprofit firms have played a major role in management of correctional facilities housing juveniles for many years (e.g., Bureau of Justice Statistics 1989), until fairly recently the role of the private sector in adult corrections was inconsequential (e.g., Logan 1990; McDonald 1990). Even in recent decades private sector involvements have been limited to the delivery of specialized services in such areas as food preparation, education, medical treatment, some prison industry programs, vocational training, and the management of small, nonsecure facilities like work release and restitution centers (e.g., Camp and Camp 1984; Mullen, Chabotar, and Carrow 1985; Hackett et al. 1987). Since the mid-1980s, however, a growing correctional crisis closely linked to an explosion in the size of our prisoner population gave rise to a belief that the private sector could and should play a greater role in the operation of the nation's jails and prisons.

Slowly at first but later with rapidly growing momentum, jurisdictions all across the country enacted legislation authorizing full-scale privatization of local, state, and federal correctional facilities (Calvert Hanson 1991). A private corrections industry swiftly took form. Indeed, corporations that did not exist only a decade ago—firms like Concepts, Inc., the Corrections Corporation of America, Eden Detention, Inc., Esmor, Inc., the GRW Corporation, Management and Training, Inc., Pricor, Inc., the U.S. Corrections Corporation, and the Wackenhut Corrections Corporation—quickly grew to a point at which some of them operated facilities housing a larger number of prisoners than did the correctional systems of nearly one half of the nation's state departments of corrections. This rapid growth is continuing. By the close of 1991, for example, private corrections management firms will be responsible for the operation of sixty or more secure adult correctional facilities in roughly a dozen states. Those facilities will house some 20,000 local, state, and federal prisoners, and the value of their contracts with government is very likely to exceed a quarter of a billion dollars.[1]

In this analysis our purpose will be to examine the emergence, the present status, and the future potential of the private sector as a provider of correctional management services. We will begin with a very general overview of some of the problems which gave rise to a willingness on the part of government to explore the value of correctional privatization. We will then devote separate attention to the swiftness with which the innovation was accepted and the developing body of evidence regarding the degree to which privatization has yielded benefits in the form, for example, of decreased correctional costs and enhancements in the quality of correctional services.

A Historical Review of the Growing Crisis in Corrections

Regardless of where one travels in the United States and of whether one's attention focuses on the status of local, state, or federal correctional facilities, one finds abundant evidence that the nation's correctional systems are in the midst of a deepening crisis. The crisis was created by a fairly broad array of influences whose presence began to become obvious by no later than the mid-1970s. Legislative bodies across the nation moved to toughen their sentencing philosophies and practices (e.g., Gross and von Hirsch 1981). Police and prosecutors began to adopt a more aggressive stance towards offenders.[2]

Support for various rehabilitative strategies began to diminish in the face of evidence that few if any change-oriented initiatives had been shown to be effective (e.g., Logan 1972; Martinson 1974; Thomas 1987). This loss of support accelerated following sharp ethical and philosophical challenges to the propriety of coercive involvement in rehabilitative programs and a closely correlated increase in the perceived value of such retributive objectives as just deserts and such utilitarian goals as incapacitation (American Friends Service Committee 1971; Morris 1974; Fogel 1975, Fogel and Hudson 1981; Gross and von Hirsch 1981; von Hirsch 1985; Thomas 1987).

The effects of the above and other causal variables on the nation's correctional systems became apparent almost immediately. They are most easily illustrated by a period of unprecedented growth in the nation's jail and prison population that began around 1975 and that persists today. In 1975, for example, the number of state and federal prisoners stood at 240,211 and the confinement rate—the number of state and federal prisoners per 100,000 persons in the nation's population—stood at 113 (Jamieson and Flanagan 1989, 612).[3]

Importantly, these 1975 figures are not dramatically different from what one would find when corresponding statistics for earlier time periods are examined. The average state and federal prisoner population for the period of 1960 through 1974, for instance, was 205,745, and the average incarceration rate for the same fifteen-year period was 104 (Jamieson and Flanagan 1989, 612).

Stable prisoner populations and incarceration rates, however, swiftly became relics of our penological past. Within five years after the trend that began in 1975 materialized, the prisoner population rose by 25.50 percent to 301,470 and the incarceration rate rose by 20.35 percent to 136. Within ten years the prisoner population rose by 84.59 percent to 443,398 and the incarceration rate rose by 66.37 percent to 188. Within fifteen years the prisoner population rose by 195.60 percent to 710,054 and the incarceration rate rose by 142.48 percent to 274. Even if legislative bodies and government agencies had anticipated and planned for this explosive growth in our prisoner population—and the evidence shows that their projections and plans were substantially less than exemplary—

the burden it placed on our correctional systems almost certainly would have been more than they could reasonably have been expected to shoulder.

Our experience during any recent year is sufficient to illustrate the impossibility of the task. Between the end of 1988 and the end of 1989, for example, our state and federal prison populations increased by 82,466 inmates (Bureau of Justice Statistics 1990a), and we estimate that the nation's local jail population increased by 37,105 pretrial detainees and sentenced offenders (Bureau of Justice Statistics 1990b). Ignoring altogether the pressing need for new jails and prisons that existed at the end of 1988 as a consequence of facility overcrowding, *this one-year growth created the need for the construction and opening of approximately one 700-bed jail and one 1,600-bed prison during each and every week of 1989.* Using a conservative per bed cost estimate for this new construction of $50,000, *the capital outlay required merely to meet this new construction requirement would have been $115,000,000 per week and 5.98 billion dollars for the year.*

Not unlike each and every other year since the prisoner population explosion began in 1975, government efforts in 1989 did not meet the challenge. Since 1989 the correctional crisis has only become more acute. Numerous illustrations of this are as obvious as they are ominous, but the following are a few that immediately come to mind.

- Roughly two-thirds of the states are operating under court orders or consent decrees associated with conditions of confinement suits brought by that are closely linked to facility overcrowding. (Camp and Camp 1989, 3)

- The federal prisoner population is now at roughly 170 percent of its rated capacity. (Bureau of Justice Statistics 1990a, 6)

- Nine state systems are operating at more than 150 percent of their design capacities. (Bureau of Justice Statistics 1990a, 6)

- Fifteen states are operating at between 125 and 150 percent of their design capacities. (Bureau of Justice Statistics 1990a, 6)

- Only six states—Louisiana, Missouri, North Carolina, North Dakota, Texas, and West Virginia—report prisoner populations at or below their design capacities. (Bureau of Justice Statistics 1990a; 6), and some of these reports, as is true of Texas, are effects of compliance with court orders rather a true lack of demand for additional prison beds.

- Thousands of sentenced offenders are receiving early releases from terms of confinement long before they otherwise would be released only as a means of alleviating this overcrowding. (Camp and Camp 1989, 25)

- Many thousands of other sentenced felons are being housed in local jails that were never designed to deal with long-term prisoners purely because there is no space for them in state prisons (Bureau of Justice Statistics 1990b, 6). Because the nation's jails are confronting overcrowding problems which are nearly as acute as those of state and federal agencies, the unanticipated pressures this places on local correctional facilities has itself become a major concern.

Private Corrections Industry

Warning signs flashing as early as the 1970s made it altogether obvious that a "business as usual" approach would be entirely insufficient to meet the growing correctional crisis. It was readily apparent that innovative strategies in a broad array of areas had to be identified and pursued aggressively. This necessity-based pressure for change produced diverse results. Efforts were made, to cite only a few obvious illustrations, to foster a higher degree of integration among the component parts of the criminal justice system, to improve the quality of statistical models used to predict the effects on prisoner populations of new as well as existing sentencing policies, to devise pretrial diversion programs capable of reducing population pressures on local correctional facilities, to identify and implement such alternatives to imprisonment as intensive probation, "house arrest," and electronic monitoring, to assign a higher priority to the capital outlay needs of a correctional system that had pressing needs for an expanded population capacity, and to create early release programs capable of serving as a pressure relief mechanism when prisoner population sizes rose to impossible levels or, quite often, to levels above court-imposed population "caps."

The Influence of the Larger Economic and Political Context

The pressures mounting within the context of the criminal justice system, however, were not the only forces that were urging change in the ways government approached the delivery of essential services as we entered the 1980s. Indeed, years before the prisoner population explosion began in the mid-1970s, units of local, state, and federal government were encountering increasingly strident public demands for, on the one hand, a "downsizing" of government and of the resources made available to government agencies and for, on the other hand, increases in the number and the quality of public services government provided. Obvious illustrations of this somewhat paradoxical set of pressures and its consequences were soon to be provided by the referendum on Proposition 13 in California, the referendum on Proposition 2 1/2 in Massachusetts in 1979, and the tax reductions produced by the Economic Recovery Act of 1981.

Government, in short, was being told to do more with less. As far back as the early 1970s this "do more with less" mandate prompted growing numbers of elected officials to challenge the notion that government had the responsibility for both identifying the range of public services that were to be provided to the public *and* devising means by which government would provide those services through its own agencies. Instead, policymakers began turning to the private sector as a means of providing mandated services of the high quality at the lowest possible cost. The effect was a rapid growth in the number and the diversity of private sector firms whose futures depended on the appeal of privatization—especially on a rather simple form of privatization that involves government contracting with the private sector for services government traditionally has provided through the efforts of its own agencies and employees.

The success of the privatization movement is now a matter of historical record. Private firms began providing contract-based services in such dissimilar areas as building maintenance, day-care services, solid waste collection and disposal, wastewater treatment, medical services, public transportation, and vehicle maintenance. By 1972 the dollar value of local-level contracts with the private sector alone had reached twenty-two billion dollars, and by 1982 the value of these contracts is estimated to have reached sixty-five billion dollars (National Commission for Employment Policy 1988, 8). This rapid growth in the involvement of the private sector as a provider of essential public services persists today in large measure as a consequence of compelling evidence that the private sector is able to provide those services at a cost below that attributable to government agencies and at a quality level equal to or better than that of those agencies (e.g., Savas 1982; Touche Ross 1987; President's Commission on Privatization 1988).

The Birth of the Correctional Privatization Movement

As we entered the 1980s pressures for changes in traditional methods of delivering correctional services were growing both within and beyond the limits of the nation's correctional systems. The only missing ingredients were (1) entrepreneurs who had access to the capital required to cover construction and start-up costs, (2) experienced correctional administrators who were willing to exchange the relative security of public sector careers for the potential benefits of becoming a part of a new industry, (3) a willingness on the part of government to experiment with a novel method of delivering correctional services, and, in the vast majority of American jurisdictions, (4) enabling legislative which expressly authorized contracting for correctional management services.

Precisely when and where these missing ingredients materialized in such a way as to give birth to the correctional privatization movement is not altogether clear. A few small contracts were awarded by federal agencies and by at least one state agency to such firms as Dismas House, Eclectic Communications, Inc. and Behavioral Systems Southwest in the early 1980s (Press 1990; Calvert Hanson 1991). Important as these early contract awards may have been in setting the stage for what was soon to follow, it would be inaccurate to suggest that the true beginnings of the private corrections industry are traceable to these efforts. Instead, were we asked to point to the "fathers" of the correctional privatization movement, we would point to Thomas W. Beasley and Doctor R. Crants and their decision to form the Nashville-based Corrections Corporation of America (CCA) in 1983.

To be sure, CCA arrived on the correctional scene at an especially opportune time. Initial experiments with private facility management had been successful, support for enabling legislation already had begun to mount, and the prisoner population explosion had reached crisis proportions. CCA, however, joined the embryonic private corrections industry with multiple advantages no other firm enjoyed. It had been able, for example, to obtain substantial working capital, to persuade a number of experienced and highly regarded correctional administrators to move from the public to the private sector, to establish a division of labor within its corporate structure which called for senior business and senior corrections executives to exercise decision-making powers in their respective areas of expertise, and, not least consequentially, to benefit from Tom

Beasley's flamboyant, charismatic presentation of himself, of CCA, and of the private corrections industry CCA was in the process of forming.

Almost immediately following the highly visible entry of CCA into the private corrections industry, the correctional privatization movement began to gather momentum—even though it almost simultaneously began to stimulate opposition from such diverse groups as the National Prison Project of the American Civil Liberties Union, the National Sheriffs Association, the American Federation of State, County, and Municipal Employees (AFSCME), and the American Bar Association. Within three years, for example, CCA obtained contracts to manage local jails in Bay County, Florida (1985), Hamilton County, Tennessee (1984), and Santa Fe County, New Mexico (1986) as well as federal facilities in Houston, Texas (1984) and Laredo, Texas (1984). Eclectic Communications, Inc. received a contract from the California Department of Corrections to manage a parole violator facility (1986). Pricor, Inc. obtained a contract to manage a local jail in Tuscaloosa, Alabama (1986). The U.S. Corrections Corporation obtained a state-level contract for a facility in Kentucky (1986).

Given the fact that change has seldom come swiftly in the adult corrections arena and the fact that antiprivatization efforts were becoming increasingly aggressive by the mid-1980s, these initial contracting experiences were of vital importance to those who saw potential in the private sector option. Those proponents of privatization were not disappointed. The initial contracting efforts demonstrated that private corrections firms bring construction projects to fruition substantially faster and at a significantly lower cost than could government agencies, that the transition from public to private management of "takeover" facilities could be accomplished smoothly, that the per diem costs of private management of correctional facilities yielded important cost savings, and that the quality of services private firms provided were equal to and often better than those of government (e.g., Camp and Camp 1984; Mullen, Chabotar, and Carrow 1985; Hackett et al. 1987; Brakel 1988; Logan and McGriff 1989; and Logan 1990).

The stage having been firmly set by what already had transpired and the growth in national prisoner populations placing unrelenting pressure on correctional systems throughout the nation, the volume of enabling legislation and contracting decisions made between 1986 and the present proved to be substantial (Calvert Hanson 1991). Today correctional privatization is both a legal and a contracting reality in Alabama, California, Florida, Kansas, Kentucky, Louisiana, Oklahoma, New Mexico, Tennessee, and Texas. Some of these jurisdictions and such other jurisdictions as Colorado, New York, and Washington have become the sites for privately managed secure facilities that house federal prisoners for the Federal Bureau of Prisons, the Immigration and Naturalization Service, and the U.S. Marshals Service. The number and the geographical distribution of private correctional facilities are certain to expand. For example, under the terms of an agreement with the U.S. Marshals Service, the Corrections Corporation of American is moving forward with its plan to construct and then manage a 440-bed facility for maximum security prisoners in Leavenworth, Kansas. Additionally, a growing number of jurisdictions—including Nevada, Virginia, West Virginia, and Wyoming—have recently passed enabling legislation, and still more enabling legislation is under active consideration as this essay is being written (e.g., Nebraska, North Carolina, and Pennsylvania).

Evaluating the Performance of the Private Sector

The successes of the private corrections industry have been dramatic. A decade ago the industry simply did not exist. Today private firms are managing minimum, medium, and maximum security adult facilities housing female as well as male prisoners in jurisdictions all across the nation. Questions remain, however, regarding whether the private corrections industry has overcome the obstacles it confronted when it began to take form and whether the promises the industry made from the beginning have been kept. Indeed, since 1985 one or both of us have appeared before or worked closely with groups of local- or state-level elected officials in such dissimilar jurisdictions as California, Florida, Illinois, Iowa, Louisiana, Michigan, Nebraska, New Mexico, Pennsylvania, Virginia, Wisconsin, and Wyoming. They repeat the same core set of questions and concerns time and time again. Is the delegation of facility management responsibilities to a private firm constitutional? How will the legal liability exposure of government be affected by decisions to privatize? Will privatization have an adverse effect on the legal rights of confined persons? Can privatization really yield cost savings to government? Will cost savings only be possible because of decreases in the quality of correctional services that are provided? Will the accountability of a private corrections firms be lower than that of a government agency?

No effort to evaluate the potential value of correctional privatization can or should ignore these common and pressing concerns. Although our responses to each question necessarily will be abbreviated, in what follows we will provide answers that are supported by the best available evidence.

The Constitutional Question

Very early in the privatization debate critics contended that the debate would have no practical significance. They were persuaded that any effort by government to delegate full-scale facility management responsibilities to the private sector would be defined by the courts as being unconstitutional. The management and operation of correctional facilities, they argued, involves the exercise of the police powers of the State, powers that must be seen as being inherently governmental in nature and, therefore, as being nondelegable (Field 1987; Robbins 1988a, 1988b).

Any effort to evaluate privatization on this constitutional level poses major difficulties for at least two reasons. One of these reasons is that the nondelegation doctrine upon which this challenge to privatization is based must be assessed in terms specific to each American jurisdiction. Some jurisdictions define the power of branches of government to delegate their powers rather broadly. In the federal jurisdiction, for example, the courts have not invalidated any delegation of powers to the private sector on federal constitutional grounds since the 1936 United States Supreme Court case of *Carter v. Carter Coal Company* (298 U.S. 238). Some state courts, however, have interpreted their state constitutions in such a way as to assign a good deal more significance to the nondelegation doctrine. Florida and Virginia are widely recognized as illustrations of these "strict delegation" jurisdictions. Their courts demand that any delegations of power be based both on explicit expressions of legislative intent and similarly explicit legislative limitations on the exercise of delegated powers. This reality, in turn, does much to explain why the privatization statutes Florida enacted in 1985 and Virginia enacted in 1991 are substantially more detailed than any existing federal statute.

Difficulties with this first aspect of the constitutional issue notwithstanding, no jurisdiction in the United States that has sought to forge a sound enabling statute has encountered a serious constitutional obstacle. We do no wish to trivialize the constitutional concern, but any problems that do exist call for little more than drafting statutes in such a way as to comply with existing provisions of applicable constitutional law. The less than troublesome nature of the drafting task is reflected by the fact that no successful constitutional challenge to any piece of enabling legislation has been reported to date.

The second and in some ways more difficult component of the constitutional issue is narrower in its focus. It pertains to definitions of what powers government may and may not delegate to a private corrections firm. To be sure, a theoretical position can be advanced in support of the thesis that few powers of the State are immune from delegation to a private party on constitutional grounds (e.g., Thomas et al, 1988; Logan 1990). The special concern of both critics of privatization and more than a few of its proponents, however, is with the ethical and the constitutional propriety of a profit-motivated private party being delegated powers that permit it to make determinations regarding who will be imprisoned, the duration of a period of imprisonment, various types of adjustments in sentence lengths (e.g., awards of "good time" and early release on parole), and alterations in the conditions of confinement that are linked to disciplinary actions (e.g., placement in solitary confinement and transfers for disciplinary reasons to a facility which has a higher security classification). The concern, of course, flows from a fear that profit motives might improperly shape decisions in such areas as these.

Suffice it to say that this aspect of the constitutional question has not proven to be problematic. Existing statutes bolstered by language contained in all privatization contracts prohibit private corrections firms and their employees from making final determinations that could have an adverse effect on the liberty interests of prisoners. Thus, for example, private firms have no power to determine who will or who will not be committed to their facilities, to shape determinations of when those who are committed to their facilities will be released, or to control disciplinary processes whose outcome could alter significantly the conditions of confinement.

The Legal Liability Question

There probably is no unit of government that has considered correctional privatization that has not also sought to resolve questions regarding what if any effect privatization would have on its legal liability exposure. The question raises especially complex legal issues that cannot be pursued here in any detail. Two facts, however, do deserve some emphasis.

First, the dominant source of legal liability exposure in the correctional context is linked to constitutional tort actions, especially actions brought by prisoner plaintiffs under 42 USC Section 1983. Because these Section 1983 suits ordinarily must allege that a state official has caused a deprivation of a right secured by the Constitution, some prisoners' rights advocates were concerned that prisoners housed in a private correctional facility might lack a legal means of attacking any substandard jail or prison conditions they might encounter. This understandable concern, however, was largely pushed into the background when the United States Supreme Court, in the important case of *West v. Atkins* (487 U.S. 42 [1988]), held that private parties who contract with government to provide constitutionally mandated services could be named as defendants in Section 1983 suits.

Second, as a consequence of the statutes of many jurisdictions and, to the best of our knowledge, all privatization contracts, the liability exposure of government has been reduced by indemnification requirements. Indemnification clauses insert a "liability buffer" between government and the activities of a private corrections firm and its employees. The private firm guarantees that it will shoulder the liability costs—including litigation costs, attorney fees, costs associated with the settlement of pending cases, and damage awards—that are linked to the manner in which it discharges its contractual responsibilities. This has the dual benefit of decreasing the preexisting financial burden on government and of serving as an important incentive for the private corrections firms to conduct their operations as efficiently and effectively as they can.

The Prisoners' Rights Question

Another significant and entirely appropriate question requiring careful evaluation by those considering correctional privatization involves how privatization might affect the legal rights of confined persons. The source of this concern will be obvious. Profit motives could encourage an unscrupulous private firm to disregard the rights of prisoners to proper food, medical services, and so on. Such a firm, to quote Ira Robbins' familiar complaint, might be "more interested in doing *well* than in doing *good*" (Robbins 1988a, 4, emphasis in original). Were such a possibility to become a reality, would the effect of privatization be to undermine the legal remedies prisoners could pursue?

Because many if not most of those who have followed the correctional privatization movement have some special expertise in the legal aspects of privatization, this question is remarkable if for no reason other than the fact that it has received so little systematic attention. Indeed, only one person has addressed the issue in any detail (Thomas 1991a, 1991b). In both analyses Thomas documents how interpretations of constitutional law and of 42 USC Section 1983 limit the access of prisoners housed in government-managed correctional facilities to various forms of legal remedies (e.g., compensatory and punitive damage awards). He then explains how these limitations apply only when government agencies and their employees operate correctional facilities and, more importantly, how they do not apply in privatized facilities.

For example, when prisoners housed in traditional state correctional facilities bring Section 1983 actions in federal courts, judicial interpretations of the Eleventh Amendment prevent them from seeking compensatory or punitive damages from the state agencies that may have been responsible for deprivations.[5]

This limits such plaintiffs to a quest for prospective injunctive relief. Private corrections firms, however, enjoy no Eleventh Amendment immunity from damage suits brought under Section 1983. Thus, while prisoners confined in both traditional and privatized state correctional facilities can rely on Section 1983 when they seek prospective injunctive relief, only those confined in privatized correctional facilities are in a position to seek compensatory and, when appropriate, punitive damage awards.

This, of course, does not mean that private facilities will necessarily be managed in a more satisfactory fashion than public facilities. However, it does mean that those who suffer constitutional deprivations while confined in a private rather than a public facility will enjoy more effective means of responding to those deprivations. This, in turn, means that private corrections firms have a greater incentive to meet all constitutional requirements and that they will be held to a higher standard of accountability if they fail to do so.

The Quality Question

The premodern record of private jails and prisons in America is rather bleak. However, so, too, is the record of public correctional facilities during the same historical period. More importantly, the private prisons and jails that emerged during the 1980s bear so little resemblance to their earlier counterparts that they must be judged on their own merits and in comparison with their contemporary governmental alternatives. Because the modern era is only a decade old, it is difficult to form such judgments on the basis of sound research. Still, there have been three studies so far that systematically evaluate the performance of private facilities for adults and that provide comparisons either to previous governmental operation of the same facility or to a separate but reasonably comparable governmental facility.

In the first study, Samuel J. Brakel (1988), then a researcher for the American Bar Association Foundation, surveyed inmates at Silverdale—the Hamilton County (Chattanooga, Tennessee) Penal Farm—operated by the Corrections Corporation of America. Brakel, a former Special Master with experience in the oversight of prisons operating under court orders or consent decrees, administered a questionnaire covering all the topics that might be found in a comprehensive consent decree, such as conditions of confinement, programs and services, due process procedures (e.g., disciplinary procedures, grievance mechanisms, protections of rights of access to legal assistance, and release procedures), and relations with the outside world.

Brakel found that the private prison was more highly rated by inmates on its physical improvements, upkeep, and cleanliness; staff competence and character; work assignments; chaplain and counsellor services; requests and grievances; correspondence and telephone; and outside contacts. Other areas had a balance of positive and negative evaluations (e.g., safety, security, classification, medical care, food, education, discipline, and legal access). Two areas received mostly negative ratings: recreation and release procedures (but the latter remained under county, not private, control). Six prisoners who had been in the prison under the previous administration by county employees were able to make, collec-

Potential of Correctional Privatization 227

tively, twenty-eight explicit before-and-after comparisons. Of these, twenty-four favored the private prison and four favored the previous county administration.

It might be argued, of course, that Silverdale was a case of a shabby county operation that had nowhere to go but up and, therefore, that the private operation could not avoid appearing to be better. However, when prisoners with the relevant experience compared the private operation to a local city jail and to the state penitentiary, those comparisons also strongly favored the private prison. Moreover, the private company made its improvements while decreasing costs to the county (Logan and McGriff 1989), so the results could hardly be regarded as preordained.

A second study, sponsored by the National Institute of Justice and conducted by the Urban Institute, compared private and public operation of a roughly matched pair of minimum security adult prisons in Kentucky and two matched pairs of secure treatment facilities for juveniles in Massachusetts (See chap. 15). In Kentucky, the Marion Adjustment Center, a minimum security prerelease facility owned and operated by the U. S. Corrections Corporation under contract to the State of Kentucky, was compared to the Blackburn Correctional Center, a minimum security prison under state operation. Using data from surveys of staff and inmates and official government records, empirical indicators of performance were identified in four broad areas: conditions of confinement, internal security and control, social adjustment and rehabilitation, and management. More similarities than differences were found between the public and private prisons,[6] but where differences did exist they usually favored the private over the public prison. The ratio of comparisons favoring the private prison per each one favoring the state prison was 2.6 overall, with a ratio of 1.5 on the dimension of social adjustment and rehabilitation, of 2.4 each on the dimensions of conditions of confinement and internal security and control, and of 6.0 on the dimension of management issues. For the matched pairs of state and private juvenile facilities in Massachusetts, comparisons favored the private operations even more strongly than was the case in Kentucky.[7]

Summarizing the data for both states, the Urban Institute concluded that "[f]or a substantial majority of these performance indicators, the privately operated facilities had at least a small advantage. By and large, both staff and inmates gave better ratings to the services and programs at the privately operated facilities; escape rates were lower; there were fewer disturbances by inmates; and in general, staff and offenders felt more comfortable at the privately-operated facilities" (see chap. 15). Greater staff experience and higher wages at the state facilities did not lead to higher performance. "By and large," commented the Urban Institute researchers, "staff in the privately operated [facilities] appeared to be more enthusiastic about their work, more involved in their work, and more interested in working with the inmates than their public counterparts." Regarding management issues, the privately operated facilities appeared to be more flexible and less regimented, with staff subject to less stringent controls. These elements seem to have made life in the privately operated correctional facilities somewhat more pleasant for both inmates and staff. Note, however, that the privately operated institutions in Kentucky and in Massachusetts were required to follow the same basic rules as the publicly operated facilities" (See chap. 15).

A third study by Charles H. Logan, funded by the National Institute of Justice, the National Institute of Corrections, and the Federal Bureau of Prisons, compared the quality of confinement in three multiple security level women's prisons: (1) a privately operated facility for all of New Mexico's female prisoners, (2) the state-operated prison holding virtually that same population one year before, and (3) a federal prison for women (Logan 1991). "Quality of confinement" was defined and measured along eight dimensions: security, safety, order, care (mostly medical), activity (programs), justice, living conditions, and management. Data from institutional records and surveys of inmates and staff produced 333 empirical indicators of the eight dimensions of quality for the state and private prisons, and 131 of these also were available for the federal prison. Results of all possible pairwise comparisons between prisons were summarized for each prison on each dimension in a comparative score called the Prison Quality Index.

In short, the private prison outperformed its state and federal counterparts on all dimensions except care (where the state scored slightly higher) and justice (where the federal prison matched the private).[8] Using the federal prison as a standard of good quality, the conclusion was that both the state and private prisons were good quality institutions and that each prison had different areas of strength and weakness. However, on most dimensions the state was able to improve the quality of confinement for its female felons by contracting for the private operation of their prison.

Importantly, it cost the State of New Mexico $80 a day per inmate to operate the state correctional facility for women during its last year of operation. The fee paid to the Corrections Corporation of America the following year for operation of the newly constructed private prison was $69.75. Neither of these two figures included costs of construction or debt retirement. Thus, for a 12.8 percent lower operating cost, New Mexico received a higher quality of prison operation by contracting with a private provider. Other and much more thorough research that we will discuss in the next section of this analysis also supports the expectation of cost savings as a result of contracting for the operation of correctional facilities.

The above and other evidence has been so persuasive that even some critics have been favorably impressed. The most striking recent example of this comes from comments made by Sheriff James A. Gondles, Jr., the executive director designee of the American Correctional Association. In 1989 Sheriff Gondles published an article in *The National Sheriff* in which he strongly opposed the concept of jail privatization (Gondles 1989). In 1991, however, he participated in an ACA accreditation audit of New Mexico's only women's prison. The prison was designed, constructed, and is now managed by the Corrections Corporation of America. Noting that this was his first direct experience in a privatized correctional facility, Sheriff Gondles said that he was "impressed with the professionalism of the staff" and called the prison "the brightest, the cleanest—and for the most part, the happiest" correctional institution he had ever seen. The CCA facility, he concluded, "can meet any correctional institution in the nation—for men or women—head-on." Sheriff Gondles' enthusiasm was shared by other members of the ACA audit team. When the audit was complete, for example, Sigmund L. Fine, the director of the Adult Corrections Department for Minnesota and the chairperson of the accreditation group, announced that of the 495 standards audited, the prison fell short on only four. Each of those four was linked to noise associated with the operation of air conditioning equipment. Overall, Fine observed, the CCA facility scored 100 percent on all mandatory standards and 99.20 percent on all nonmandatory items (Cibola County, New Mexico *County Beacon*, 1 March 1991, 1-2).[9]

The Cost Question

A realistic expectation of cost savings as a result of contracting is probably in the range of 5 percent to 15 percent. Savings to particular jurisdictions might be greater under certain circumstances, such as when a contractor uses subcontracts to other jurisdictions to fill a facility that would have been under-utilized if run by the government or when an improved operation saves the government the cost of a large lawsuit. As a general expectation, however, we would use the figure of 5 to 15 percent.

This estimate is derived in large part from a study done for the National Institute of Justice and is based on data provided by the County Auditor of Hamilton County, Tennessee (Logan and McGriff 1989; Logan 1989). Because a county auditor is in a unique position to identify and estimate interagency and other indirect costs, that study was unusual in its thoroughness. The study focused on the experience of a facility managed by the Corrections Corporation of America.

Specifically, in 1984, CCA assumed management of the Hamilton County Penal Farm, a 350-bed minimum-to-medium security county prison located near Chattanooga. The facility was inherited in a state of deterioration and neglect and required extensive renovation by CCA. In addition, Hamilton County is located in a region of the country has relatively low correctional costs, and Hamilton County was already spending less on its prison than other jurisdictions in the same region were spending on their facilities. Because the county already was among the lowest of the low spenders, this facility provided a fairly severe test of a private contractor's ability to lower costs still further while simultaneously renovating the physical plant, expanding capacity, and improving the quality of operations, all of which it did accomplish.

Consistently conservative assumptions were used to estimate all the direct and indirect costs the county would have incurred if it had retained or resumed operation of the facility itself. The assumptions were conservative in the sense that they were designed to err in the direction of underestimating the costs of county operation. These costs were then compared to the costs of contractual operation, which included both the contractor's fee and all the direct and indirect county costs that continued to exist in addition to that fee (e.g., the cost of contract administration and monitoring). The study concluded that, over the three years examined, the county reduced its costs of corrections by at least 4 percent to 8 percent per year, and a cost savings estimate of 5 percent to 15 percent would be easy to defend.

This study is not alone in its demonstration of cost savings. There have been several others. One of these deserves mention because it, too, was particularly thorough and careful in its methodology (Texas Sunset Advisory Commission 1991). The study to which we refer is found in a 1991 report by the State Auditor's office to the Sunset Commission of the State of Texas. Historically, the cost of corrections has been lower in Texas than in most other states, yet that state pursued even greater cost reductions by contracting four 500-bed prisons to two private vendors— the Corrections Corporation of America and the Wackenhut Corrections Corporation. The Texas Auditor's figures show that the two private companies have run their prisons at between 10 percent and 15 percent less than what it would cost the state to run those exact same prisons.[10]

Unfortunately, studies comparing the quality and costs of public and private prisons are few in number. A high priority should be assigned to independent research on both topics. Importantly, however, all of the available evidence supports the hypothesis that private management of correctional facilities is significantly less costly than is public management. The same body of research reveals that cost savings can be realized without any sacrifice being made in terms of the quality of correctional services that are provided. Indeed, the research evidence to date reveals that operating costs can be significantly reduced at the same time that the quality of correctional services is being enhanced.

The Accountability Question

Critics of correctional privatization often hypothesize that contracting decisions will undermine the accountability of and governmental control over correctional facilities. The core contention appears to be that traditional methods of delivering correctional services place the ultimate responsibility for those services on the shoulders of elected representatives and thus permit the electorate to remove from office those who discharge their responsibilities in an inefficient or ineffective fashion. The implication is that contracting somehow undermines an important chain of accountability and control.

This criticism has an especially hollow ring (Logan 1990, 194-210). The true structure of traditional government-managed departments of corrections is radically different from what the critics seem to imagine. Multiple layers of unelected government officials commonly exist between elected officials in the executive and legislative branches of government and those who actually deliver correctional services. When inefficiency or ineffectiveness does exist, it is exceedingly difficult to detect and, even were one or both to be detected, it is substantially more difficult to place responsibility directly at the feet of those who are elected. Working down the ranks from middle management to lower management to line staff, public employees become progressively less politically accountable. Most government employees enjoy civil service protections that make them virtually immune to being fired. At the extreme of nonaccountability, when government employees, including correctional officers, go on strike, the first thing they demand—and typically get—is amnesty for their illegal action. Moreover, and quite apart from questions of accountability to the electorate, the very nature of government is such that one finds few incentives that encourage or reward efficiency and effectiveness and, perhaps consequently, few efforts to measure whether essential public services have been provided in an efficient, effective manner.

The irony, of course, is that one of the most obvious advantages of contracting is that it significantly enhances accountability and control. The most obvious illustration of how this happens is provided by the terms of contracts linking the public and private sectors. Those contracts define the obligations of private corrections firms in far greater detail than do the quite general legislative mandates public corrections agencies are obliged to follow. Contracts identify goals, standards, and criteria against which the performance of contractors is measured. They define the sanctions that may be imposed on the contractor if its obligations are not met satisfactorily. They provide for adjustments in the terms of the contracts should the need for adjustments arise. Further, whether because of statutory or contractual language, a government contract monitor is commonly if not invariably required to assess contract compliance on a continuous basis. No analogous representative of government is so pervasively or so powerfully represented in any public corrections facility.

There is more, of course, to accountability than the legal accountability we discussed previously and the political accountability we have addressed here. Private corrections firms also confront forms of economic accountability one does not find in the public sector. As a result of economic competition, private corrections firms are subject to both direct and indirect market mechanisms of control. They are directly accountable to the contracting units of government who are their customers. Additionally, one must take into account the role played by their competitors, investors, stockholders, and insurers. Competition, comparison, information, and accountability: each follows naturally from the one before. Competing firms provide comparative information about themselves and hold one another to account on matters of quality and cost. Insurers impose discipline through premiums that reflect independent and objective assessments of risk. Stockholders and investment advisors evaluate both the current status and future prospects of companies. This information affects such important variables as stock valuations, the ease with which firms have access to the capital markets, and the cost of the capital they obtain. These variables shape the future of any company. For example, stock prices anticipate the future. A private corrections firm headed for scandal, lawsuits, or uninsurability as a result of mismanagement will see its stock begin to fall. Moreover, if employees are also stockholders, this distributes the supervision motive to where it is likely to do the most good.

In short, a careful comparison of public sector corrections agencies with private sector corrections firms that focuses on the important issue of accountability would necessarily find greater economic, legal, and political accountability when correctional services are provided by the private sector. Thus, it is perplexing to note that critics of privatization so often mention the accountability issue. Doing so appears to serve no purpose other than placing them on very thin ice.

The Future Prospects for Correctional Privatization

The private corrections industry is less than a decade old. Although private corrections firms like Concepts, Inc., the Corrections Corporation of America, Eclectic Communications, Inc., Esmor, Inc., Pricor, Inc., the U.S. Corrections Corporation, and the Wackenhut Corrections Corporation have experienced remarkably rapid growth and have been evaluated with considerable enthusiasm by contracting units of government, it is exceedingly difficult to predict what the future holds in store for these and the growing number of other firms which comprise the industry. Many of the advantages such firms enjoy today, for example, are closely linked to pressures associated with an unprecedented rate of growth in the nation's local, state, and federal prisoner populations. It is impossible to imagine that the rate of increase in those populations we have witnessed during the past fifteen or so years will be tolerated for much longer. Cost considerations alone are almost certain to force policy decisions that will diminish rates of growth or perhaps even decrease the total size of the prisoner population. This, in turn, would have the effect of decreasing the intensity of the demand for both public and private correctional services, and decreased demand almost certainly would place a heavier burden on the private sector than it would on the public sector. After all, resistance to correctional privatization has been weakest when privatization initiatives have focused on the management of new facilities and strongest when they have focused on the transfer of existing facilities from public to private management. Thus, it would not be unreasonable to predict that a formidable barrier to the continued success of the correctional privatization movement will be encountered when the prisoner population peaks or begins to subside.

We reject any such prediction because we see it as being too myopic. To be sure, when the private corrections industry began to take form during the mid-1980s, the road to initial success and subsequent rapid growth was paved by the acute problems government faced as its best efforts to meet a correctional crisis caused by rapid prisoner population increases proved to be inadequate. It is altogether probable that the concept of correctional privatization would have remained undeveloped and unexplored had these problems not materialized. The forces that give rise to new methods for providing goods or services, however, often are only weakly linked to the reasons why those new methods remain attractive over time. The "staying power" of new methods is driven by the ability of those methods to provide something of value. In the case of correctional privatization, value means an ability to provide excellent correctional services at the lowest possible cost. Value is necessarily assessed in a comparative fashion—which includes comparisons between different private sector firms as well as between the public and private sectors.

The importance of value being best pursued by choosing between alternatives must not be underestimated. By the close of 1991 approximately sixty secure private correctional facilities housing some 20,000 prisoners will have become a reality. Dozens of points of comparison will thus be in place. How they came to be will be far less relevant than the fact that they will exist. Their existence means that the noncompetitive monopoly government enjoyed until a decade ago exists no longer. Not so unlike the fall of Humpty Dumpty, it is exceedingly unlikely that there will be any set of circumstances under which that monopoly will be restored. Too many units of government have experienced and have found value in the private alternative for any return to a "business as usual" approach to be seen as being acceptable. As long as fair comparisons reveal that private corrections firms can respond swiftly, flexibly, efficiently, and effectively, the public demand for the services they provide will continue to grow even if the nation's prison population does not.[11]

Our favorable assessment of the future of the correctional privatization movement, of course, should not be interpreted to mean that private corrections firms can remedy all that now ails the field of adult corrections. They cannot and will not. Correctional privatization is not now and never will become a panacea for the problems confronting the nation's correctional system. It is nothing more and nothing less than an alternative means by which government can provide an essential public service.

Importantly, however, the best available evidence reveals that existing privatization efforts have confronted no consequential constitutional barriers, have reduced the legal liability costs contracting units of government previously confronted, expanded the scope of legal remedies made available to prisoners, have decreased correctional costs in the areas of both construction and facility operation, resulted in quality improvements in correctional services provided, and enhanced the ability of government to control and to be accountable for its correctional facilities. These are important and impressive achievements by the private sector. They are achievements that have enabled correctional privatization to move from a point at which it was a novel experiment to a point at which it is an accepted way of delivering correctional services in many jurisdictions. The question is thus no longer whether government should privatize in the correctional arena. Today government must shoulder the burden of explaining why it chooses not to pursue an alternative whose merit has been proven.

Our own view is that this dramatic change in American corrections is altogether healthy. It demands that government look beyond the public or private identity of those who wish to provide correctional services and that we focus instead on which alternative provider of those services can deliver excellent services at the lowest possible cost. The day when adult corrections could be thought of as a noncompetitive governmental monopoly has passed. The day has come when our jails and prisons will be managed by whoever can handle the task most efficiently and most effectively. Whether fair competition between public and private providers of correctional services results in a particular correctional facility being managed by one or the other seems altogether inconsequential. What is consequential is that the modern correctional era encourages competition, demands accountability, stimulates creativity, rewards success, and creates choices. Sometimes the winner in the competition will be the private sector. Sometimes the winner will be the public sector. Always the winner will be the public interest.

Notes

1. The total value of private contracts for the management of secure adult facilities is difficult to estimate with precision. Nonetheless, on 1 November 1991 the Corrections Corporation of America, which is the largest private corrections management firm in the United States and which also manages an adult facility in Queensland, Australia, released its quarterly report for the period ending 30 September 1991. The report reveals that the end of the quarter found 5,134 prisoners in CCA-managed facilities and that CCA's revenue per compensated manday (i.e., its average per diem rate) was $38.56. If this per diem rate were applied to the 20,000 prisoners we expect will be housed in private facilities by the close of 1991, then the estimated value of all contracts would be $281,488,000.
2. For example, federal statistics reveal trends in the number of court commitments to state prisons per 1,000 arrests for selected serious felonies (i.e., murder, nonnegligent manslaughter, forcible rape, robbery, aggravated assault, and burglary). In 1975 there were twenty-six sentences of imprisonment per 1,000 arrests. By 1988 this statistic had increased by 96.15 percent to fifty-one (Bureau of Justice Statistics 1990a, 7-8).
3. The usefulness of confinement rate statistics may not be immediately obvious to some readers. It should be emphasized that the number of prisoners per capita is not a valid measure of "punitiveness." Thus, claims that the United States has the highest imprisonment rate and therefore is the most punitive society in the world are invalid. The United States has an extremely high crime rate. This, of course, is what creates the potential for large prisoner populations. When the number of prisoners is divided by the number of crimes known to the police—and even more so when it is divided by the number of arrests or convictions—the standing of the United States in "punitiveness" plummets dramatically. Nonetheless, for whatever reasons and with

Potential of Correctional Privatization 237

however much or little justification, the imprisonment rate does tell us something about our demand for imprisonment, and it is the mismatch between demand and supply that is at the heart of today's crisis in corrections. Whether the mismatch is the result of too much demand or too little supply is not addressed here. Since the mid-1970s, however, there is strong evidence that willingness to incarcerate has risen much more rapidly than have reports of serious crime. In 1975, for example, the Federal Bureau of Investigation recorded 11,256,600 reports of serious felonies (i.e., murder, nonnegligent manslaughter, rape, robbery, aggravated assault, burglary, grand larceny, and auto theft). This produced a reported crime rate per 100,000 citizens of 5,281.7 (Jamieson and Flanagan 1989, 427). The corresponding figures for 1985 were 12,430,000 reports and a crime rate of 5,206.5. Thus, during this decade of experience the volume of reported crime rose by only 10.42 percent and the crime rate actually decreased by 1.42 percent. During the same time period the number of state and federal prisoners increased by 99.74 percent and the incarceration rate rose by 80.18 percent (Jamieson and Flanagan 1989, 612).
4. The overcrowding problem has become especially acute in urban areas which house a majority of the nation's local pretrial detainees and sentenced offenders (Bureau of Justice Statistics 1990b, 6). Federal statistics reveal that 54.15 percent of the 339,633 prisoners are housed in local facilities with design capacities of 250 or more. Those with capacities in the range of 250-499 report that they are operating with prisoner populations equal to 107 percent of their capacities, those with capacities of 500-999 are operating at 116 percent of their capacities, and those with capacities of 1,000 or more are operating at 126 percent of their capacities.
5. It should be noted that the Eleventh Amendment does not stand as a barrier to efforts bring damage suits under Section 1983 in which specific state correctional officials are sued in their individual capacities. Often, however, the core cause of class action suits challenging unconstitutional prison conditions is a general policy that gave rise to, for example, overcrowding, unconstitutional disciplinary policies, or improper medical treatment. In such circumstances, the true responsibility for constitutional deprivations is the State itself and not merely an individual state official. Nonetheless, the Eleventh Amendment precludes plaintiffs from seeking monetary damage awards that would have to be paid from state funds.
6. Of 191 performance indicators comparing the state and private prisons, 70 percent produced differences that either failed to achieve statistical significance or were not testable (Urban Institute 1989, Table ES-6 of the Executive Summary).
7. In Massachusetts the ratio of comparisons favoring the set of private juvenile facilities over their matched state counterparts was 8.3 overall, with a ratio of 5.5 on the dimension of management and staffing, of 7.0 on the dimension of conditions of confinement, of 10.0 on the dimension of social adjustment and rehabilitation, and of 15.0 on the dimension of internal security and control (See chap. 15).
8. These findings were sensitive to the sources of data used in the measures of quality. Using data drawn only from the inmate surveys, the state prison scored higher than the private prison on all dimensions of quality except activity (programs like education, work, and education). In the Urban Institute's study, male inmates in Kentucky and Massachusetts were not as positive toward the private facilities as were staff, but their evaluations were not so much lower as to rank the private facilities lower than the public ones, as happened in New Mexico. However, in the New Mexico study, the inmates' marginally more negative evaluation of the private prison was outweighed by the far more positive comparisons based on the staff

surveys and the institutional records data. Thus, across all measures and data sources in New Mexico, the private prison ranked first in the Prison Quality Index scores.
9. It is worth emphasizing that the accomplishments of those responsible for the management of CCA's Grants, New Mexico facility have been found in many other private correctional facilities. The demanding national accreditation standards of the American Correctional Association are such that facilities seeking accreditation must obtain audit scores of 100 percent on all mandatory items and no less than 90 percent on all nonmandatory items. Prevailing private corrections industry standards routinely require that private facilities achieve accreditation within one to two years of beginning operation. We are aware of no private facility that has completed the review process but which has failed to receive accreditation. Many private facilities have received remarkably high audit scores on nonmandatory standards as well as the required 100 percent on all mandatory standards. Illustrations include CCA's Bay County, Florida county jail, accredited on 16 January 1989 with an audit score of 99.4 percent; CCA's Houston Processing Center, accredited on 22 February 1989 with an audit score of 97.5 percent; CCA's Sante Fe, New Mexico county jail, accredited on 15 August 1989 with an audit score of 98.2 percent; CCA's Cleveland, Texas Pre-Release Center, accredited on August 19, 1990 with an audit score of 97.5 percent; CCA's Venus, Texas Pre-Release Center, accredited on 16 January 1991 with an audit score of 99.7 percent; the Eclectic Communications, Inc. Baker, Texas Return-to-Custody Center, accredited on 12 August 1990 with an audit score of 99.20 percent; the Eclectic Communications, Inc. Hidden Valley Ranch Return-to-Custody Center, accredited on 12 August 1990 with an audit score of 98.74 percent; the Eclectic Communications, Inc. Leo Chesney Return-to-Custody Center, accredited on 13 January 1991 with an audit score of 99.39 percent; the Wackenhut Corrections Corporation Kyle, Texas Pre-Release Center, accredited on 12 August 1990 with an audit score of 93.0 percent, and the Wackenhut Corrections Corporation Bridgeport, Texas Pre-Release Center, accredited on 4 May 1991 with an audit score of 98.43, and two facilities operated in Kentucky by the U.S. Corrections Corporation which are expected to receive ACA accreditation by the end of 1991.
10. Whether it is 10 or 15 percent depends on whether computations include the state and local tax benefits that are derived from the private operations.
11. Although recent developments certainly are not independent of pressures caused by growing prisoner populations, it is worth noting that the immediate future of the private corrections industry impresses us as being very bright. As this chapter is being completed, for example, formal requests for proposals issued by units of local, state, and federal government would, if they result in contract awards to the private sector, result in the private management of facilities in Arizona or California, Florida, Tennessee, and Virginia within which approximately 4,000 prisoners would be housed.

References

American Friends Service Committee. (1971) *Struggle for Justice: A Report on Crime and Justice In America*. New York: Hill and Wang.
Brakel, Samuel J. (1988) "Prison Management, Private Enterprise Style: The Inmates' Evaluation." *New England Journal on Criminal and Civil Confinement* 14: 175-244.

Bureau of Justice Statistics. (1989) "Children in Custody, 1975-85: Census of Public and Private Juvenile Detention, Correctional, and Shelter Facilities." Washington, DC: U.S. Department of Justice.

_____.(1990a) "Prisoners in 1989." Washington, DC: National Institute of Justice.

_____.(1990b) "Census of Local Jails." Washington, DC: National Institute of Justice.

Calvert Hanson, L.S. (1991) "The Privatization of Corrections Movement: A Decade of Change." *Journal of Contemporary Criminal Justice* 7: 1-28.

Camp, G.M. and C.G. Camp. (1984) *Private Sector Involvement in Prison Services and Operations*. Washington, DC: National Institute of Justice.

_____.(1989) *The Corrections Yearbook, 1989*. South Salem, NY: Criminal Justice Institute.

Field, J.E. (1987) "Making Prisons Private: An Improper Delegation of a Governmental Power." *Hofstra Law Review* 15: 649-75.

Fogel, D. (1975) *We Are The Living Proof: The Justice Model for Corrections*. Cincinnati: Anderson Publishing Company.

Fogel, D. and J. Hudson, editors. (1981) *Justice As Fairness: Perspectives on the Justice Model*. Cincinnati: Anderson Publishing Company.

Gondles, J.A. (1989) "Jail Privatization." *The National Sheriff*: 40-45.

Gross, H. and A. von Hirsch, editors (1981) *Sentencing*. New York: Oxford University Press.

Hackett, J., H. Hatry, R.B. Levinson, J. Allen, K. Chi, and E. D. Feigenbaum. (1987) *Issues in Contracting for Private Operation of Prisons and Jails*. Washington, DC: National Institute of Justice.

Jamieson, K.M. and T.J. Flanagan, editors. (1989) *Sourcebook of Criminal Justice Statistics*. Washington, DC: National Institute of Justice.

Logan, C.H. (1972) "Evaluation Research in Crime and Delinquency: A Reappraisal." *Journal of Criminal Law, Criminology and Police Science* 63: 378-87.

_____.(1989) "Proprietary Prisons." In L. Goodstein and D. MacKenzie, eds., *The American Prison: Issues in Research and Policy*, 45-62. New York: Plenum Press.

_____.(1990). *Private Prisons: Cons and Pros*. New York: Oxford University Press.

_____.(1991) *Well Kept: Comparing Quality of Confinement in a Public and a Private Prison*. Washington, DC: National Institute of Justice.

Logan, C.H. and B.W. McGriff. (1989) "Comparing Costs of Public and Private Prisons: A Case Study." *NIJ Reports* 216: 2-8.

McDonald, D.C., editor. (1990) *Private Prisons and the Public Interest*. New Brunswick, NJ: Rutgers University Press.

Martinson, R. (1974) "What Works? Questions and Answers about Prison Reform." *The Public Interest* 35: 22-45.

Morris, N. (1974) *The Future of Imprisonment*. Chicago: University of Chicago Press.

Mullen, J., K.J. Chabotar, and D.M. Carrow. (1985) *The Privatization of Corrections*. Washington, DC: National Institute of Justice.

National Commission for Employment Policy. (1988) *Privatization and Public Employees: The Impact of City and County Contracting Out on Government Workers*. Washington, DC: National Commission for Employment Policy.

President's Commission on Privatization. (1988) *Privatization: Toward More Effective Government*. Washington, DC: President's Commission on Privatization.

Press, A. (1990) "The Good, the Bad, and the Ugly: Private Prisons in the 1980's," In D. McDonald, ed., *Private Prisons and the Public Interest* 19-41. New Brunswick: Rutgers University Press.

Robbins, I.P. (1988a) *The Legal Dimensions of Private Incarceration.* Washington, DC: American Bar Association.

_____.(1988b) "The Impact of the Delegation Doctrine on Prison Privatization." *UCLA Law Review* 35: 911-52.

Savas, E.S. (1982) *Privatizing the Public Sector.* Chatham: Chatham House Publishers.

Thomas, Charles W. (1987) *Corrections in America: Problems of the Past and the Present.* Beverly Hills, CA: Sage Publications.

_____.(1991a) "Prisoners' Rights and Correctional Privatization: A Legal and Ethical Analysis." *Business and Professional Ethics Journal* 10: 3-45.

_____.(1991b) "How Correctional Privatization Redefines the Legal Rights of Prisoners." *The Privatization Review* 6: 38-58.

Thomas, C.W. and L.S. Calvert Hanson. (1989) "The Implications of 42 U.S.C. Section 1983 for the Privatization of Prisons." *Florida State University Law Review* 16: 933-62.

Thomas, C.W., L.Lanza-Kaduce, L.S. Calvert Hanson, and K.A. Duffy. (1988) *The Privatization of American Corrections: As Assessment of Its Legal Implications.* Gainesville, FL: Center for Studies in Criminology and Law.

Texas Sunset Advisory Commission. (1991) "Information Report on Contracts and Correctional Facilities and Services." Chapter 5 in *Recommendations to the Governor of Texas and Members of the Seventy-Second Legislature.* Austin: Texas Sunset Advisory Commission.

Touche Ross and Company. (1987) "Privatization in America." Washington, DC: Touche Ross and Company.

von Hirsch, A. (1985) *Past or Future Crimes: Deservedness and Dangerousness in the Sentencing of Criminals.* New Brunswick, NJ: Rutgers University Press.

Contributors

Editors

DR. GARY W. BOWMAN has been associate professor of economics at Temple University since 1973. His research focuses on applications of microeconomics including public and managerial decisions and policy in such areas as privatization, regulation, and antitrust. He has published approximately fifteen articles and headed funded research projects from the National Science Foundation and other sources.

DR. SIMON HAKIM has been with Temple University since 1975, and is currently professor of economics. He has published over thirty scientific articles and has edited four books as well as having conducted funded research projects for governmental agencies, and private companies. His work centers on analysis of criminal behavior, police operations, and privatization of justice institutions.

DR. PAUL SEIDENSTAT has been on the faculty of Temple University since 1967 and is currently associate professor of economics and director of the graduate program. He has been principal investigator for several research projects for federal government agencies local governments as finance director and financial advisor. His research has been in the area of state and local government finance and management and urban and environmental economics and he has published a book and several articles in these fields.

Authors

BARBARA AUERBACH, Criminal Justice Associates, Philadelphia, PA

PAUL J. BROUNSTEIN, president, Prism Enterprises, Inc., Gaithersburg, MD

WARREN E. BURGER, Chief Justice, U.S. Supreme Court (retired)

WAYNE H. CALABRESE, vice president, Business Development, Wackenhut Corporation, Coral Gables, FL

WARREN I. CIKINS, senior staff member, Brookings Institution, Washington, DC

LINDA G. COOPER, vice-president of legal affairs, Corrections Corporation of America, Nashville, TN

NORMAN R. COX, president, N.R. Cox Associates, Ft. Worth, TX

ALEXIS M. DURHAM III, director Criminal Justice Program, Texas Christian University, Fort Worth, TX

HARRY P. HATRY, director, State and Local Research Program, The Urban Institute, Washington, DC

MICHAEL JANUS, associate warden, Federal Correctional Institution, Milan, MI

DANA JOEL, director of policy for state projects, Citizens for a Sound Economy, Washington, DC

ROBERT B. LEVINSON, special projects manager, American Correctional Association, Laurel, MD

CHARLES H. LOGAN, associate professor of sociology, University of Connecticut & visiting fellow, Federal Bureau of Prisons

TIMOTHY S. MAGUIGAN, administrator, Tuscaloosa Metropolitan Minimum Security, Detention Facility, Tuscaloosa, AL

TODD MASON, staff reporter for the *Wall Street Journal*

ROBERT D. MCCRIE, assistant professor Department of Law & Police Science, John Jay College of Criminal Justice, The City University of New York, New York, NY

H. LAWS MCCULLOUGH, director of Corporate Relations and Communications, PRICOR, Murfreesboro, TN

WILLIAM E. OSTERHOFF, professor, Department of Justice & Public Safety, Auburn University at Montgomery, ALA

JUDITH SCHLOEGEL, vice president, Division of Inmate Programs Prison Rehabilitative Industries and Diversified, Enterprises, Inc. (PRIDE), Clearwater, FL

Contributors

HAROLD J. SULLIVAN, associate professor and chair, Department of Government, John Jay College of Criminal Justice, New York, NY

CHARLES W. THOMAS, professor of criminology & director, Center for Studies in Criminology and Law, University of Florida, Gainesville, FL

Index

AFL-CIO, 39, 61
American Federation of State, County & Municipal Employees, 40, 61
Auburn, New York, 24
Auburn prison, 35, 43

Banishment, 77
Bay County Jail, 60, 68
Bechtel, 28
Best West International, Inc., 56
Blackburn Correctional Center, 68, 84, 227
Blum, 146
Blum v. Yaretsky, 148, 150
Board Of Public Labor (Texas), 37
Buckingham Security Ltd., 64, 65
Build-Operate-Transfer Agreement, 21
Bureau of Justice Assisstance, 96
Bureau of Prisons, 59

Capital depreciation, 79
Carl (Sonny) Emerson, 172
Carter v. Carter Coal Company, 222
Certification, 93, 96
Charles H. Logan, 53
Chief of Police Ken Swindle, 159
Comprehensive Drug Act, of 1986, 80
Contract inmate labor, 116
Corporation for Prison Industries, 100
Corrections Corporation of America, 27, 29, 34, 42, 48, 57, 59, 65, 68, 70, 84, 131, 129

Detention Services, 168
Deviant behavior, 80
Diversified Managerial Services, 165, 166
Don Hutto, 65, 167, 199, 231

Eckerd Foundation, 40
Economies of scale, 78
Effectiveness, 79
Eighth Amendment, 149

Factories within fences, 18, 91, 94, 105, 119
Flagg, 151, 152
Florida Pine Company, 386
Free Venture Model, 92

Hamilton County Penal Farm, 230
Hardy Mc Collum, 159
Houston Detention Center, 57
Huger & Jones, 44

Immigration & Naturalization Service, 57, 59
Iron triangle, 81

Jeremy Bentham, 40
Job Training Partnership Act, 98, 100
John D. Donahue, 55
Josiah Barber, 43

Labor law of 1842, 36, 38
Law Enforcement Assistance Administration, 116
Leased inmate labor, 116
Lease/purchase agreement, 16
Leasing system, 24
Low-balling, 67, 68, 78

Margaret Thatcher, 54
Marion Adjustment Center, 57, 59, 66, 67, 68, 176, 227
Marquis de Beccaria, 22
McCauley, 44, 45
McHatton, Pratt & Company, 36
Medina v. O'Neill, 69, 146, 148
Merrill Lynch & Shearson Lehman, 16
Milonas v. Williams, 147

National Center for Innovation & Correction, 94
National Council of State Legislatures, 193
Newgate prison, 38
Nullen crimen sen lege, 80

245

N-Group Securities Inc., 164, 165, 166

Odam Correctional Center, 145
Okeechobee Boy's School, 78
Orlando Sentinel, 52

Pauley Jail Building & Manufacturing Co., 117
Perfect competition, 66
Pricor, 28, 157
Prison Industries Enhancement (PIE), 92, 93
Prison Quality Index, 228

RCA Services, 33
Rendell-Baker v. Kohn, 141, 146
Request for proposal (RFP), 60, 182, 183, 184
Research & Policy Committee, 123
Ronald Reagan, 54
Rutherford County Tennessee Adult Detention Center, 158

Salvation Army, 86
Samuel James, 44
Senator Charles Percy, 91, 93, 95, 97, 100
Sheriff James A. Gondles, Jr., 229
Silverdale Detention Center, 59, 60, 68
Symbolism in corections, 76, 80, 87

S.C. Williams, 36

Targeted Jobs Tax Credit, 98, 100
Teen Trax, 161
Tennessee Coal & Iron Company, 42
Tennessee Valley Authority, 16
Texas Penal Code, 41
The Limits Of The Criminal Sanction, 80
Thomas Jefferson, 20
Trans World Airlines, 158
Tuscaloosa Metropolitan Minimum Security Detention Penalty, 158, 160

Upper East Tennessee Regional Juvenile Detention Center, 160
U.S. Attorney General's Task Force on Violent Crimes, 121
U.S. Corrections Corporations, 66, 67, 68, 69, 70
U.S. Department of Justice, 91

Ventura Center Training School, 56

Wackenhut Corporation, 28, 231
West v. Atkins, 145, 146, 148, 224

Zavala County, 163, 164, 167, 168, 169, 174
Zephyr Products, 97